ECHOES OF TRAUMA AND SHAME IN GERMAN FAMILIES

ECHOES OF TRAUMA AND SHAME IN GERMAN FAMILIES

The Post–World War II Generations

LINA JAKOB

INDIANA UNIVERSITY PRESS

This book is a publication of

Indiana University Press
Office of Scholarly Publishing
Herman B Wells Library 350
1320 East 10th Street
Bloomington, Indiana 47405 USA

iupress.indiana.edu

Manufactured in the United States of America

Cataloging information is available from the Library of Congress.

ISBN 978-0-253-04824-0 (hardback)
ISBN 978-0-253-04825-7 (paperback)
ISBN 978-0-253-04827-1 (web PDF)

1 2 3 4 5 25 24 23 22 21 20

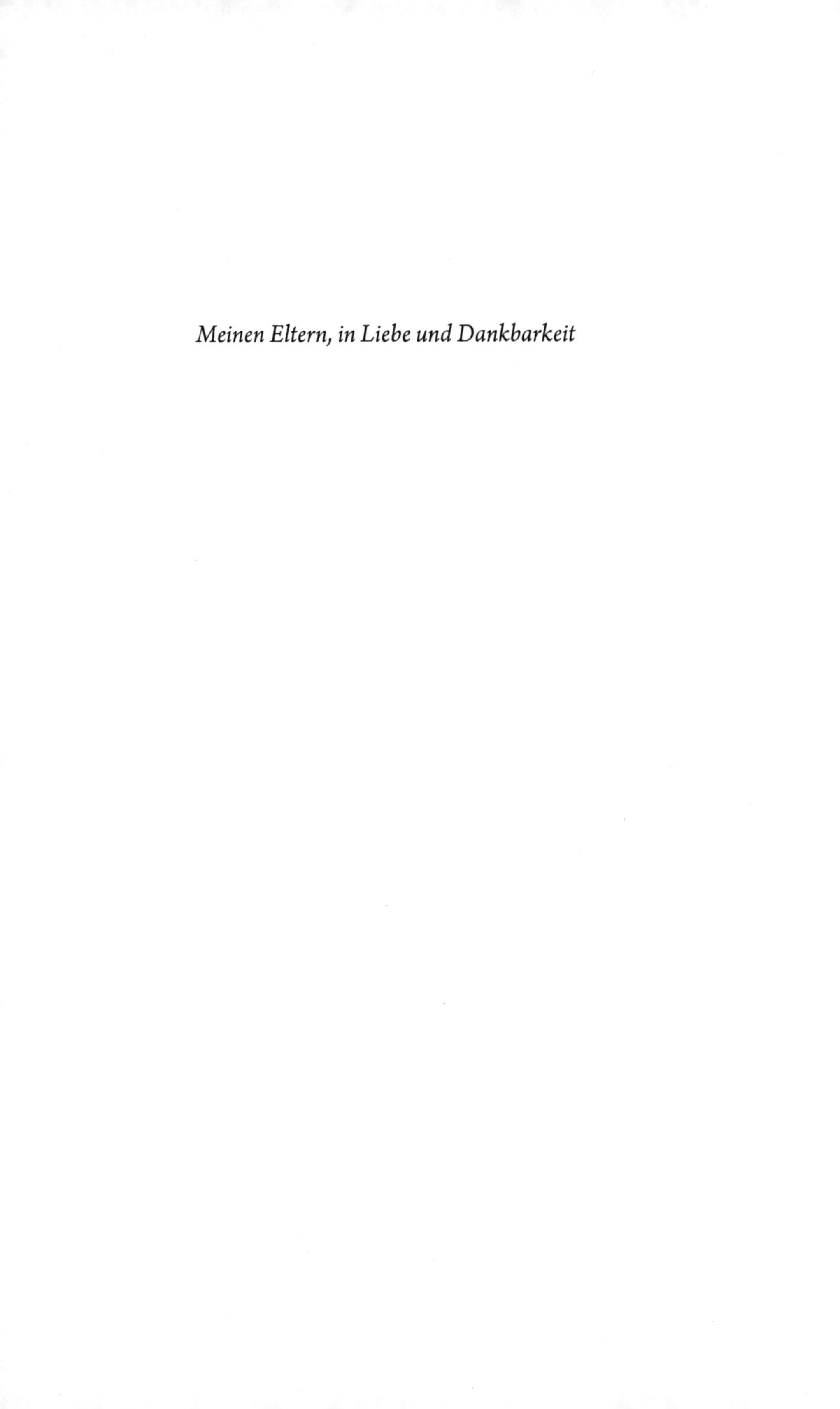

Meinen Eltern, in Liebe und Dankbarkeit

CONTENTS

ACKNOWLEDGMENTS

I HAD AN ENORMOUS AMOUNT of support in researching and writing this book. I am incredibly grateful in particular to the following:

To all my German Kriegsenkel interview partners for spending time with me and for trusting me with your stories. I hope I did them justice.

To the anthropologists at the Australian National University, in particular to Francesca Merlan for her unwavering enthusiasm and intellectual support from the very first to the very last minute, and to Ana Dragojlovic and Carly Schuster for taking the time to comment on my work.

To Jennika Baines and Allison Chaplin from Indiana University Press for their encouragement and expert guidance through the publication process, and to the two anonymous reviewers for their kind and constructive comments, which greatly helped to improve the final manuscript.

To Ben Hillman for convincing me that giving up a steady job to pursue a PhD was a good idea, and to Lee-Anne Henfry, Soraya, and Lucia for distracting me with pedicures and Peppa Pig stories when I desperately needed a break.

To my meditation friends Catherine Sinclair, Wilhelmina von Buellen, Karen O'Connell, and Anne Beyers for reminding me that there was a higher inspiration behind my quest; and to Eva-Marie Matuschka and Verena Flück for faithfully cheering me on from a distance.

To Louisa Cass for proofreading my draft thesis and for caring enough to challenge some of my views.

To my parents, Katrin and Richard Jakob, and my brothers, Jens and Lars, for sharing this journey with love, curiosity, and interest; and my sister Micha, for making this time into so much more of an adventure than I could ever have imagined.

To my husband, Luigi Tomba, for the encouragement, patience, and enormous emotional, financial, and practical support, and for taking me out for peppermint tea to reassure me that all my ups and downs were "perfectly normal" for an insecure scholar; to Jack, the cat, for keeping me company on lonely winter days; and to Tom Cliff, Lina Tan, and later Abraham for looking after Jack—and us.

Lastly, to my grandparents, Hedwig and Sigismund Jakob and Hilde and Josef Schaefer, for inspiring me to start this quest with your stories as much as with your silences and secrets. Grandpa Jupp, I know you would have loved to talk to me about my research over a glass of grappa—or two.

ECHOES OF TRAUMA AND SHAME IN GERMAN FAMILIES

INTRODUCTION

GRANDPA JUPP AND THE BLIND SPOTS IN THE FAMILY HISTORY

On April 25, 2011, I stumbled into the Anzac parade in Sydney, the annual commemoration for Australian and New Zealand soldiers who served their country in wars, conflicts, and peacekeeping operations since World War I.[1] It was not something I had ever considered watching before, not even after becoming an Australian citizen in 2007. There they were, hundreds of veterans of all the recent and not so recent wars Australia had participated in, proudly marching past a cheering crowd. They were mostly men, of all ages, some in uniforms, their chests decorated with medals, grouped behind the banner of their respective army units. The younger ones had recently returned from assignments in Iraq or Afghanistan. The older ones, World War II, Korea, and Vietnam war veterans, were on crutches or in wheelchairs pushed along by their families, still smiling and shaking hands all around. There were groups of army nurses on vans waving at the spectators, and classes of schoolchildren playing the national anthem with brass instruments and bagpipes, enticing the crowd to sing along. Witnessing this celebration of patriotism and war, I felt extremely uncomfortable. In my mind I cannot associate war with anything other than senseless violence, death, and destruction. How could this be such a cheerful event? What struck me the most were the young people—the children, grandchildren, and great-grandchildren of veterans—who took part in the parade. Many of them were carrying photos and wearing the medals of their ancestors, their youthful faces lit up with pride. I could not help but wonder what it would have been like for me, as a little girl in Germany, to proudly march in a parade commemorating World War II, carrying a photo of my grandfather in the uniform of the German *Wehrmacht,* my chest decorated with the Iron Cross Second Class he received in 1941 for personal bravery in the battle against the Soviet Union. As for many Germans of my generation, for me this is inconceivable. There were no parades, of course. If I had walked the streets like that in the city where I grew up, people would have called me a neo-Nazi or a Holocaust denier.

When Nazi Germany unconditionally surrendered on May 8, 1945, it left scenes of utter devastation: between fifty and seventy million people had perished worldwide, more than half of them civilians. It is now almost seventy-five years since the end of the war. The last war criminals are being tracked down and put on trial, and the last remaining survivors are traveling to Auschwitz and other concentration camps to commemorate the six million lives lost in the Holocaust. At least three generations have passed since Germans invaded the countries of their European neighbors. Over many of the past seven decades, the German population was trying to come to terms with the unspeakable crimes committed in their name. Books and documentaries about the Holocaust have shaped how past, current, and most likely future generations of Germans feel about themselves, their families, and their national identity. Clearly, commemoration of the past, family traditions, and transgenerational transmission mean something very different in the German context. The fact that our grandfathers participated in World War II is not a source of pride and inspiration but an enduring legacy of shame.

I have been interested in my family history all my life. Stories from the war were a topic in my conversations with all four grandparents, but particularly with my mother's father, Josef "Jupp" Schaefer, who, in spite of heavy smoking in his earlier life and heavy drinking in his later years, lived until he was almost one hundred years old. Jupp was a soldier during World War II, stationed first in France and later sent east when Germany declared war on the Soviet Union in 1941. "We have to defeat the Russian colossus," he wrote in his Christmas letter to the family in 1941, sitting in a bunker somewhere in Russia. One of my grandmother's letters to him from April 1945 read, "We have to fulfill our duty until the very last moment." The Red Army captured my grandfather before the letter could reach him. Jupp survived the Russian winters and harsh conditions in the prisoner-of-war (POW) camp. He came home, skinny and defeated, one day in May 1948, nearly ten years after he had first left. Like many teenagers of my generation, I asked my grandparents a lot of questions: "Did you support Hitler?" "Did you know about the Holocaust?" Like many others I was often frustrated when their responses seemed evasive. However, my grandmother willingly talked about everyday life during the war. Sitting in her living room, she gave me vivid descriptions of how she had to get up most nights to take the children to an air-raid shelter. How she had to push away the constant fear that she would never see my grandfather again, and how she stole potatoes and coal to feed the family after the collapse of the Nazi regime. My grandfather told lively stories from his time in the Russian POW camp, how they rolled cigarettes with *Pravda* paper, recited Goethe in improvised poetry clubs, and struggled to survive on thin vegetable soup and stale bread. All in all, I was pretty confident that I knew a lot about my family's experiences during the war. Somehow, I never noticed the gaps, in particular that there were almost no stories about my grandfather's time as a soldier.

Around 2009, my father told me about a conversation he had had with my grandfather shortly before his death. It was late at night and my grandfather, as on most nights, was drinking. The conversation turned to the war, and Jupp confessed that all his life he had felt guilty that when he was a radio operator with the *Wehrmacht* in Russia, he was sent away from his military unit on several occasions. Each time there was an attack by the Soviet Army, and many of his comrades who had stayed behind were wounded or killed. He survived by sheer luck. This is of course a secondhand story, but when I heard it, I was stunned. What my grandfather had shared sounded a bit like survivor's guilt to me, a psychological phenomenon that I had only ever heard about in the context of the Holocaust. Was it possible that he had not just been a soldier and therefore one of the perpetrators of World War II's atrocities but that he, at the same time, had also been traumatized by his war experience? It dawned on me that I had missed something crucial in our many conversations. More and more questions arose. If he was in fact traumatized, how did this affect his life and that of his family? What about all the other Germans of that generation and their experiences of active combat? Or the civilians, who lived through bombardment, death, destruction, and forced displacement? What about their children and grandchildren? Could it be that the sense of heaviness that I had observed so often in Germans of my generation was not only the result of a collective legacy of guilt and shame for the crimes committed during World War II, as I had always assumed, but also a consequence of the fact that some of the traumatic experiences of our grandparents and parents were transmitted to us? Why had none of this ever occurred to me before? The scarce results of an initial literature search on the topic led me to believe that I was not the only person who had blocked out this aspect of her family history. Even psychologists and psychoanalysts are now publicly rubbing their eyes, asking themselves how it was possible that the war had been absent from their private practices for most of the postwar years.

In 2012, after having lived abroad for twenty years, I traveled to Berlin to explore these questions with other Germans of my generation. By the time I got there, a small scene of people had started to gather in a handful of self-help groups and internet forums to talk about their family histories and the impact of World War II on their own lives. They called themselves *Kriegsenkel*—grandchildren of war.

Meeting with people of my age in Berlin, I was struck by the level of discontent and depression that dominated many of our conversations. Many of my interviewees felt an indistinct sense of malaise overshadowing their lives, for which, up until that point, there seemed to be no convincing explanation. There was Andrea, the social worker, who had to take two years off work because of severe burnout, and Anja, whose panic attacks prevented her from leaving the house even to take her son swimming. There was Karoline, who had fallen into despair after a number of relationship breakups, and Martin, the talented artist, unable to ramp up the courage to put together an exhibition with his paintings. There was Boris, whose father had been unable to control his violent outbursts and who was now struggling to manage his own, and Katarina, who still felt so enmeshed with her depressed mother that she found it difficult to build her own independent life. Many had previously accessed psychotherapy, yet often without satisfactory results.

All of these could easily be viewed as quite generic psychological issues common in many Western societies. However, a few years earlier, two popular books with life histories of this particular generation had been published: Anne-Ev Ustorf's (2008) *Wir Kinder der Kriegskinder: Die Generation im Schatten des Krieges* (We children of the war children: The generation in the shadow of the war) and Sabine Bode's *Kriegsenkel: Die Erben der vergessenen Generation* (War grandchildren: The heirs of the forgotten generation), first published in 2009. The authors directly link their interviewees' present psychological challenges to their families' experiences during World War II.

Most Germans who are now seniors were confronted with violence, loss, death, and destruction at a young age. As children they had spent nights in shelters during air raids, fearing for their own lives and those of their families, sometimes finding their homes destroyed when they returned in the morning. Many had lost their fathers or older brothers in the war or had waited years for them to return from a POW camp after 1945. Others had fled with their families from their homes in Eastern Europe, carrying their few belongings in bags and after a long and dangerous journey arriving in Germany as unwelcome refugees. For most of the postwar years, the war generation had tried to put those memories behind them. Many established successful careers, enabled by the "economic miracle" (*Wirtschaftswunder*) of the 1960s in West Germany, or contributed to building a new socialist society in the eastern part of the country. On either side of the wall, people put all their effort into providing the next generation with the stability and financial security that they themselves had missed out on. They were trying to forget the past, not wanting to be reminded of the pain and the shame attached to it. Yet, looking back, many of the people I met in Berlin had sensed that there was something not quite right in their predominantly middle-class homes, without having been able to put a clear name to this perception. Joy and laughter seemed to be missing, and depression was frequently named as the dominant mood, a lack of levity and happiness that seemed to jar with the outward display of ordinariness and stability. Their parents (and often grandparents) seemed to be carrying an emotional burden. They showed behaviors and had reactions that the children could not understand. Mothers in particular were often described as cold and emotionally unavailable, with little empathy for the children's small, everyday problems. "Stop whining. You don't know how lucky you are" was a common response. Some fathers became violent when something interrupted their fixed routines, or they scared their families with unpredictable outbursts. Boris still vividly remembered how, when he was about six years old, his father suddenly jumped up during one particularly harmonious family dinner. He ripped the tablecloth, food, and dishes from the table and yelled at his mortified family, "This is what an air raid feels like!".

Anne-Ev Ustorf's and Sabine Bode's books both argue that in this atmosphere of "pathological normalcy" ("*Pathologische Normalität,*" Radebold 2000), unresolved World War II experiences, predominantly traumatic memories but often mixed with aspects of perpetratorship, were passed on to the children. These experiences were seen as causing a broad range of issues, from depression, anxiety disorders, and burnout to relationship breakups and career problems. The books were groundbreaking because they brought the question of a possible transgenerational impact of World War II into the German public for the first time. Since then, a small Kriegsenkel movement has gained momentum. Growing numbers of Germans have embarked on journeys to explore the indirect impact of World War II on their lives. Interested people now meet in support groups that have formed in many German cities. Designated websites and Facebook groups provide information and networking opportunities and encourage the sharing of life histories. The media has covered the topic in newspaper articles, TV and radio programs, and talk shows. Psychotherapists offer specialized services to help alleviate the problems associated with transmitted war trauma.

Why are people who were born in the 1960s and 1970s suddenly discovering the war as a determining influence on their lives? Why are they asking those questions only now? Why do they understand their suffering in this particular way? How do they address it and with what result? This book explores these questions. Drawing on extensive ethnographic interviews and participant observation and engaging with a broad range of scholarship from the fields of history, anthropology, sociology, and psychology, the book traces how the Kriegsenkel movement emerged at the nexus between public and familial silences about World War II. It critically discusses how this new collective identity is constructed and addressed entirely within the framework of psychological discourses and Western therapeutic culture. It is based on insights into the subjective experiences of the descendants of German families who lived through World War II, and it weighs in on the broader international debate about the construction of second-generation survivor identities. It is also a case study of how descendants manage emotional suffering resulting from a war in which their country was the main perpetrator.

APPROACHES TO TRANSGENERATIONAL TRANSMISSION OF TRAUMA

Today it is widely accepted that traumatic experiences such as war, violence, or mass loss can have a lasting impact on generations born long after the actual events. Anthropologists Fassin and Rechtman (2009, xi) note, "Trauma has become a major signifier of our age. It is our normal means of relating present suffering to past violence. It is the scar that a tragic event leaves on an individual victim or on a witness—sometimes even on the perpetrator. It is also the collective imprint on a group of a historical experience that may have occurred decades, generations, or even centuries ago."

How survivors pass on traumatic experiences to their families has been explored across a number of different disciplines, such as memory studies (Hirsch 2008; Hirsch and Spitzer 2006), anthropology (Argenti and Schramm 2010; Crapanzano 2011; Feuchtwang 2011; Kidron 2003, 2009a, 2009b, 2012), and neurobiology (Yehuda 2006; Yehuda and Bierer 2007). However, the so-called "psy sciences"—psychology, psychoanalysis, and psychiatry—have contributed the most comprehensive body of research under labels such as *transgenerational, intergenerational, multigenerational,* or *cross-generational transmission of trauma,* or *secondary traumatization.*

A common understanding is that if the eyewitness generation does not work through their trauma, preferably in therapy, they will likely pass it down to their children, affecting the descendants' mental, emotional, and physical health. The often cited "conspiracy of silence" (Danieli 1998, 4) between the survivors and the societies in which they live is perceived as impeding the process of mourning and the psychological integration of trauma. It is furthermore claimed that the chain of transgenerational transmission can only be broken if the person to whom trauma has been passed gains an awareness of these influences and can remove them from the psyche (Volkan, Ast, and Greer 2002).

Researchers working with Holocaust survivor families were the first to raise questions about the long-term psychological impact of extreme traumatization. In the 1960s children of survivors started to seek psychological treatment in Canada and later in the United States and Israel. By 2000, clinicians and researchers had described and debated the intergenerational influence of the Holocaust in more than five hundred books and articles (Kellermann 2008). Findings were mixed and ultimately remained inconclusive. While clinical studies often reported a range of symptoms transmitted over the generations, empirical research often found no evidence that children of Holocaust survivors were more prone to psychopathology than the rest of the population. However, they were showing an increased vulnerability to post-traumatic stress disorder (PTSD) and several other psychiatric illnesses, and those who were adversely affected by their emotional legacy were found to suffer more deeply than their peers (Danieli 2007). Kellermann (2008) points to a clinical subgroup of descendants who were afflicted with severe "second-generation syndrome." Identified symptoms include not only a predisposition to develop PTSD but also difficulties separating from the parents, personality disorders or neurotic conflicts, bouts of anxiety and depression during times of crisis, and more or less impaired occupational, social, and emotional functioning. In countries such as the United States and Israel, descendants themselves gathered around an identity as second-generation Holocaust survivors with a sense of shared psychological distress.

In the 1980s and 1990s, investigations into the intergenerational effects of trauma were extended to other contexts, such as war, genocide, repressive regimes, suppression of indigenous populations, domestic violence, and infectious diseases.[2] Despite a lack of evidence for a pathological "second-generation syndrome," empirical research based on mental health practitioner accounts reported a range of complaints commonly observed in patients from families who had lived through war and violence. These included children of Vietnam veterans in the United States (Rosenheck and Nathan 1985; Rosenheck and

Fontana 1994), of Dutch collaborators with the Nazi regime (Lindt 1998), and of World War II survivors from the Dutch East Indies (Aarts 1998). While such studies do not claim to present an authoritative list of common psychological symptoms, they do point to the existence of a second-generation profile—a similar way in which descendants in their respective countries tend to struggle as a result of their parents' trauma. This may also, as in the case of the Dutch collaborators with the Nazi regime, include difficulties resulting from a family history linked to perpetratorship. (I will come back to this in more detail in chap. 3.)

In Germany research on the intergenerational impact of World War II on the non-Jewish majority population has only recently started to emerge. Yet similarly, psychotherapists have observed that certain issues are commonly found in members of the Kriegsenkel generation. The list includes a deep-seated sense of loneliness, a depressed view of the world, negative attitudes toward life, and problems with self-worth (Alberti 2010); difficulties with separation and individuation from parents (Bachofen 2012); and an insecure sense of identity and higher levels of anxiety (Lamparter and Holstein 2013).

The main purpose of this body of work, situated in the realm of the "psy sciences," is to ascertain a causal link between the parental trauma and the children's psychological problems, to capture symptoms, and to suggest interventions to alleviate the descendants' emotional suffering. As an anthropologist, I take a different route. My research is built around the descendants' subjective experiences of growing up in families that lived through World War II. My aim is to understand why the German Kriegsenkel explain their emotional suffering in this way and to what effect. Rather than using them as diagnostic tools, I take psychological models of transgenerational transmission as narratives, and they form part of my analysis.

Transgenerational Transmission as the Cornerstone of a Kriegsenkel Identity

Until around 2000, the war did not commonly feature as a topic in German psychotherapeutic practices. Psychoanalyst Hartmut Radebold speaks of "therapy without history," which did not consider the historical context to be of any importance in the treatment of mental illness (Radebold 2012). Since then, a number of studies on the occurrence of PTSD in German seniors have been published, and post-traumatic stress disorder is available as a psychiatric diagnosis for the war generation. However, in 2012–13, there was no equivalent when it came to their children and grandchildren. Being a Kriegsenkel was not linked to any clearly defined symptoms or a recognized mental health condition. My interviewees' claim that the roots of their problems stretched all the way back to the war was still frequently dismissed as far-fetched or as the grievance of middle-class complainers looking for yet another therapeutic concept to let them blame their families for their failures in life. With psychological research, therapeutic practices, and broad public acknowledgment still lagging, my book explores how the Kriegsenkel took matters into their own hands to legitimize their suffering by "diagnosing" themselves as sufferers of transmitted war trauma (chap. 3). In particular, the popular Kriegsenkel books advanced to something akin to informal diagnostic manuals. Any problems described in the life histories were pointed to as belonging to a collective Kriegsenkel profile and, ultimately, a "shared illness identity." Anthropologist Kristin Barker (2002, 284) defines this term as "an understanding of self, and affiliation with others, on the basis of a shared experience of symptoms and suffering." As was observed for cases of contested or emerging illnesses for which the status as a legitimate condition is still controversial, a self-help community gathered to confer legitimacy and validation and offer emotional support. Kriegsenkel met in self-help groups, workshops, and weekend seminars or on Facebook and designated websites to share their family histories and to compare their psychological difficulties with those of their peers. I believe that through this process of sharing and comparing, a cluster of symptoms for a new psychological profile was slowly being negotiated and associated with a Kriegsenkel identity. Although the continuous broadening of categories of mental illness and the constant creation of new disorders and syndromes have been criticized as "pathologizing" and "medicalizing" the problems of everyday life (Furedi 2004; Kutchins and Kirk 1997), it was clear that Kriegsenkel framed their struggles as an emerging mental health condition. The main driving force behind their push toward medicalization was more than just a validation of suffering. With a clear diagnosis and a shared illness identity also comes a promise for healing. "I am grateful that I finally found out why I am having such difficulties in my life and why everything was so strange at home. I hope that now I will finally be able to work through all of this," one woman shared.

I would like to stress that I am not trying to prove or dispute that a Kriegsenkel identity exists or whether it should be recognized as a psychological condition. My research merely seeks to describe the construction of this identity and explore why some people take on and choose to wear this particular mantle. This does not mean that I see my interviewees' psychological problems as imagined or made up. I share Leslie Irvine's (1999) view that, while narratives of suffering are socially constructed, suffering itself is always real for the person experiencing it.

Kriegsenkel Identities and Therapeutic Culture

A typical Kriegsenkel journey always starts from a state of psychological suffering. Often, after previous attempts to identify the root of their emotional issues and address them with a therapist, my interviewees discovered the Kriegsenkel books or a feature on the topic in a magazine or on TV. For most, this caused an extremely emotional "eureka moment" as the link between their own problems and the war was established. Next, they commonly looked around for others, yearning to connect with like-minded peers. The activities of the emerging self-help community helped break through social isolation and affirmed the newly found Kriegsenkel identity. Psychotherapists and other healers offered specialized therapy sessions and workshops to help people work through their inherited emotional burden. Many Kriegsenkel tried approaches that extended beyond traditional psychotherapy to hypnosis, creative writing, artistic expression, genealogy, and family constellation seminars.[3] The expressed goal was to come to terms with the emotional legacy of World War II, to find a sense of acceptance and closure, and to move toward a happier and emotionally healthier future for themselves and their children. All of these elements firmly link the German Kriegsenkel into the framework of contemporary Western therapeutic culture. In chapter 4, I draw on sociologist Eva Illouz's (2008) work to show how Kriegsenkel identities are constructed, explored, performed, and managed entirely in accordance with the norms of therapeutic discourses and self-help culture.

There is a broad consensus that therapeutic culture has exerted an unparalleled influence on modern Western (and increasingly global) societies. Psychological thinking has long transcended the relationship between an individual and a therapist, spilling over into almost every aspect of private and public life. Illouz (2008, 7) explains that therapeutic discourse "has come to constitute one of the major codes with which to express, shape, and guide selfhood." Sociologists have critiqued the rise of counseling and therapy culture as fostering moral collapse (Furedi 2004; Lasch 1991; Rieff 1966), as encouraging extreme individualism (Lasch 1991), and as creating a "new faith" (Moskowitz 2001) to fill a need that was once addressed by religion. Some authors claim that, rather than alleviating emotional suffering, therapeutic culture ends up creating or perpetuating the very pain it is trying to cure, either by fostering a culture of emotional vulnerability and victimhood vis-à-vis the challenges of modern life (Furedi 2004) or by setting vague benchmarks of emotional health, self-actualization, and happiness against which individuals invariably find themselves falling short (Illouz 2008). From my observations among my German interviewees, I would agree that having been socialized to understand one's problems in therapeutic terms reinforces a sense of victimhood rather than strengthens aspects of resilience and agency. Many of the Kriegsenkel I spoke to understood themselves to be the emotional casualties of their dysfunctional families, and they would wholeheartedly subscribe to concepts of the self as fragile and constantly at risk of being traumatized. Yet at the same time, making the Kriegsenkel journey was experienced as unequivocally positive. Therapeutic culture was seen as offering the tools to understand and overcome suffering, which was subjectively experienced as effective and empowering. For the German Kriegsenkel there was never a question, critique, or alternative: therapeutic culture is just how you do things!

A Broad Approach to Transgenerational Transmission

An important goal of this book is the search for a broader understanding of the processes of transgenerational transmission of trauma. A number of different models can help explain how these processes occur (these will be explained in more detail in chap. 5). Psychoanalytical approaches, for example, claim that traumatic experiences are unconsciously passed on from one generation to the next: "Transgenerational transmission is when an older person unconsciously externalizes his traumatized self onto a developing child's personality. A child then becomes a reservoir for the unwanted, troublesome parts of an older generation. . . . It becomes the child's task to mourn, to reverse the humiliation and feeling of helplessness pertaining to the trauma of his forebears" (Volkan 1997, 43).

Sociocultural and socialization approaches, on the other hand, emphasize the conscious and direct influence parents have by modeling behavior and raising children with their views of the world. Julia Dickson-Gómez (2002, 417) found traces of a "traumatized world view" in the children of *campesinos* who survived the civil war that raged in El Salvador from 1980 to 1992. Although they were born long after the event, the children still showed a fundamental mistrust of the police, neighbors, and politicians. Furthermore, family systems models account for the fact that both conscious and unconscious transmission of trauma always take place in a particular family dynamic. Holocaust survivor families, for example, were said to behave like "tight little islands," as highly closed systems where the parents were very focused on their children. The children in turn were deeply concerned with their parents' welfare, leading to problems regarding separation and individuation (Kellermann 2001b,

260). Lastly, biological and epigenetic research traces the physical changes that trauma leaves behind in the eyewitness generation and in their offspring. Parental trauma can create a genetic or biochemical predisposition in the children, making them more vulnerable to stress and PTSD (Yehuda 2006; Yehuda et al., "Vulnerability to Posttraumatic Stress Disorder,"1998; Yehuda and Bierer 2007). Mainstreamed by therapeutic culture, these models provided the basic concepts and vocabulary into which the Kriegsenkel tapped to explain why and how their parents' and grandparents' war experiences affected them.

I do not claim to be an expert in the extensive literature on traumatology. Like my German interviewees, I understand these models mainly in their simplified form, condensed to their basic structure and "truth rules" (Irvine 1999, 85). Yet, as we delved deeper into their life histories, many aspects of the stories they shared did not seem to neatly fit. Or rather, the subjective perceptions of growing up in German families that lived through World War II were messier than these models seem to account for. My interviews suggest that transmission is not always a linear process, handing experiences neatly down from generation to generation. While the parents were always described as the main source of the inherited difficulties, the grandparents (and sometimes members of the extended family) also often had an important and direct influence on the lives of the Kriegsenkel. Secondly, the effects of past trauma in descendants can also not necessarily be traced back to a distinct source in the family or to a distinct event, as overlapping traumas can affect the same family. There is also no clear demarcation between traumatic and nontraumatic aspects of World War II experiences, with only the "unresolved" ones handed down the family line as was often assumed. Even parents who were described as having adjusted well after the war raised their children on the basis of experiences formed during that time and passed on their attitudes and worldviews.

I suggest in chapter 5 that an approach derived from affect theory may present an alternative way to conceptualize how a difficult past affects families. Teresa Brennan (2004) explains that affect theory understands human beings as fundamentally open systems, constantly interacting with and being influenced by other people and the environment around them. Rather than pathologizing the interaction between the generations, this approach would understand as natural and unavoidable that all affects, positive and negative, flow between any people who live in close physical proximity. Instead of separating traumatized (or unhealthy) and normal (or healthy) content, I propose that the transmitted affects from the war should be normalized as an integral part of the overall transfer that invariably happens as part of child-rearing.

Following the psychoanalytical model, my German interviewees furthermore tended to picture their problems as an unwanted parcel of undigested experiences left over from the war, handed down by their families and weighing heavily on their present lives. Yet, as we explored their perceptions in more depth, many of the examples that were brought forward revolved around a sense of lack or gap. Many people were feeling pain because of what had not been transmitted by their family, or what was more broadly felt to be missing as a result of World War II. Chapter 6 traces the dynamic role of these gaps and absences in Kriegsenkel narratives. I focus in particular on experiences of forced migration and the absence of a *Heimat* (homeland) and also on the breaks and gaps in family relationships that come with having a high-level Nazi perpetrator in the family. Commenting on concepts from the *Anthropology of Absence* (Bille, Hastrup, and Sørensen 2010a), I explore how places and people that are not present are still felt to have a major impact on a person's life and how the Kriegsenkel are ultimately able to exert agency over what is missing.

As a final point, psychological models tend to conceptualize and treat transgenerational transmission of trauma as a collection of symptoms of psychological distress. My research, on the other hand, highlights how the broader sociopolitical environment crucially influences whether and how suffering is constructed, experienced, and addressed. Germany, as a "perpetrator" country, provides a particularly good case study for this.

NAVIGATING WARTIME SUFFERING IN A "PERPETRATOR COUNTRY"

How does a society manage the psychological damage resulting from a war for which their country was directly responsible? The first part of the book traces how Germany tried to come to terms with the responsibility for the war and the Holocaust as well as with its own losses. As discussed in chapter 1, until the reunification in 1990, both German states excluded most aspects of wartime suffering of the majority population from their respective culture of public commemoration, for different ideological reasons. The socialist government of the German Democratic Republic (GDR) understood itself as the heir of the communist resistance against Hitler and therefore as belonging to the "victors of history" rather than to the perpetrators. It consequently rejected all accountability for Hitler's rise to power and the crimes committed in the German name. The memory of the brave communists who had died in the antifascist resistance took center stage in commemorative practices. West Germany (and from 1990 the reunited country), on the other hand, accepted historical responsibility for the crimes committed under the Nazi regime. In particular since the 1960s, official commemorations stressed the need to remember the Holocaust and to ensure that history would never repeat itself. "All of us, whether guilty or not, whether old or young, must accept the past. We are all affected by its consequences and liable for it," former president Richard von Weizsäcker said in his programmatic speech on May 8, 1985. For most of the postwar years, publicly speaking of German victimhood was largely considered a moral taboo. Up until around 2000, when a flood of memories of wartime suffering suddenly swept into the public sphere, the German population was coming to terms with its losses in private. From a moral perspective, this "humiliated silence" (Connerton 2008) was without a doubt the only appropriate response out of respect for the millions of victims of the German aggression. From a psychological perspective, on the other hand, societal silences come at a cost. Public recognition is deemed essential in helping populations deal with consequences of war and mass loss (Danieli 1998). Regarding the case of the Soviet Union, where any mention of the massive loss of life during the Stalin era was systematically excluded from public narratives, historian Catherine Merridale (1999, 75) observed: "Personal grief had no wider framework, no mirror, in which to observe itself gradually diminishing."

It is sometimes argued that parents and grandparents felt less constraint in sharing their stories of wartime suffering and hardship in the safety of the family home. However, as chapter 2 explains, in the majority of Germany families I heard about, the war was not much of a topic around the dinner table either. While there was rarely complete silence, information and stories about the past tended to be patchy, fragmented, and unreliable. Taboos, secrets, and an unwillingness to openly talk about painful or shameful memories left the younger generation without a clear sense of the familial history. The public culture of commemoration reached into the private sphere, shaping family conversations. In West Germany in particular, discussions at home tended to focus on the older generations' attitudes toward the Hitler regime, while the difficult or traumatic aspects of their experiences were played down or blocked out altogether. Overlapping layers of silences, gaps, and blind spots contributed to a situation where questions of the long-term influence of World War II on the mental health of the German majority population remained hidden from both public and private awareness. This helps explain why the subject matter was taken up with such surprise and emotional intensity.

The center part of the book, chapters 3, 4, and 5, illuminates how the topic of the intergenerational impact of the war, once it had moved into public view, was explored entirely within the framework of psychological discourses and funneled into the realm of therapeutic culture to be worked through. A common critique of therapeutic culture is that by defining problems as individual and personal it fosters a "narcissistic over occupation with the self" (Lasch 1991, xv), while at the same time discouraging social and political action (Moskowitz 2001). My exploration shows that the Kriegsenkel indeed understood "being affected by World War II experiences" as an entirely personal problem. It was traced back to the childhood family and addressed in private therapy or explored with groups of peers. A striking characteristic of the Kriegsenkel movement is its complete absence of any broader social goals and ambitions. All of this could well be viewed as political disengagement and narcissistic self-concern. However, framing problems as psychological is also a strategy to navigate a political environment where the issues in question are still considered sensitive. By choosing to define their suffering as a shared illness identity, the Kriegsenkel were able to stay clear of the controversies around German victimhood and Holocaust memory. Therapeutic culture and practices provided safe spaces where concerns could be explored without fear of repercussions.

Chapter 6 brings the focus back even more sharply to how Germany's changing sociopolitical environment affects the perception of emotional suffering. In Charlotte's story, I trace how each of the three generations of the same family experienced the loss of their *Heimat*—their ancestral home—at the end of the war. For Charlotte's grandparents, the new postwar borders made a return to their old houses impossible, and the notion of home for them was surrounded by nostalgia, pain, sadness, and longing. For her parents, *Heimat* turned into a dirty word, an unwelcome reminder of the Nazi "blood and soil" ideology and the aggressive territorial expansion of the *Lebensraum* (living space) for the German ethnic community. Rather than a painful lack, the disconnection from their ancestral homeland was accepted as a political necessity. For most of her life, Charlotte had no awareness that something was missing at all. Only after reading the Kriegsenkel books did she notice diffuse feelings of homelessness and lack of attachment, and she started to feel a painful yearning for a sense of rootedness and belonging. The collapse of the Soviet Union and the emergence of more positive attitudes toward German national identity allowed her to search for a reconnection with the "lost home." By making the journey into the regions where her grandparents had once lived, Charlotte was able to transform the absence into a kind of presence and find a home inside herself that filled the void.

Lastly, Germany's responsibility for World War II and the Holocaust also directly affects family relationships. Rainer and Paula (chap. 6) were both trying to find a way to come to terms with the fact that their grandfathers were well-known Nazi officials and war criminals. As the grandson of the commander of Auschwitz, Rainer was terrified that he may have inherited his grandfather's "evil genes." He broke with his family and publicly denounced his grandfather's crimes. Accepting the moral responsibility imparted by the German culture of commemoration, he devoted his life to ensuring that the Holocaust will never be forgotten. Paula, on the other hand, was cautiously trying to look for a new connection with her deceased grandfather, acutely aware of the taboos she was breaking and conducting her exploration largely in secret. While these were extreme examples, many Kriegsenkel were also haunted by the (known or suspected) crimes of their grandparents and often their parents' denial. This led to varying degrees of separation, and sometimes ties were severed altogether. Kurt, one particularly angry man, explained, "You can't just sit down with these people on a Sunday and play cards, and the next day you ask them about the war, and they just tell you some bullshit lies."

A NOTE ON METHODOLOGY

This book draws on more than eighty life-history interviews with fifty-four Germans of the Kriegsenkel generation undertaken over thirteen months in 2012 and 2013 in Berlin. In addition, I collected information through participant observation among the emerging Kriegsenkel support community as well as in interviews with book authors, psychotherapists, and organizers of the Kriegsenkel support groups and websites.

My interviewees were predominantly well-educated professionals in their forties and early fifties (most of them having been born in the 1960s and 1970s), with a strong representation of therapeutic, social, and administrative professions. Of these interviewees, 63 percent (34) were women and 37 percent (20) men, 67 percent (36) were born in West Germany and 33 percent (18) in the East. Some of their grandparents had been actively involved with the Nazis, and many (to their grandchildren's knowledge) belonged to the group of so-called "bystanders," neither actively supporting nor actively resisting the Hitler regime. Two people from families of victims of the Third Reich also participated (the story of one of them, Kerstin, will be told in chap. 4). People volunteered for my project for different reasons.[4] Some had been interested in their familial history for most of their lives and were keen to share their experiences or frustrations about their attempts to break through their families' silence. Others had only recently discovered the topic through the Kriegsenkel books or an article in the media and wanted to explore in more depth how World War II still affected them today. Eight were the siblings of my primary participants. They often had a fascinatingly different view about growing up in the same family. I conducted the biographical interviews in a semistructured format, with open-ended questions. They lasted between ninety minutes and two hours, roughly following a list of topics I tried to cover with each person (see the appendix for a more detailed interview structure and sample questions). I met more regularly with around a dozen people, first in 2012 and then again in 2013. We went to support group meetings and other Kriegsenkel activities together and stayed in touch by email or telephone between catch-ups. I was able to track their exploration of the topic over eighteen months, fascinated to see their attitudes and stories evolve over time. Many of the case studies told in more detail in my later chapters belong to this core group.

During our interviews, we often covered a person's whole life span from childhood and adolescence to the present day. In this process of retelling and analyzing the family history, complex and diverse layers of memories were drawn together to explain current emotional struggles. Some explanations were based on direct observations of the family's behavior, closer to the present or retrieved further back from childhood and adolescence. The main point of reference, however—World War II—lay well before the times of their births. All were at least secondhand narrations of events, with some stories being even more steps removed, where the grandparents' war experiences had been retold by the parents at some point. In many cases there was not enough openly shared information, and what happened to the family during the war could only be sensed and inferred. I was often surprised when someone seamlessly drew together as "historic truth" facts they had learned from their family or a historical archive with what they found out during a family constellation workshop or a session with a hypnotherapist.

In addition, my interviewees had only recently come to consider the psychological impact of the war on their families and by extension themselves. They had previously attributed their emotional problems to other causes. They were "re-writing the past," as Ian Hacking (1995) described in the context of multiple personality disorder (now called dissociative identity disorder): they were superimposing new ideas and creating new causal connections between past events that were not experienced in that way at the time. Today *trauma* is a widely accepted term to express the long-term scarring of the psyche following catastrophic events. Yet Germans who experienced World War II directly did not conceive of themselves as "traumatized" at the time. The common understanding was that "war was just what happened to everyone" (Radebold 2008, 49) and that people would simply get over it with time. *Trauma* was not widely used as a concept in postwar Germany, not even by psychiatrists. Historian

Svenja Goltermann (2010) presents a fascinating analysis of 450 medical files of returned Wehrmacht soldiers who had sought psychiatric help in the late 1940s and 1950s. Many patients reported extreme anxiety, unsettledness, a sense of guilt, and fear of punishment because they had killed other human beings. Yet their doctors viewed this as a passing state of mind, which they expected to disappear after a few weeks or months. Psychiatrists shared a widely held belief that a mental illness could not be triggered by external events, provided there was no physical damage, and that if a war veteran remained troubled longer term, it was only a reflection of bad character.

The idea that traumatic experiences can be transmitted to the next generation is also a relatively new concept. Kriegsenkel might have felt that something was not quite right with their families, but it is only now that they have begun to reexamine their childhood memories through the lens of transgenerational transmission of trauma. These were new concepts imposed on past events and memories, providing a new template to renarrate biographies that would have been told differently only a few years ago. At the point of each interview, my interviewees presented a complex, richly textured, multilayered matrix of memories varying in temporality and factuality, drawn together under new psychological labels. The interviews were produced in "joint production" with an active role played by myself as the interviewer (Maynes, Pierce, and Laslett 2008, 100). My questions and probing contributed to the crafting of the narrative and sometimes led to new insights for my interviewees.

It is not my main concern to elicit an elusive historic truth. By its very nature, human memory is a rather unreliable source of information about past events (Assmann 2006a). It is a widely acknowledged fact in memory studies that an unfiltered account of historic events does not exist and that "the past is mediated by, rather than directly reflected in personal memory" (Radstone 2005, 135). The act of remembering is influenced by a number of factors, including the prevailing conventions of remembering and the person's social context, beliefs, and aspirations (Freemann 2010). While the memories therefore were not to be considered true reflections of the past, it was the subjective presentation of my interiewees' life histories at the time of the interviews and the retrospective reflections on growing up in families affected by war that I was most interested in. They form the basis of my analysis.

A few words on terminology. For reasons of simplicity I use the term *Kriegsenkel* for all members of this particular generation, although not all of my interviewees were familiar with the term or identified as such. As I will explain in chapter 3, technically everyone whose parents were children during World War II is a Kriegsenkel. However, only people who feel that they are suffering as a result of their upbringing tend to use this label for themselves. Also, in spite of some criticism of the concept of *transgenerational transmission of trauma*, I will nevertheless use it as my key term because it facilitates widespread, shared understanding of the topic. To allow for the inclusion of the aspects of nontraumatic content as well as aspects of perpetratorship, I will predominantly speak of transgenerational transmission of World War II *experiences*. Unless stated otherwise, all translations from German to English are mine.

AN "ANTHROPOLOGIZATION" OF SUFFERING?: ON GERMANS AS VICTIMS

Before launching into the subject matter, I would like to express one final caveat, which is of personal importance to me. In this book I will talk extensively about the wartime suffering of the majority population of Germany, as these experiences lie at the heart of the Kriegsenkel movement. However, writing about the suffering of a nation that was directly responsible for the Holocaust is still a sensitive issue. Much opening up on the topic has happened in Germany in recent decades, but some critics remain suspicious of the shift in public attention. In 2008, Jewish German journalist Henryk M. Broder said, "Everything the Germans had to go through during the war and after the war was mere discomfort compared with what the Nazis did to their victims. . . . In a world in which everyone wants to be a victim even the grandchildren and great-grandchildren of the perpetrators want to stand on the right side of history" (Crossland 2008).

Historian Dan Diner (2003) criticizes recent public debates' as "dehistorization" in favor of an "anthropologization of suffering" (*"Anthropologisierung des Leidens"*). He warns against the tendency to portray German wartime suffering as merely a human experience in the most general sense, thereby stripping it of its moral and political context and pushing aside the historical circumstances and responsibilities that caused the suffering in the first place.

These are important concerns. As a German brought up and socialized in the public culture of commemoration of my time, I share much of the uneasiness around the topic, and having my research perceived as an attempt to exonerate Germans of their crimes would go entirely against my personal convictions. At the same time, I also believe that all stories, including the painful and shameful ones, need to be told if we really want to come to terms with and "master the past," as individuals and as a society more broadly. Historian Michael Rothberg (2009, 3) critiques the idea that the public sphere is a scarce resource, where different collective memories compete for preeminence in a zero-sum struggle for recognition and where the memories of one group invariably block out those of others. I believe that today it is possible to paint a more multifaceted picture of the German past, in which Germans committed unspeakable acts of violence and suffered enormous losses, without creating false equivalences and without one set of memories diminishing the other.

NOTES

1. The acronym *Anzac* stands for Australian and New Zealand Army Corps. More info at https://www.awm.gov.au/commemoration/anzac-day.

2. For a large collection of articles about these topics, see Yael Danieli, *International Handbook of Multigenerational Legacies of Trauma* (1998); also Janine Altounian, "Putting into Words, Putting to Rest and Putting Aside the Ancestors" (1999); and Julia Dickson-Gómez, "The Sound of Barking Dogs" (2002).

3. For more information about family constellations, see Family Constellations. n.d. Hellinger sciencia. Accessed November 9, 2019. https://www.hellinger.com/en/home/family-constellation/.

4. Around half of my core participants were recruited through the two Kriegsenkel information and support websites, which allowed me to post my project information and contact details. The other half came through personal networks and snowballing. The selection of my interviewees was guided by people's interest in exploring the topic, and it is not a representative sample of the German population. All interviewee names were changed to protect their identity unless they explicitly requested that their real name be used.

ONE

BETWEEN "MASTERING" AND "SILENCING" THE PAST

Public Commemorations of World War II

IN MARCH 2012, a group of Germans in their forties and fifties got together in the picturesque university town of Göttingen for a two-day workshop entitled "The Children of the War Children and the Long-Term Impact of the Nazi Terror." The meeting, organized by the little-known Association for Psychohistory and Political Psychology (Gesellschaft für Psychohistorie und Politische Psychologie), appeared to be just another inconspicuous conference on a slightly convoluted topic. Yet it turned out to be surprising in a number of ways. First, there was the attendance. The annual meeting of the association usually attracts around 30 or 40 people, mainly its core membership. This time, 170 people—the majority from the general public—registered, exceeding not only all expectations but also the logistical capacity of the organizers and their venue. People were put on waiting lists, and quite a few who decided to try their luck were turned away at the door. In the end, 130 bodies were squeezed into the conference facilities at the Göttingen observatory.

Then there were the reactions from the audience. What I had expected to be a rather cerebral exchange about the long-term impact of World War II on German society unfolded into a highly emotional event. Psychoanalysts and psychotherapists delivered papers on topics like "Emotional Rubble: The Postwar Generation Overshadowed by the Trauma of War," or "Idyllic Worlds: How the War Grandchildren Unconsciously Give Up Their Own Lives," while members of the Kriegsenkel generation—the war grandchildren—presented their life histories. The speakers vividly sketched out what it was like to grow up in a German family who had lived through World War II. They painted a depressing picture. They showed the Kriegsenkel as a generation raised by parents who were frugal and hardworking. They portrayed parents who had rebuilt their lives from the ruins, focusing all their attention on providing financial security for their children, while being emotionally absent, unable to provide warmth or show emotion. They depicted mothers who told their children to eat everything on their plate and to stop whining about their "little" problems and unpredictable fathers who could lose their temper at any given moment when something upset their painstakingly safeguarded emotional stability and daily routines. They described children who felt responsible for their emotionally fragile parents, unable to build their independent lives, and quiet grandparents shrouded by an impenetrable veil of silence about the past. All of this together had created an atmosphere of foggy heaviness hanging over many otherwise picture-perfect German homes of the 1960s, 1970s, and 1980s.

In previous years, the waiting rooms of the psychotherapists presenting at the conference had started to fill with people who were struggling to find their path in life, in spite of the fact that they had grown up in times of peace, stability, and (mostly) prosperity. They were wrestling with emotional problems such as depression, anxiety, or a general sense of hopelessness and lack of belonging. They had difficulty separating themselves from their parents and starting their own lives. They were struggling to build committed relationships and successful careers. For many of these issues, therapists were unable to clearly identify the cause of suffering, and therapeutic interventions often failed to produce the desired results. The psychologists were starting to look for potential sources further back in the family history—all the way to the events of World War II. Could it be, the psychologists were now asking, that what their patients' parents and grandparents had witnessed in World War II had left them damaged or even traumatized? Had the bombardment of German cities, the nights spent in air-raid shelters, the deaths of family members, and the loss of homes and belongings left much bigger psychological scars in these generations than was previously known or even suspected? Had these scars and the "emotional rubble" (*Seelische Trümmer*, Alberti 2010), pushed aside by the intense effort of economic reconstruction after 1945 and buried under a sense of guilt and shame about the crimes that Germans had committed, affected not only the mental health of the eyewitnesses but also the emotional well-being of their children and grandchildren? Had the survivors inadvertently and unconsciously passed down their unresolved emotional baggage, and could this be an explanation for the psychological problems of the Kriegsenkel?

The audience listened in teary silence as memories of their childhoods came back to life. Question times were dominated by expressions of relief and empathy and by listeners' own stories. Again and again someone would stand up and, choking with emotion, say something like, "I have never ever looked at myself and my family in this way before. Now, finally, I understand why my parents were the way they were and why I have been struggling all my life. I always felt that there was something wrong with me. Now, I can see where it all came from, and that there are other people out there who are just like me. For the first time, I don't feel alone anymore." Each time, 130 people clapped in support.

Sunday afternoon, on the train back to Berlin, exhausted and overwhelmed by the intensity of the previous two days, I pondered on what I had just witnessed. One thing was obvious: what had made the event so emotional was that this was a new topic for the audience, one that had come as a big revelation. It offered a fresh lens through which people reconsidered not only their own lives but also those of their parents and grandparents. The memory of the war had always been there—as a constant presence in public commemorations, history lessons at school, and TV documentaries. Yet its psychological impact had somehow been blocked from view. They had not been able to grasp it. Having grown up in Germany, I intuitively understood why the conference participants were so surprised by the sudden discovery of the connection between World War II and their own emotional issues. Up until that moment, Germans (not only of this particular generation) related to the war in two distinct ways: either as a historical event that had little or no impact on their own lives or as a national and familial legacy of perpetratorship, guilt, and shame. It had never before been considered that not only had the eyewitness generation participated in or condoned the crimes of the Nazi regime but the war had also psychologically scarred them, creating lasting emotional damage that they then passed on to their children and grandchildren.

Why did it take more than sixty years before Germans started to even think about these issues? Three main factors may help explain. First, for different ideological reasons, the culture of commemoration in East and West (and later the reunited) Germany largely excluded the suffering of the non-Jewish majority population from public discourses about World War II. In the West the emphasis was on the responsibility for the Nazi war crimes and the Holocaust, while the East German regime focused on building a socialist future rather than looking back to the past. Without the stimulation of a broader public discussion, the aspect of the German losses in World War II history did not feature prominently in people's awareness, and so they were not systematically considered.

Second, conversations between the different generations in German families tended to be dominated by silences, disjointed anecdotes, accusations, and denials. This disrupted communication left the younger generations with only sketchy knowledge about what had happened to their family during the war, and it did not allow them to understand how they may have been affected later on.

Lastly, the mainstreaming of psychological knowledge about the multigenerational impact of traumatic events is a very recent development. This knowledge is a crucial element for the construction of Kriegsenkel life histories and the understanding of the enduring emotional legacy of World War II more broadly. While they may have experienced suffering, the German eyewitness generation of World War II did not consider themselves traumatized after the war, and research on the effects on their children and grandchildren is only just starting to emerge.

The culture of commemoration of a country—the way a nation remembers, describes, and relates to its past—is relayed in public policies and political debates, memorials and museums, rituals of commemoration, and the media (Moller 2003). The construction of any national history is invariably a selective representation of the past, emphasizing certain aspects while simultaneously omitting and "silencing" (Trouillot 1995) others. Ashplant, Dawson, and Roper (2000, 7) point out that the commemoration of war in particular is often a key element used by the state "for binding its citizens into a collective national identity." What makes the German case complicated in this regard is the fact that Nazi Germany had started World War II and was directly responsible for an enormous loss of human life worldwide. Consequently, there were no victories or heroes to celebrate (although East Germany did to a degree, as I will explain). Both German states had to find a way to break with the past and distance themselves from the actions of the Nazi regime.

The public mourning of Germany's losses consequently (and rightly, I believe) had to take a large step back behind the consideration for the crimes committed. At times it disappeared almost entirely from public view. Journalist Sabine Bode suggested in 2006 (271) that the only dignified way to publicly remember and mourn the destruction of German cities and the loss of life was for the population to gather on the night of May 8 and stand in silence. She observed that all too often local politicians still could not find the appropriate words to say. Using anthropologist Paul Connerton's (2008) "seven types of forgetting," this chapter highlights the shifting and often contradictory ways in which Germans publicly talked about World War II. It traces the tension between the responsibility for the Holocaust on the one hand and the wartime suffering of the civilian population on the other.

FROM THE "DESIRE TO FORGET" TO THE SINGULARITY OF THE HOLOCAUST: THE WAR IN WEST GERMAN PUBLIC DISCOURSES BEFORE 1990

After the capitulation of the National Socialist regime in May 1945, Allied and Soviet forces occupied Germany. In 1949 two separate states were founded, the German Federal Republic (FRG) in the West and the German Democratic Republic (GDR), ruled by the Socialist Unity Party (Sozialistische Einheitspartei Deutschlands, SED), in the East. Until Germany's reunification in 1990, the two states had very different ways of coming to terms with and "mastering the past" (*Vergangenheitsbewältigung*, Herf 1997, 8).

The Postwar Years: Between the "Desire to Forget" and "Humiliated Silence"

From the late 1940s to the mid-1960s, as it focused strongly on rebuilding the country, the West German government assumed political responsibility for the war and committed to reparations to the Jewish victims and the state of Israel. In 1945 and 1946, Allied tribunals sentenced many of the most prominent members of the political, military, and economic leadership of the Nazi regime at the Nuremberg trials.

At the same time, public policy, commemoration, and the media also drew attention to two groups of Germans who were experiencing the consequences of the defeat: the millions of Germans expelled from Central and Eastern European countries and the approximately 1.5–2 million soldiers still held in Russian POW camps. Mass organizations representing veterans and expellees (*Vertriebenenverbände*) emerged as political actors in this first postwar period, influencing government policy to consider their interests (Moeller 1996). Although the government paid lip service to the great suffering inflicted by Germans, and although the Nuremberg trials made details about Nazi crimes widely known, the Jewish victims remained largely faceless in the political rhetoric and consciousness of the German people. US historian Robert G. Moeller (2005, 2006) points out that statistics and numbers representing the deportation and murder of much of the European Jewry did not inspire as much empathy as the vivid descriptions found in popular movies, memoirs, and novels. There were stories of German women fleeing from the advancing Russians and of brave German soldiers fighting at the eastern front—victimized first by the Nazis and then by the Red Army in POW camps. Moeller's German colleague Ruth Wittlinger (2006) adds that by sentencing a few Nazi leaders, the Nuremberg trials encouraged a view of the past where the German population had been the victims of a criminal group at the top, which had led the German people astray. This view allowed the majority of the population to firmly shift the main responsibility to the political elites. Susanne Vees-Gulani (2008) found that literary texts about the first postwar years portray a population refusing to believe in or admit to the German atrocities. Over time, outright denial gave way to passivity and indifference.

With the "denazification" (1946–51), an unprecedented yet half-hearted attempt was made to rid German society of any remnants of National Socialist ideology and expel former Nazis from positions of power. There was always suspicion that it was largely a pro forma activity. It was seen as something superficially imposed by the Allied forces, who had a strong interest in returning Germany to "normality" as a bulwark against the communist Eastern bloc, rather than as a phase of true reeducation and acceptance of responsibility for past crimes. Older Germans commonly referred to the denazification documents as *Persilscheine*, making reference to a popular washing powder (Persil) famous for its exceptional "whitewashing" capacity and ability to produce superior "cleanliness" (Nowak 2012). Appalled that only 0.5 percent of all six million denazification proceedings resulted in a "guilty" or "very guilty" verdict, writer and publicist Ralph Giordano (1987, 90) denounced the widespread denials of the war generation's support for Hitler as their "second guilt" (*Zweite Schuld*). As a teenager I often asked myself where the tens of thousands of people who had been involved in the deportation and murder of the Jews had gone. No one ever spoke of them. No one seemed to know anyone, let alone be related to anyone, who had taken part.

While Giordano condemns these silences and the desire to forget as an attempt to escape uncomfortable memories and confrontational questions, Connerton puts forward a more accepting view. He refers to early postwar Germany as an example of "prescriptive forgetting" (Connerton 2008, 61–62). Connerton argues that in order to restore cohesion to civil society and to rebuild the legitimacy of the new West German state, the Adenauer government needed to turn the persecution and punishment of convicted Nazis into a forgotten issue by the early 1950s.

It was the generation of the Kriegsenkel's grandparents, a generation who had actively participated in the war and had generally supported the Hitler regime, that was affected by the sociopolitical environment of the late 1940s and 1950s, with its official lip service to the acceptance of responsibility for the war on the one hand and the strong desire to forget the past and one's involvement on the other. Their unwillingness to confront the past later became an issue of intense conflict with the next generation. On a political level, there was the protest movement of 1968. On a familial level, there was tension between the war generation and their children. What makes this situation (and the transgenerational dynamic) even more complex is the fact that this unresolved relationship with the Nazi crimes was paired with what Connerton (2008, 67) calls "humiliated silence." The Allied air raids of German cities had left as many as six hundred thousand civilians dead and more than eight hundred thousand wounded. More than five million German soldiers were killed before the shooting stopped, over half of them on the eastern front (Moeller 2005). Around twelve to fifteen million ethnic Germans either were expelled or had left their homes in Eastern Europe to escape the advancing Red Army in spring 1945. As many as two million are believed to have died from violence, starvation, and disease in the process (Naimark 2010). Connerton (2008, 68) expresses surprise that, for many of the postwar years, almost no one in Germany publicly talked about the bombardment and destruction of German cities and that "a colossal collective experience was followed by half a century of silence." He sees the "economic miracle" and the quick reconstruction of the country as a covering up of the past. It concealed all visible signs of not only physical but also emotional destruction, an attempted effacement of painful and shameful memories. Such silencing, Connerton concludes, can be seen as a type of repression, but it may at the same time be an essential survival strategy.

Although public speeches in the postwar period mentioned to some extent the fate of the expellees and the prisoners of war, there was little focus on the mental and physical difficulties of the larger civilian population. Most families were left to their own devices to cope with fathers and grandfathers who had returned physically and psychologically damaged or to grieve for those who had not returned at all.[1] Millions of Germans had to privately come to terms with the loss of their homes and livelihoods in the Eastern European countries in the wake of the German defeat. Victims of rape and other forms of violence had to deal with the loss of their physical and emotional health on their own. While hard to fathom from today's standpoint, this solitary suffering was the norm at the time—across the globe. It was only at the end of the 1980s that psychological support started to be provided in the context of humanitarian aid, immediately treating populations traumatized by war and mass loss (Goltermann 2017).

From a moral standpoint, "humiliated silence" and a reluctance to publicly emphasize German wartime suffering were undoubtedly the only attitudes to appropriately show respect for the victims of the Nazis. From a psychological perspective, though, the picture looks different. Researchers and mental health practitioners have pointed to the importance of public recognition to help populations deal with the traumatic consequences of war, violence, and mass loss. French psychologist Erika Apfelbaum (quoted in Wajnryb 2001, 72) explains that individuals need to construct themselves in a way that links personal and collective memory. She highlights (in the context of the Holocaust) that public silencing is harmful for the individual as it delegitimizes personal history. Historian Catherine Merridale (1999, 1996) conducted interviews in countries of the former Soviet Union, where the communist regime had systematically suppressed public mention of the massive loss of human life during the Stalin era. Although the Russians she interviewed would share their stories of suffering and hardship with family and friends, they had no way of processing their losses in the context of society at large.

According to psychologist Yael Danieli (1998, 7), an individual's identity involves a complex interplay of multiple spheres or systems, including the biological and intrapsychic; the interpersonal, familial, social, and communal; the ethnic and cultural; the religious and spiritual; and the political, national, and international. For a trauma to be integrated, it must be addressed in all the affected systems, including on the level of society. Danieli stresses the importance of public acknowledgment of trauma for the healing process. She speaks for Holocaust survivors and other victims of gross human rights violations rather than for the much more morally complex situation of a perpetrator country, such as Germany in World War II. On a strictly psychological level, the argument is still applicable. In the context of the Vietnam veterans (also at least partly considered "perpetrators"), for example, it was often pointed out that negative public opinion vis-à-vis the US engagement in the war and a lack of recognition hindered the soldiers' psychological adaptation after their homecoming and contributed to their ongoing mental health issues (see for example Lifton 1973).

From the Late 1960s to the Early 1990s: The Need to "Master the Past," the Centrality of Holocaust Memory, and the Exclusion of Wartime Suffering

With a new generation coming of age in the 1960s, different accounts of the Third Reich and World War II appeared. Younger historians no longer attributed the war to a small group of Nazis acting alone but to a National Socialist ideology that had been widely supported by the German people. The reasons for Hitler's rise to power, the Nazi war crimes, and the Holocaust took center stage in the public culture of commemoration. In 1969, Willy Brandt, who had fought against the Wehrmacht in the Norwegian resistance, became the first Social Democratic chancellor after 1945. His *Ost-Politik* heralded a new era of foreign relations with Eastern European countries and set the tone for the national memory for the next thirty years. Brandt believed it to be essential to publicly acknowledge and express remorse for the Nazi crimes. He famously fell to his knees in front of the memorial for Jews killed in the Warsaw ghetto (Vees-Gulani 2008). In political speeches, public commemorations, and history books, a new version of the past—in which German suffering and losses were the appropriate price to pay for the pain the nation had inflicted—became the dominant public narrative (Moeller 1996).

At the same time, the left-wing student movement of 1968 protested against the continuities between the Third Reich and the FRG, claiming that almost the entire bureaucratic, military, and political elite of the Nazi regime had found equivalent or better careers in the new state. Publicly, as well as at home with their families, young people demanded answers from their silent parents about their involvement in, or tacit support for, the atrocities of World War II, and they strongly identified with the victims of the Holocaust (see Jureit and Schneider 2010). Psychoanalysts Margarete and Alexander Mitscherlich's widely read book *The Inability to Mourn: Principles of Collective Behavior* (1967) criticized their fellow Germans for being in denial about their collective and personal responsibility for the crimes committed by the Nazi regime. This psychological mechanism had left them incapable of mourning the loss of Hitler, whom they had supported in overwhelming numbers, and also of feeling empathy for the millions of victims. The so-called "generation of '68" was born roughly between 1935 and 1950. In terms of age, these are the mothers and fathers of my interviewees. However, only Charlotte's parents, whose story will be told in chapter 6, directly participated in the protest movement. Most others came from predominantly conservative middle-class families, where the parents tended to condone the grandparents' silence and denials rather than challenge them.

By the end of the 1960s and up until today, the public focus in West Germany had clearly shifted. The dominant view of National Socialism and World War II has been one in which Germans were—if not collectively guilty—certainly collectively accountable for the war and the Holocaust. Public commemorations stress the need to remember the past and impart to the younger generations the moral responsibility to ensure that history will never repeat itself. The US TV miniseries *Holocaust*, broadcast in 1979, contributed to a change in public opinion. Almost half of the population over fourteen years of age watched at least part of the series. Viewers followed the struggle and suffering of the Jewish German Weiss family through the war and into the concentration camps. For the first time victims were turned into living, breathing people with individual histories instead of abstract statistics and piles of withered corpses. In the mid-1980s right-wing historians tried to juxtapose the murder of the European Jews with the mass murders under Stalin in an attempt to relativize the Holocaust in the "historians' controversy" (*Historikerstreit*). They were vehemently criticized and marginalized by the vast majority of academic voices, which affirmed the historic significance and singularity of Auschwitz.[2] Talking about German suffering and claiming any kind of victim status was deemed suspicious and was denounced as a denial of responsibility for the crimes committed. In his famous speech of May 8, 1985, commemorating the fortieth anniversary of the liberation from the Nazi regime, then president Richard von Weizsäcker confirmed that German crimes against humanity must remain at the center of public memory into the future:

> There is no such thing as the guilt or innocence of an entire nation. The vast majority of today's population were either children then or had not been born. They cannot profess guilt of their own for crimes that they did not commit. . . . But their forefathers have left them a grave legacy. All of us, whether guilty or not, whether old or young, must accept the past. We are all affected by its consequences and liable for it. The young and old generations must and can help each other to understand why it is vital to keep alive the memories. (von Weizsäcker 1985)

This has since remained the normative framework for German national memory, into which all the other memories have to be integrated (Assmann 2006b). At the same time, acknowledging the horrors of what Germans had done and accepting moral responsibility had all but closed off the space in which it was permissible to publicly discuss German losses. While some historians do not fully agree—as some accounts of wartime suffering can be found throughout the postwar period (for example Moeller 1996, 2005; Niven 2006a; Wittlinger 2006)—publicly speaking of German victimhood was largely considered a moral taboo from the late 1960s to the late 1990s.

It is daring to label West Germany's culture of commemoration of this time as "repressive erasure" (Connerton 2008), because the label has connotations of totalitarian regimes. Researchers have denounced the suppression of open debates about past mass losses in relation to the political purges under Stalin in the Soviet Union (Baker and Gippenreiter 1998; Merridale 1999, 2010) and to the crimes of the military junta in Chile under Pinochet (Becker and Diaz 1998). During the "Great Leap Forward" of the late 1950s and early 1960s in

China, tens of millions of people starved to death because of natural catastrophes compounded by economic mismanagement and political fervor. More than fifty years on, the Chinese Communist Party still has not officially acknowledged the massive loss of human life or publicly commemorated the victims (Feuchtwang 2011). However, "repressive erasures" do not necessarily have to take violent forms but can signify the existence of a master historical narrative that people are expected to internalize and that, while highlighting some aspects of history, at the same time neglects or deliberately edits out others (Connerton 2008, 60). Over the years, a number of public scandals have underscored that the officially sanctioned version of the German past is indeed quite prescriptive. Striking the wrong chord in a public speech or choosing words carelessly can easily derail or at least tarnish political, academic, or intellectual careers. One such example was the affair around Phillip Jenniger's controversial speech in November 1988, commemorating the fiftieth anniversary of the Kristallnacht (the Night of Broken Glass). Jenninger, then president of the German Parliament, attempted to explain the reasons behind the popular support of National Socialism. He failed to dissociate himself clearly from the ideas he outlined, calling them "fascinating," and his monotonous voice was perceived as not carrying enough empathy for the victims. More than fifty members of parliament walked out in protest, and the ensuing political storm forced Jenninger to resign, ending his career in politics (Fischer and Lorenz 2007, 240–42).

"We Never Talked about the Destruction": History Lessons in West German Schools in the 1970s and 1980s

A country's culture of commemoration is not only communicated in public policies and political debates, memorials and museums. It also filters into history books and lessons at school, where the aim is to impart knowledge about historical events to the younger generation and to cultivate certain attitudes vis-à-vis their nation's past. German studies scholar Rainer Bendick (2001, 541) explains that history books "relay patterns of perceptions and interpretation of the past, that are foundational to a society. . . . With their help, the next generation is expected to learn an understanding of history, which correlates with the self-image of the society in which they as adults will one day assume responsibilities."

Most Kriegsenkel were of high school age in the late 1970s and 1980s, and what they learned about National Socialism, World War II, and the Holocaust largely mirrored the public narratives of the time. Many of my West German interviewees remembered their history lessons quite clearly, although they had taken place almost thirty years earlier. The dominant impression was that National Socialism and the war were talked about a lot in the *Gymnasium*, which, belonging to middle-class families, the majority of them had attended.[3] Their teachers, especially the younger and more left-leaning ones who had received their training around the time of the protest movement of 1968, had put in great effort to teach their pupils about the widespread popular support for Hitler and about the horrors of the Holocaust. Students watched documentaries about the liberation of Auschwitz in class or visited concentration camps on school excursions. The message about the indescribable cruelty Germans were capable of hit home and left a deep impression on their developing attitudes toward their national identity. Brigitta, born in 1966, summarized her memories: "In the last few years of school, we only ever talked about the war. That was when the guilt came. For my sense of identity, it was very dark and gloomy. We were watching all these documentaries, the liberation of Auschwitz and so on. When I think back to my history lessons, those images are all I ever see."

Many Kriegsenkel read Anne Frank's *Diary of a Young Girl* in German literature class and watched documentaries about World War II or the episodes of the *Holocaust* miniseries on TV at home. Images of emaciated faces peering from behind barbed wire and of earthmovers pushing piles of dead bodies into mass graves are impossible to forget. Eva-Marie, born in 1967, reflected: "Every morning when I turn on the shower, I think about how the Jews were gassed, and that the Nazis experimented on them with boiling hot and freezing cold water. I think about these things very often, about the physical pain. I must have been fourteen or so when I watched the first documentaries, without any forewarning. Before that time, the world was still a good place."

Not everyone reacted in the same way or shared the same memories of the history lessons. Some said that World War II was such a constant and repetitive topic at school that they got to a stage of being "completely fed up with it." Others felt that although the war had been dutifully "worked through," it was not really discussed or analyzed in depth. Their teachers were often older, of the war generation themselves, and uncomfortable with the topic. They had avoided moving beyond a dry presentation of historical facts, which failed to reach their students emotionally. Sanna, born in 1974, admitted: "History lessons at school were really boring; they did not have anything to do with me at all. You had to read those fifteen-odd pages, and you had to learn things by heart for the exams, but I can't even recall those facts anymore now."

A handful of people said that they could not remember that the war had been a topic at school at all, either because it had not been part of the curriculum or because they had no recollection of it. While the latter explanation is plausible, given the long time span that has passed and the unreliability of human memory, history lessons were indeed not uniform for all schools. In West Germany, responsibility for the education system lies primarily with the *Länder*, (the states), each deciding on its own educational policies and school curricula.[4] Because the Kriegsenkel went to the *Gymnasium* at different times and in different parts of the country, it is quite possible that in some schools "history lessons had stopped at a time just before the war started," as a few of them claimed.

However, while each person remembered a degree of working through the war and Holocaust at school slightly differently, some aspects of their reports closely resembled one another. The focus always lay on the reasons for Hitler's rise to power, the factual history of World War II, and the systematic murder of six million Jews and countless other people in the concentration and extermination camps. Some teachers were more invested than others in imparting the message that the past needed to be remembered and that another Holocaust should never be allowed to happen again. This narrative always carried a moral weight and could not easily be questioned. "I always had the sense that there was no other option than to think of it [the war] as something very bad. You were quasi brainwashed to think like that. That was definitely the right thing to do, but . . ." Tom, born in 1969, summed up this sentiment, his hushed voice and uneasy look revealing his discomfort with admitting his conflicted emotions.

It went all but unnoticed that some aspects of World War II were missing from the history lessons altogether. Not one person recalled being told about the impact of World War II on the German civilian population, the bombing of German cities, or the expulsions from Eastern Europe. Before we were scheduled to meet for our first interview, Nora, born in 1959, went on the internet to look at photos of her hometown in 1945. She could not recall ever having seen images of her city in ruins before: "During *Heimatkunde* [local history and geography] lessons at school, we talked about rocks and things like that, but not about the destruction. Maybe they did not want to burden us kids with these things. But those photos of the destroyed city, I have the sense that I saw them for the first time last week."

Leafing through around 50 of the 100 to 150 different history books that were used in West German schools between 1949 and 2000, historian Bodo von Borries (2004) found that World War II took up on average about twenty pages, with a separate chapter on the persecution of the Jews and the Holocaust. Only one textbook used in schools in the 1970s and 1980s included some information about the bombing of German cities, and it also excluded information about the expulsions from the East and the violence inflicted by the Red Army in

1944–45. The calculations about German war casualties were "rather conservative" (Borries 2004, 403). As in other areas of society, in history books and history lessons the suffering of the German majority population took a step back to leave space for the consideration of the immeasurable pain the Germans had inflicted on their victims.

Most Kriegsenkel I interviewed firmly subscribed to the version of the past they had been inculcated in. They had deeply internalized the moral responsibility for their forebears' crimes and commitment to the Holocaust memory. The wartime suffering of their own families and of the German population more broadly remained in the background. Even if they may have had some factual knowledge, it did not fully reach their consciousness.

"ZERO HOUR" AND THE "VICTORS OF HISTORY": WORLD WAR II IN EAST GERMAN PUBLIC MEMORY

In East Germany, public narratives about World War II and National Socialism diverged from those of the West, and a substantially different view of the past was relayed to the population. However, while "victim" and "perpetrator" binaries were demarcated quite differently, they also ended up with a similar double phenomenon as in the early postwar period in the West: an even more pronounced exculpation from the crimes of the Nazi regime on the one hand coupled with a silencing of significant aspects of wartime suffering of the majority population on the other. Unlike in the West, however, the East German government upheld the same view of the past until the fall of the Berlin Wall in 1989.

The GDR was founded in October 1949, a few months after its West German counterpart. The new government under Walter Ulbricht comprised members of the former Communist Party. Persecuted by the Nazis, they had fled to the Soviet Union before the war and were now returning from exile as the self-proclaimed "victors of history" (Danyel 1995a, 32). The new political elite understood themselves as the heirs of the communist resistance against Hitler, directly treading in the footsteps of the victims and not the perpetrators of the Nazi regime. National Socialism was interpreted as an expression of fascist class rule against which the communists had battled. The memory of those who had died in the antifascist resistance took center stage in commemorative practices (Danyel 1995b). People like Ernst Thälmann, a communist leader imprisoned by the Nazis and killed in the Buchenwald concentration camp in 1944, were upheld as paragons of virtue to inspire current and future generations. At the end of the induction ceremony for the Young Pioneers, the Communist youth organization, each child received a red flag symbolically soaked with the blood of the many victims of the struggle for socialism (Moeller 2005).

With a founding myth constructed around communist martyrdom and the final victory over the Nazi regime, the East German government consequently rejected all political responsibility for Hitler's rise to power and the crimes committed in the German name. Although the East Germans in no way denied the Holocaust, the Jewish victims were often subsumed under the general term of "victims of fascism" (Danyel 1995b), and the Holocaust tended to be cited as a particularly cruel expression of fascist terror, without any distinctive significance or singularity. The end of the war was celebrated as "*Stunde Null*" ("Zero Hour"), the beginning of a new era with a clean slate, looking toward a brighter, socialist future. As in the West, the focus here too was on recovering economically and building a new and better society from the ruins. The gaze was firmly fixed on the future, not dwelling on the past. As in the West, people were expected to come to terms with the physical and emotional damage left by the war largely on their own.

However, as was the case in the Federal Republic immediately after the war, the general population was granted a certain measure of victimhood, portrayed here too as a group of powerless victims, in this case of "fascist seduction" (Moller 2003, 46). People were now given the chance to erase these past mistakes and to contribute to the building of the new Germany. The denazification measures were abandoned even more swiftly than in the other part of the country. The GDR saw itself as the "better Germany." It firmly pushed the main responsibility for World War II to the West, an alleged "paradise for war criminals" where fascism had lived on beyond 1945 (Moller 2003, 54). This view safely placed the perpetrators on the other side of the wall and exonerated the East German population from much of the collective guilt and responsibility that was so prominent in the West from the late 1960s. "We really did not work through what happened. It was always the Nazis who started the war, but it was never mentioned that the Nazis might also have been your neighbors. Millions of people had been ecstatic about Hitler, but suddenly everyone was an antifascist," Daniel, one of my East German interviewees, born in 1964, reflected.

From the beginning of the 1950s, annual ceremonies were held in Dresden, where in February 1945 American and British air raids had destroyed most of the city and had killed twenty-five thousand people. In the spirit of the Cold War, the bombing was explained as proof of the aggressiveness of the Western Allies promoting their fascist-imperialist interests. Susanne Vees-Gulani (2008) argues that by portraying bombing as a fascist act, East Germany equated the destruction of Dresden with the crimes committed under the Nazi regime and strengthened the idea of East Germans as victims.

There was a stern official silencing of all violence attributed to the Soviet Army. The soldiers of the Red Army were presented as having come to East Germany as communist heroes, friends, and liberators of the people. German expellees (*Vertriebene*) from the East were labeled more neutrally as "resettlers" (*Umsiedler*). In their speeches GDR politicians completely denied the fact that the Red Army had often forced those "resettlers" to leave their homes at the end of the war. Similarly, they did not mention the rape of German women and girls (Niven 2006b). These were not minor issues: around 4 million people had been "resettled" in East Germany after the war (Moeller 1996), and most of the estimated 1.9 million rapes were attributed to the Red Army (Radebold 2008). In my interviews with East Germans, the "communist brothers" were frequently referred to with cynicism and palpable anger.

Connerton (2008, 60) would probably label both the rejection of all responsibility for the rise and crimes of the Hitler regime and the official silencing of the violence of the Soviet Army as examples of "repressive erasures." While the government of the GDR selected certain things to be remembered, others were edited out of the master historical narrative, as was the case in the West. Although in the Federal Republic questions of how to "master the past" (Herf 1997) continued to be the topic of public debates and the attitudes toward the Third Reich and the Holocaust changed quite radically from the late 1960s, in East Germany the interpretations of National Socialism and World War II remained stable. The decades from the mid-1950s until the collapse of the GDR in 1989 are described as a time of "calcification" ("*Versteinerung*"; Moller 2003, 50) of the antifascist culture of commemoration.

However, in contrast to the official culture of commemoration relayed by politicians and the state media, a kind of "counter-memory movement" (Moller 2003, 55) emerged in East German literature. Widely read books like Christa Wolf's *Kindheitsmuster* (Patterns of childhood, 1976) or Jurek Becker's *Jakob der Lügner* (Jakob the Liar, 1969) challenged the official party line and asked critical questions about the true relationship between the population and its support for National Socialism.[5]

"We Did Not Have Any Nazis Here": History Lessons in the 1970s and 1980s, East German Style

The East German state centrally managed and controlled the education system. From 1963 until the fall of the Berlin Wall in 1989, Margot Honecker, the wife of

Erich Honecker—chair of the SED Central Committee and head of state—was the minister for education. School curricula were uniform across the country. All students were expected to learn the same content. Only one history book was used up to year ten across the state, and it was revised regularly every eight years (Borries 2004). Political socialization was an integral part of education and of at least equal importance as the transmission of factual knowledge.[6] It is therefore not surprising that what my East German interviewees remembered from their history classes mirrored the official narrative. Students learned about the "imperialists" who had started the war, the communist resistance against Hitler, and the "liberation from fascist rule" by the "communist heroes." Karoline, born in 1967, explained: "We were told that it had all been very terrible, but now it was over. The Russians were our friends, they had saved us, and now everything was fine. It did not impress me much, but it did have something comforting. It was good that things had turned out this way."

Children and teenagers in the East also learned about the horrors of the Holocaust, and their teachers strongly condemned the Nazi crimes. Although they were as shocked by the images as their Western counterparts, many reported feeling distant from the crimes committed by their forebears. On the one hand, this distance arose because history was often taught only in broad and abstract ideological terms without any personal stories to which the students could relate. On the other hand, children in the GDR were brought up in the consciousness that they were the heirs of those heroic antifascist Germans, who had stood on the "right side of history." Christiane, born in 1966, remembered: "We watched those Russian war movies, where the Germans were always the bad guys, but that had nothing to do with me of course, because I was in the East."

Analyzing the content of school history books in both German states, Borries (2004) revealed that in the GDR the war took up around fifty pages—many more than in the West. Here, the focus was on the fight between the "imperialists" and the "socialists" and Hitler's war against the Soviet Union. The exploitation and genocide committed against the Russian people were described in grueling detail. The main responsibility, however, it was argued, lay with the Nazi regime, the upper class, and the capitalists, and not with the German population or the common soldiers. As a consequence, my East German interviewees did not absorb the same sense of shame and responsibility in relation to the war and Holocaust. Children going to school in the East were often under the impression that all the Nazis had fled to live in the West. It did not occur to them that their grandparents might have supported the Nazi Party. The East German Kriegsenkel I met seemed to carry less collective guilt as a result. "We knew that the Germans had started the war," Cornelia, born in 1964, said, "but the communists were the good guys of course, they were against the Nazis, and they had neither started nor continued the war, and so the question of guilt simply did not exist." For her, and for many others who grew up on the other side of the wall, those issues only came to consciousness after 1989.

While not feeling morally responsible, Cornelia was still emotionally affected by the Holocaust. More routinely than their West German counterparts, East German schoolchildren visited concentration camps on school excursions or for working bees to learn about those who had died in the antifascist struggle, a struggle that the younger generation was enlisted to continue. Cornelia recalled how as a relatively young child she had visited the Sachsenhausen and Buchenwald concentration camps and had watched documentaries about the Holocaust. As for many other teenagers, East and West, the experience was overwhelming, and the teachers did not provide any emotional support or space for discussion. Cornelia felt left alone with "all this horror and all these images."

Yet history lessons, documentaries, and official speeches were not the only sources of information about the past. Although it was illegal, many East Germans watched West German TV programs at home and consequently had access to differing views on the history of World War II. However, I still had the impression that most of the people I spoke to at the time accepted the GDR interpretation of past events. Other research comes to different conclusions. In 1987, a group of researchers from an East German institute in Leipzig anonymously questioned around two thousand East Germans (roughly the same age as my interviewees) about their views on National Socialism and World War II. They found that some of the responses strikingly contradicted the state-sanctioned narrative promoted by the schools. The team believed that the political education of the GDR had been ineffective. Its content had not been internalized, nor did it have much credibility in the eyes of young people (Moller 2003, 85–87).

Martin, born in 1966, fits with these findings, but he was the exception in my group. History lessons at school were "too stupid, too black and white" to convince Martin's questioning teenage mind. He did not buy the teachers' claim that all soldiers were fascists or Nazis, because his grandfather had been with the Wehrmacht and he, as far as Martin knew, was neither. Martin also had access to other sources of historical information from an early age. His father brought home history books from the university library for him to read. These books, which were printed in the West and were not publicly available in the GDR, painted a different picture of the war, a picture that Martin found more sophisticated and more believable.[7]

There was one particular topic on which his peers also questioned the official version of history presented by their teachers: when it came to the image of the Soviets as friends and liberators. The vast majority of rapes and other acts of violence the Red Army committed at the end of the war had happened in the territory that later became the GDR. Knowledge about these crimes circulated among friends and family, quietly and behind closed doors. A number of East German Kriegsenkel had an awareness of what had happened to the women in their neighborhoods or families. They found the official image of the virtuous communist heroes confusing at best. Parents would strongly impart to their children that these topics had to be kept in private and should not be mentioned outside the walls of the family home.

Although in the West students could in theory have questioned the way World War II was presented in class (though no one I talked to actually did), voicing dissent was riskier in the East. The official version could not be challenged without consequences. Alfred (born in 1963) recalled that one of his friends had dared to mention that Russian soldiers had raped his grandmother and that the boy had been "taken away" by the teacher. His sister Anna (born in 1965) was absolutely certain that had she raised her hand in history class to ask "What about all that injustice the Russians have done to us?" their parents would have gotten arrested. Aspects of German wartime suffering, which did not fit into the officially sanctioned narrative, were excluded from East German history classes as much as from West German ones. As in the broader East German community, this exclusion mainly concerned topics around the violence of the Red Army and the expulsions from Eastern Europe. Other topics, like the bombing of East German cities toward the end of the war, were not as tabooed and silenced. However, the information often remained abstract and intangible. A number of my interviewees confirmed that, growing up in the East, they had no real awareness of German civilian or military casualties. Daniel remembered how around the age of twenty he visited a war memorial and was stunned by the sudden realization that in fact "a lot of German civilians had perished, and not just Wehrmacht soldiers. Suddenly it became clear that this was not just a case of the 'bad Nazis' and the 'good Russians' but that this was my own history too."

In summary, at the time the Kriegsenkel went to school and started to read books and to watch TV in the 1970s and 1980s, what they learned about the war, National Socialism, and the Holocaust was quite uniform and prescriptive in both German states. Looking back thirty years later, people from either side of the wall said that they had largely accepted and internalized the narratives about World War II they were presented with. While different messages were relayed in terms of German perpetratorship, both parts of the country were united in that most aspects of German wartime suffering were either excluded from the curriculum altogether or marginalized to an extent that they did not leave any lasting impressions. This erasure did not encourage students to integrate aspects of German victimhood in their understanding of World War II history. Most of my interviewees, whether they were born in the East or in the West, had no awareness of that at all. This lack of knowledge explains the surprise about the discovery of the Kriegsenkel topic in recent years.

OPENING THE SPACE: THE REEMERGENCE OF GERMAN WARTIME SUFFERING IN THE NEW MILLENNIUM

With the fall of the Berlin Wall and the collapse of the GDR in 1989, the era of state antifascism expired as well. From 1990 the memory culture of the newly reunified Germany continued in line with the established West German precept without much public debate.

One significant event of the 1990s was the *War of Annihilation: Crimes of the Wehrmacht* exhibition, which was touring Germany and Austria from 1995 to 1999 and then again from 2001 (Heer and Stiftung Hamburger Institut für Sozialforschung 1997). The exhibition gave rise to heated debates because it showed that responsibility for the mass murder of the Jewish population did not simply lie with an inner circle around Hitler and the special units of the SS but that the regular soldiers of the Wehrmacht had taken an active part in these crimes. Millions visited the exhibition or read about it in the media, and many were shocked by its message. A second milestone was the debate surrounding Daniel Goldhagen's 1996 book *Hitler's Willing Executioners.* Goldhagen suggested that antisemitism had been widespread among ordinary Germans and that they had killed Jews willingly, rather than under compulsion. Both of these events stressed German perpetratorship, widening its space within the broad population rather than allowing the crimes to be externalized to a small clique of Nazis.[8]

While the general focus and tone of official commemorations remained the same, with the beginning of the new millennium a flood of memories of German wartime suffering suddenly appeared in the media, books, movies, and TV documentaries. The main works setting this new trend include Günther Grass's novel *Im Krebsgang* (*Crabwalk,* 2002), which tells the story of the sinking of the *Wilhelm Gustloff,* a passenger ship carrying German refugees in 1945. Five thousand people lost their lives when a Russian submarine torpedoed the ship in the Baltic Sea. There were also Winfried G. Sebald's *Luftkrieg und Literatur* (2001, published in English in 1999 as *On the Natural History of Destruction*) and Jörg Friedrich's *Der Brand* (*The Fire,* 2002), both turning public attention to the carpet-bombing of German cities and its devastating effect on the population. Lastly, the anonymous diary *Eine Frau in Berlin* (*A Woman in Berlin*, 2003) gives a painfully laconic autobiographical account of the systematic rape of German women by Russian soldiers in occupied Berlin in 1945. In *Crabwalk*, Grass claims that tales of German wartime suffering had long been excluded from a mainstream commemorative culture, allowing Germans to express collective shame only for what the Nazis had done to others but leaving them no space to mourn their own losses. Aleida Assmann (2006b) argues that while the exclusion of the victim narrative was never as complete as Grass stated, the emotional intensity of these accounts and their wide social resonance across different generations were indeed unprecedented.

One major contributing factor was that with the German reunification in 1990, the Cold War era had come to a conclusion. The new, less antagonistic international political landscape allowed for a move beyond the entrenched victim-perpetrator dichotomies (Moeller 2005). Simultaneously, worldwide reconciliation movements and truth commissions in countries such as South Africa, Peru, and Chile also aimed to transcend these narrow definitions and treaded new paths in an attempt to heal past violence. Besides, it was also a time when members of the war generation were retiring from their professional careers and were starting to look back on their lives. Memories that had previously been pushed aside reemerged with unprecedented emotional intensity. Social memory, as Aleida Assmann (2006b) notes, follows biological rhythms: where one generation is superseded by the next and in the liminal phase, memories can assert themselves with great emphasis. As the last generation of eyewitnesses came closer to passing away, personal memories of wartime survival and hardship that had been confined to the space of private conversations were swept into the public sphere and mediatized on a large scale. While the appropriateness of speaking of German suffering continued to be debated among historians and intellectuals (see, for example, Diner 2003), there was a clear sense that the taboo that had surrounded the topic in previous decades had been lifted. A space had cautiously opened up, in which it had become more acceptable to publicly discuss the traumatic impact of World War II on the German majority population without immediately causing suspicion of minimizing the Holocaust.

DISCOVERING THE ENDURING PSYCHOLOGICAL IMPACT OF THE WAR: THE "WAR CHILDREN" AND THE "WAR GRANDCHILDREN" MOVEMENTS

In the early 2000s Germans first started to systematically reflect on the possible long-term impact of traumatic war experiences on the majority population.

In the late 1990s psychoanalysts and psychotherapists had increasingly noticed occurrences of burnout, depression, flashbacks, panic attacks, and other anxiety disorders among their elderly patients. These people had been children at the time of World War II, and many of them were already in their sixties when they first showed (or sought help for) psychological symptoms. Many had led unremarkable lives until then and were retiring from successful professional careers. Psychoanalyst Hartmut Radebold was the first to come to the conclusion that childhood experiences of war could be the cause behind the psychological disorders among his elderly patients (Radebold 2000, 2004, 2005, 2008). They were labeled the *Kriegskinder* (war children) generation.

Until that time, psychotherapists did not ask their patients about the war or National Socialism at all (Ermann 2007; Heimannsberg and Schmidt 1992; Radebold 2012). Psychiatrist Philipp Kuwert, who offers therapy to German seniors suffering from war trauma, commented in 2008: "We're only now able to examine the suffering and listen to what people here went through without being suspected of trivializing the Holocaust . . . If I had done this work 20 years ago I would probably have needed a bodyguard" (in Crossland 2008). Historians, psychologists, and other social scientists began to investigate the issue of war childhoods—often their own. The growing interest culminated in the 2005 war children convention in Frankfurt am Main. Around six hundred people attended to discuss their findings and share personal stories. The meeting marked the beginning of the Kriegskinder's emergence as a distinctive and recognized generation (Wierling 2010). A wealth of studies on the topic emerged in the following years (for example, Ermann 2007; Grundmann, Hoffmeister, and Knoth 2009; Hondrich 2011; Janus 2006; Radebold 2000, 2004, 2005; Seegers and Reulecke 2009). The overarching claim is that, largely unnoticed until that time, the difficult experiences of World War II had a major and lasting impact on a person's biography. These war children are the parents of my interviewees, the mothers and fathers of my generation. How growing up with them affected the generation of the Kriegsenkel—the war *grand*children—was the question raised in a subsequent wave of psychological exploration.

As mentioned in the introduction, journalists Anne-Ev Ustorf and Sabine Bode published the first popular books about the Kriegsenkel generation in 2008 and 2009. They introduce the life histories of Germans born roughly between 1955 and 1975 to parents and grandparents who experienced the war firsthand. The authors portray them in their struggles to find a clear direction in life and a sense of identity and belonging. They suffer from depression, burnout, and anxiety disorders; some feel blocked in their careers, and others have a general sense of going through life with the hand brake on. Their problems are set in direct relation to their families' unresolved war experiences, which are implied to be at the root of these psychological issues. Ustorf's and Bode's books were the first to raise the topic of the transgenerational impact of World War II, and a number of newspaper articles and radio programs covered the issue while I was in Berlin. Since then a small war grandchildren movement has gained some momentum. Interested people now meet in support groups that have formed in many German cities, while websites and Facebook groups provide information and networking opportunities. A number of therapists have gathered around the scene, offering weekend workshops and individual therapy to alleviate the problems resulting from a perceived transgenerational transmission of war experiences.

GERMANY IN 2012: THE END OF ALL TABOOS?

The Germany that I encountered in 2012 was noticeably more relaxed with its history and national identity than the country I had left twenty years earlier. That summer during the UEFA European Football Championship, Berlin was drowning in a sea of German flags. They were everywhere: on T-shirts, scarves, and hats; stuck to cars, trucks, and bicycles; and painted on people's faces. Hundreds of thousands gathered around big public screens to cheer on the national team. President Joachim Gauck said in a newspaper interview that coming generations would be less burdened by the guilt of their forefathers and that it had now become possible again to feel pride in Germany's political achievements (Hildebrandt and Di Lorenzo 2012). Stand-up comedians no longer shied away from impersonating Hitler to mock German tidiness and obsession with rules and regulations, and a store even had a comic book entitled *Hipster Hitler* on display. Timur Vermes (2012) published his best-selling satirical novel *Er ist wieder da* (Look who's back). It features Adolf Hitler waking up on a park bench in modern-day Berlin, his clothes still drenched with the gasoline used to burn his body in 1945. Hitler becomes a star on TV and YouTube while, to everyone's amusement, promoting very much the same ideas as in his last incarnation. All of the above would have been unthinkable two decades ago. None of the activists of the war grandchildren scene or the authors I interviewed were criticized for bringing the topic of transgenerational transmission of war trauma into the public sphere. Nor were there any attempts to instrumentalize their views to equate the suffering of the majority population with that of Holocaust survivors and their descendants. Yet there were also signs that the reluctance to publicly speak about German victimhood had not completely disappeared and that the issue of how to "correctly" talk about the war was still emotionally charged.

People still chose their words carefully in public, and a deeply engrained sense of discomfort remained. Journalist Merle Hilbk called it a kind of "knee-jerk reaction" that makes Germans automatically pull away from the subject.[9]

In addition, while it had become more acceptable to discuss German wartime suffering, the culture of commemoration as such had not changed. In 2010, historian Ulrike Jureit and sociologist Christian Schneider found that the past and in particular the Holocaust have to be remembered according to a rigid formula that is not open for debate, which they call "prescriptive remembering" ("*Normiertes Erinnern,*" Jureit and Schneider 2010, 33). This way of remembering, the authors claim, does not capture the entire range and complexity of experiences during the time of National Socialism and World War II, as it still excludes certain aspects of the past. For example, it prohibits the sharing of positive memories that some older people still have of everyday life under National Socialism. Jureit and Schneider conclude that the culture of commemoration is still inflexible, with sanctions imposed on those who deviate from the narrowly defined path.

At the same time, when I returned to Berlin in summer 2013, large posters with a photo of Auschwitz and the slogan "Late. But not too late! Operation Last Chance" accompanied me on my walks through the boiling hot city. The Simon Wiesenthal Center in Jerusalem was offering rewards of up to 25,000 euros for information that would help track down the last surviving war criminals so they could be put on trial before their deaths.[10] The posters were a stark reminder that, close to seventy years after the end of World War II, many Holocaust victims were still waiting for the murderers of their families to be brought to justice.

The Germans I met were only slowly adapting to the new openness. They still felt more comfortable sharing their family stories in private or in the safe space of a support group rather than under the scrutiny of the public eye. However, in the more diverse public culture of 2012–13, the space had opened up wide enough to enable my interviewees to look back on their lives through new eyes, and to allow for experiences of wartime suffering and trauma to be discussed and integrated into their family histories. It was the first time that many of them had looked at their families from this angle: "It would never have occurred to me that my parents and grandparents were traumatized," one woman said in an interview with Bremen's *Weserkurier*, "and that had a lot to do with shame, because they belonged to the generation of the perpetrators" (Müller 2013). While some of my interviewees mentioned the long exclusion of German suffering from public discourses in passing, it was accepted as a moral necessity without any complaints or openly voiced resentment.

It may not be the end of all taboos. However, because of the passage of time and the changed political situation of a reunited Germany and Europe, many of the silences—from "humiliated silence" and "desire to forget" to "repressive erasure" (Connerton 2008)—that have characterized the public debates in Germany at different times in the postwar years have been revoked or softened. The last members of the eyewitness generation are encouraged to overcome their "desire to forget," to break their "humiliated silence," and share their memories of World War II with an interested public. While some restrictions in the culture of commemoration remain, the "repressive erasure" of German wartime suffering has been lifted.

The next chapter moves to the space of the German family to explore how the intergenerational communication about the war was shaped. It will show how public silences around German victimhood were compounded by silences in the private realm.

NOTES

1. Sönke Wortmann's 2004 movie *Das Wunder von Bern* (*The Miracle of Bern*) gives an accurate impression of the conflicts that arose when a father suddenly returned to his family after the war and a long imprisonment in a Russian POW camp.

2. For a brief summary of the "historians' debate" and its different positions, see Fischer and Lorenz, 2007, 238–40.

3. *Gymnasium* is a form of secondary school, which students attend from the age of ten to around nineteen, and which academically prepares students for university.

4. For an overview of the West German education system, see Jürgen Baumert, Kai S. Cortina, Achim Leschinsky, and Karl Ulrich Mayer, *Das Bildungswesen in der Bundesrepublik Deutschland: Strukturen und Entwicklungen im Überblick* (2003).

5. Jurek Becker's book follows the story of Jacob Heym in the ghetto of Łódź. He lies to his fellow inmates by pretending to possess a forbidden radio, which allegedly broadcasts information about the advancing Soviet Army, helping them to keep their hopes alive. In *Kindheitsmuster* Christa Wolf travels back to the small town in Poland where she grew up as part of a large family during World War II. From her memories, she pieces together the everyday life of a typical German family during the war, and she deconstructs the often-repeated myth that the population did not know anything about the Holocaust.

6. For an overview of the education system of the GDR, see Hubert Hettwer, *Das Bildungswesen in der DDR: Strukturelle und inhaltliche Entwicklung seit 1945* (1976).

7. Martin suspected that his father might have had connections to the East German Ministry for State Security, the *Staatssicherheit* (commonly known as the *Stasi*), which could explain his privileged access to otherwise restricted information.

8. See Fischer and Lorenz, *Lexikon der 'Vergangenheitsbewältigung' in Deutschland* (2007, 288–90), for a brief introduction to the *Crimes of the Wehrmacht* exhibition and the same source, 295–97, for a summary of the Goldhagen debate.

9. Interview with Merle Hilbk, January 22, 2013.

10. See Operation: Last Chance. Accessed November 9, 2019. http://www.operationlastchance.org.

TWO

"WHY DO YOU HAVE TO DIG AROUND IN THE PAST?"

Conversations about World War II in German Families

HOLGER, BORN IN 1970, said: "In my family no one ever talked about the war. My grandfather was at the front and my grandmother was alone at home in Berlin with three small children. Half the house was destroyed, and they lived in what was left of it. It is just not possible that they did not have anything to talk about. But it was never, never, ever a topic at home."

Chapter 1 focused on the shifting public narratives about World War II. Chapter 2 now zooms into the private space of the German family. Some historians argue that, in contrast to dominant public discourses, stories of wartime suffering and hardship were very much part of everyday conversations in many German households, even during the years of public silencing (for example, Assmann 2006b; Welzer, Moller, and Tschuggnall 2002; Wierling 2010). This implies that two parallel narratives existed in the public and in the private domain, shaped by distinctly different norms around what could be shared and what was considered taboo. While this may have been true for families with a more open culture of communication, my research suggests that in the majority of German families the war was not much of a topic at all. German psychiatrist Hartmut Radebold also estimates that in around 80 percent of all families the war was "never talked about" at home, and in the remaining 20 percent either "a bit" or "too much," with parents overwhelming their children with their memories (Radebold 2012). At first glance, this is in line with the responses I received; 81 percent of my interviewees said that their family had remained silent about the war. However, this chapter will show that, beyond initial appearances, what people meant was not "complete silence" but rather "not enough talk."

Instead of dividing families into two distinctive groups of "those who talked" and "those who did not," I suggest a spectrum of family communication about World War II with varying degrees of silence and sharing. At one end of this spectrum are parents and grandparents who categorically brushed aside all curious questions about the war or who would casually drop a few emotionally charged lines into a conversation without further explanation. Or they volunteered a limited number of habitually repeated anecdotes of wartime hardship and everyday survival. Then there was the middle ground of open sharing of personal wartime stories, with incessant talking at the other end of the scale. At the core of this chapter lies a detailed mapping out of the patterns of family communication along this spectrum, seen through the eyes of the Kriegsenkel generation. For this, I enlist the help of Ruth Wajnryb's (2001) book *Silence: How Tragedy Shapes Talk*. Wajnryb, an Australian linguist and daughter of Polish Holocaust survivors, systematized the communication patterns in survivor families from the perspectives of the children. She comes to a similar conclusion that a binary division into "homes with talk, homes without talk" cannot adequately express the complexity of the intergenerational communication. She suggests that "Holocaust narrative might be placed on the continuum, from homes where communication was explicit and direct to homes where the past was hermetically sealed off" (Wajnryb 2001, 170). I am very conscious that drawing on this (and other) Holocaust research in the context of non-Jewish German families is difficult and may be offensive to some readers. I share this unease and would like to reiterate that it is in no way my intention to compare or weigh up the different experiences of suffering or to relativize the trauma of the Holocaust victims and their descendants. I do believe, at the same time, that the extensive body of research on Holocaust survivors and their families provides important analytical tools and lenses that can be applied more broadly.

The main purpose of this chapter is to give the reader an impression of how communication about World War II was (and often still is) structured in German families, what was talked about at home and how, and what was silenced and why. We will find that silences and taboos were not only established by the parents and grandparents but also often accepted and sometimes even reinforced by the younger generation, showing the latter as active players rather than passive victims in the family dynamic. The chapter also illustrates that the public culture of commemoration did in fact reach into the private sphere, shaping the dynamic between the generations and substantially influencing the dialogue about the past. Denial of responsibility from the older generation and judgment and grueling questions from the younger were not conducive to an atmosphere of trust and openness, in which difficult memories of the war could have been shared freely. Those attitudes also led to the creation of blind spots around experiences of wartime suffering, a topic that often remained absent from conversations or that was blocked from fully entering the younger generation's consciousness.

FROM CATEGORICAL SILENCE TO INCESSANT TALK: THE SPECTRUM OF FAMILY COMMUNICATION ABOUT WORLD WAR II

Three familial generations were typically involved in family conversations about World War II. The grandparents, born around 1900, who experienced the war as adults. The grandmothers were generally the main carers of the family, and the grandfathers were Wehrmacht soldiers and later prisoners of war in Russian or Allied POW camps. Secondly there were the parents, who were children or young teenagers at the time. Lastly the Kriegsenkel themselves, the grandchildren, born predominantly in the 1960s and 1970s.

After the heavy destruction of the war, life in both parts of Germany focused on rebuilding the country and securing a better future for present and future generations. In the West, many were grasping the opportunities presented by the "economic miracle." All their efforts went into working hard and creating wealth and financial stability. In the East, the focus was similarly on work. However, with the economic recovery coming much more slowly than in the West, people also focused on managing everyday life with scarce material resources. While the physical scars of the war were still visible, as gaps in cityscapes, dilapidated buildings, and overgrowing heaps of rubble, all hopes were set on the future, and little time was set aside for reflecting on the past.

The dominant family structure of the time was the "deutsche Normalfamilie" (Peuckert 2002), a nuclear family with parents and their underage children living together in the same household. In the West that mostly entailed the traditional role distribution with the father working as the main breadwinner and the mother looking after the children. In East Germany mothers commonly worked outside the home (Schneider 1994). Almost all of my interviewees grew up in these types of families; only a handful lived with a single parent after a divorce or the early death of the father. The households typically did not extend beyond two generations, with the grandparents living in separate houses and often in different cities. However, many Kriegsenkel regularly visited at least one set of grandparents or spent their school holidays with them. Having all four grandparents alive and close by was an exception. Many grandfathers had not returned from the war, and the German division had torn families apart, placing them on opposite sides of the wall, which made frequent visits difficult. Initially, the grandparents were often the main source of information about the family's past, in particular in situations where the parents were born toward the end of the war and had few memories of their own to share. In the 1980s and 1990s, the older generation had mostly passed away, and the Kriegsenkel had finished high school and left home. Opportunities to talk about the family history were limited to occasional visits, Christmas get-togethers, and other family events.

While these characteristics applied to most of the families of my interviewees, when it came to the patterns and dynamics of intergenerational communication, no two families were alike. Each one had its own unique way to negotiate the dialogue between the generations, and although I found a number of common styles and patterns, there was diversity in the individual mix. In many cases more than just one communication style was described, and some members of the family were more open than others. The younger generation's responses to what was shared and what was taboo also differed, as did perceptions among siblings.

In addition, the family dynamic sometimes changed over time and in accordance with different life cycles. Some Kriegsenkel had tried to query their parents and grandparents from childhood. Often the interest in the family history only emerged in their teenage years, when questions around identity and belonging gained in importance and a phase of intense probing began. Then the topic often withdrew into the background and other concerns—first love, education, career, marriage, and children—took center stage. In 2012, in the middle of their lives, many of my interviewees returned to the topic, while others were asking questions for the first time. This new or renewed interest was spurred by the Kriegsenkel books, by midlife crises and their associated reflections on life, or by the questions of my interviewees' own teenage children. In some cases, the parents, now in their seventies and eighties, were taking stock at the end of their lives and were a bit more willing to open up and share memories of their war childhoods with their sons and daughters.

"In My Family No One Ever Talked about the War": Silence(s)

When I asked my interviewees "Did your family talk about the war?" in more than 80 percent of all cases the answer was a definite "Nein, sie haben geschwiegen": "No, they remained silent." The way they used the German verb *schweigen* implied a conscious decision not to share certain experiences. It was judged to be a deliberate choice to withhold information. Therefore, *silence* was not seen as synonymous with *forgetting*, nor was it passive, because "the things we are silent about are in fact actively avoided" (Zerubavel 2010, 33).

However, when I probed further, it quickly became clear that the wall of silence was not as impermeable as initially asserted. Even in the case of Holger (quoted at the beginning of this chapter), who was most adamant that there was no conversation about the family history whatsoever, the past still seeped through the cracks in obscure remarks, charged reactions, and inexplicable behaviors. What many Kriegsenkel were referring to was not a complete absence of any form of communication. It was an atmosphere of secrecy, taboos, and hushed voices, of fragmented stories and disjointed anecdotes, surrounded by a conspicuous lack of willingness to share family stories and respond to questions openly and in ways that my interviewees would have found acceptable. *Silence* simply meant *not enough talk*. In English, this *schweigen* is more appropriately captured by using the term in its plural form—*silences*—to express those aspects of the past that were excluded from conversation (see Winter 2010).

"You Don't Know What Happened to Us": Obscure Remarks, Throwaway Lines, and Story Fragments

A common way to relay information about World War II in German families came in the form of obscure remarks or throwaway lines. About half (48%) of my interviewees mentioned that their parents or grandparents made sporadic and fragmentary references to the war, often weaving them into everyday conversations without any further explanation or broader context. Charlotte, born in 1966, whose story will be told in detail in chapter 6, recalled hearing her grandmother sigh that "everything used to be different and better in the past" and that "families had to flee," but as a child she had no idea what exactly that meant. Later, when she found out more about the family history, she was able to interpret these comments in light of her grandmother's flight from the Czech Republic and the fact that she had to leave her house and belongings behind to start from scratch as a penniless refugee in Germany in 1945. Reto (born in 1969) recalled remarks that "there was not enough bread," which puzzled him and left him feeling that there was more behind the story, something that his parents did not want to say. There was often an underlying emotional charge, clearly perceived behind those short and seemingly unspectacular comments, which made them stand out from the ebb and flow of mundane everyday conversations. It burned them into a person's memory so that they could still easily be recalled thirty years later. Karoline (born in 1967) articulated this particularly well:

> When my grandma was still alive, she used to rant about the Russians a lot. She must have had some terrible memories, but that all remained very foggy.

> We never found out what actually happened. But Grandma could never understand that we had Russian friends. Every time she heard about that, she got really upset and kept repeating, "You just don't know what happened to us." These moments when she said that stuck in my memory, because she said it so many times, but also because she seemed so different from her normal self, and that made me listen very carefully. She used to grumble a lot, and I never really paid much attention, but when she ranted about the Russians and how terrible it all had been, I knew I had to perk up my ears. Every time we talked about school and that we had Russian pen pals, the same tirades: "You don't know how horrible they are." But how? She would not say.

Karoline clearly felt that there was a painful story hidden behind her grandmother's outbursts, but without a context she could not make sense of them. According to Ruth Wajnryb (2001, 175–76), throwaway lines, obscure remarks, and cued messages belong to the realm of indirect communication. Meaning is construed to large extent by the listeners, who calibrate what they hear against what they know, looking for a fitting interpretation. For Karoline, who was born in East Germany, it was not until after the fall of the GDR in the 1990s, when more information about the violence inflicted by Soviet occupying forces became publicly available, that she finally found a plausible explanation for her grandmother's behavior. Boris (born in 1966) told how his parents only hinted at what he now thinks of as traumatic wartime experiences, providing fragments of stories without ever sharing them in their entirety. His mother would offer glimpses of her childhood memories in short sentences such as "There was an air raid alarm, and we went into a tunnel," but there the story ended. When he asked his father about his time as a fifteen-year-old *Flakhelfer* (antiaircraft helper or flak helper), his father would only disclose, "We were stationed in front of the Cologne Cathedral." Boris could not extract any more details of how these situations unfolded or how his parents had felt at the time. "It was like an extremely shortened witness statement," the trained lawyer said to me, his face revealing his lifelong frustration. Like Karoline, he also clearly picked up on the atmosphere behind these story fragments. Feelings of danger, panic, and fear of death lurked behind the silences that his parents fiercely defended all through Boris's childhood and adult years.

Attempts to probe deeper into the family history were typically brushed off with sentences such as "You children don't understand," or "Why do you need to dig around in the past?" Elise (born in 1961) wanted to know more about her parents' biography, but her curiosity was smothered with the categorical statement "You are much too small to understand these things." She was amazed that, even at fifteen or sixteen, she was still considered "too small" to be trusted with a more elaborate response. At some point, she just stopped asking. Similar to Wajnryb's (2001) findings among second-generation Holocaust survivors, information about World War II in non-Jewish German families often remained fragmented, patchy, and disjointed. Stories were "leaking out" (Wajnryb 2001, 178) over time, pieced together bit by bit over years of tedious questioning or inferred from obscure remarks and charged reactions. The piecemeal nature of the available information and the remaining gaps meant that in many cases these fragments never amounted to a complete story. Many of my interviewees expressed a deeply felt frustration about their families' unwillingness to share stories from the past. The process of continuous questioning was experienced as tiresome and aggravating. Some people felt that family secrets and taboos swallowed up their life-force like black holes and prevented them from letting go of the past and focusing on their own lives.[1]

"Eat Up, You Don't Know How Lucky You Are": Dicta and Life Lessons

Another common way to refer to the war came in the form of dicta and life lessons. More than 40 percent of my interviewees remembered their parents and grandparents making selective references to past times of hardship when disciplining their children or attempting to impart to them certain moral values and behaviors. Members of the war generation tended to display certain fixations that showed in everyday life. They often compulsively hoarded food and other household items like candles and oil in preparation for a possible crisis. Many refused to throw out food even long after the expiration date and forced their children to eat everything on their plates. "Food cannot be wasted" was the abiding truth. Anna's father went to the extreme to force his children to eat apple cores he had pulled out from the garbage to teach them that they "don't know what it means to go hungry." The past was woven into daily family life through those short references, purposely invoked whenever the situation called for it. "We always had to be grateful," Brigitta said, "because we had so much more than they did at the time." Complaints about what parents saw as minor inconveniences of a comfortable childhood in times of peace and prosperity were often not tolerated. Most Kriegsenkel recalled their parents telling them to "stop whining" and get on with whatever was expected of them.

Another set of common and very powerful dicta specific to German families revolved around the horrors of war. Statements like "*Nie wieder Krieg*" ("No more war") and "War is the worst thing that can happen to people" were repeated over and over again. All through their childhood and adolescence, the Kriegsenkel witnessed their parents being terrified of a third world war, from the Cuban missile crisis in the 1960s to the nuclear arms race of the 1980s.

It deeply affected their developing psyches. Brigitta is a typical example. She and her siblings were raised in a strictly pacifist spirit, not allowed to play cowboys and Indians or have toy weapons. She vividly remembered her mother's uncharacteristic bout of rage and scolding when she once caught her kids aiming at each other with the neighboring children's water guns. The fear of another war shaped the political views of both generations. Many Kriegsenkel objected to joining the Bundeswehr (the German Army), which was still compulsory at the time they finished school. A strong antiwar movement culminated at the time of the first Iraq war in the early 1990s and extended to the US invasion of Iraq in 2002, which 70 percent of all Germans opposed (Bode 2006, 119–22). The generation who had lived through the hardship and horrors of war imparted peace as the highest ideal, and many Kriegsenkel I spoke to still adhered to this belief.

Parents and grandparents also made reference to World War II to transmit life lessons, which they had learned in those difficult times, to their children and grandchildren. "You have to cherish what you have, and the most important thing you have is your life," Karsten's (born in 1966) parents often said. Martina's (born in 1967) grandparents' philosophy was that "material things don't matter, only life matters." Anna's father stressed the importance of a good education because "no one can take that away from you," while Charlotte's family took home from the war that "life is a struggle; you can only rely on yourself, not on others." Some of the lessons families tried to impart were perceived as odd. Reto (born in 1969) remembered that he had to eat a lot of onions as a child because his grandfather was adamant that onions had saved his eyesight during his years in a Russian POW camp. Jens (born in 1971) recalled that his father forced him and his sister to learn a musical instrument in case they lost their livelihood in a future war and needed a skill to make money. Here, the reference to the war was direct, deliberate, and clearly understood even if the experiences that led to these "abiding truths" were not shared in more detail.

Parents and grandparents across cultures use this kind of pedagogy, invoking past times of hardship to remind their children of how much more comfortable their life is by comparison and to impart to them the value of the most important things in life. Food almost always plays a central role in this, from Holocaust survivor homes (Wajnryb 2001) to families of survivors of the Cambodian genocide (Kidron 2009a) and those of the Dutch fighting the Nazis in the resistance (Op den Velde 1998). Similar messages were transmitted in families of Japanese Americans who were interned as alleged enemies during World War II (Nagata 1998) and in the "whip talk" (Feuchtwang 2011, 96) of Chinese parents who lived through the severe famine of the "Great Leap Forward" in the early 1960s. "Remember the days of starvation," these older Chinese warned their children when they did not want to finish their meals (Feuchtwang 2011).

In the case of the German Kriegsenkel, the younger generation sometimes consciously moved away from these lessons over the course of their lives. Quite a few still needed to have a full fridge to feel secure, but many others did not. Jens, who had just had a new baby when I spoke to him in the summer of 2012, decided that his son would never have to eat everything on his plate and would be encouraged to choose for himself whether he wanted to learn a musical instrument or not.

Disjointewd Anecdotes and Adventure Stories

Apart from those obscure remarks, throwaway lines, and food-related "whip talk," narratives about World War II in about half (48%) of my interviewees' families were restricted to the sharing of a limited number of anecdotes conveying wartime hardship, loss, and survival. Grandmothers would tell stories of foraging to feed the family, of making clothes out of curtains, of packing their belongings onto a horse cart and joining the treks heading West at the end of the war. Grandfathers shared vignettes of French wine and Russian winters and hard physical labor in POW camps. Parents' memories of their childhoods revolved around being woken up in the middle of the night, grabbing their most beloved toys, and running to air-raid shelters. They talked of being separated from their mothers during *Kinderlandverschickung*, when city children were evacuated to the countryside, and of playing in the rubble of destroyed houses looking for shrapnel pieces and bullet casings.

These stories were often told casually and in passing, without a fixed form or a clear beginning and end, shared on occasions like family gatherings, while the families watched TV or a slide show (Keppler 1994). Christiane's mother reminisced about everyday life during World War II whenever the family met, in particular around Christmas time, when "one talked about life in general."

There are a limited number of styles in which these stories were told. There were the "adventure stories," for example, emphasizing the family's resilience, bravery, and survival skills. Some parents and grandparents shared their recollections in great detail, creating in their audience the impression of entering into the world of the past, where the experiences were still extremely vivid. "My mother and grandmother were very fearful women, and when they talked about the war, it was like it was yesterday. I had the sense I was there with them," Paula (born in 1964) said. Others displayed a conspicuous lack of emotion, telling even the most horrific stories in a matter-of-fact style of delivery or with nonspecific language, which led away from personal experience ("Every woman had her turn with the soldiers").

In some cases, there was a sense of discordance, where the emotions did not seem appropriate for the scenario described. Paula remembered: "My mum always said how handsome her father looked in his Wehrmacht uniform, how shiny his boots were. She always said this with the broadest smile, and her eyes were sparkling. She probably really felt like that at the time. But my grandfather died, and all the other emotions, like her pain, you did not get to feel those. She was just beaming with joy when she talked, but that did not fit with the story, because the story was just horrible."

Similar to Wajnryb's (2001, 186) findings among families of Holocaust survivors, the stories the German Kriegsenkel heard of wartime events seemed somehow "laminated, static and unchanging." They tended to remain the same over the decades, told again and again, always using the same words. The listeners often knew them by heart. Interestingly, some psychologists view this kind of ritualistic retelling as another form of silence because the most emotionally challenging or traumatic aspects of an experience would often be left out (see Ancharoff, Munroe, and Fisher 1998; Baer and Frick-Baer 2010). There also sometimes remained a suspicion that the stories were sanitized (Wajnryb 2001, 208), leaving unexplained gaps with important information missing or certain people excluded altogether. A few times during my interviews a person would suddenly pause to say, "I just realized that this story does not make any sense at all. How come I have never noticed this before?" This fixed repertoire of anecdotes gave the younger generation at least some impression of what their parents and grandparents experienced during the war, and it satisfied their curiosity about the family history to an extent. However, those vignettes often remained scattered, disjointed, and incomplete, without ever providing a full picture. German historians Vesper and Weber (1991) claim that a coherent narrative of the familial past can only be woven once a sufficient number of anecdotes is known, allowing the listeners to thread them together without too many gaps and contradictions. Most Kriegsenkel did not know enough anecdotes. Frustration, helplessness, and sadness about this situation clearly came through in many of our conversations. So did a deep yearning for more knowledge and a sound chronology of past events, which would provide a sense of continuity and allow them to insert their own life stories into the pictures of greater family chronicles.

Taboo Topics: Soldiers, War Crimes, and Sexual Violence

As mentioned at the beginning of this chapter, German researchers often claim that aspects of wartime suffering, while largely excluded from public narratives, found an alternative space of expression in the private conversations between family members. The examples given above showed that some stories of personal loss and hardship did indeed have a place in the family communication—at least in those families where anecdotes from World War II were shared. However, even in these cases the stories often revolved around a limited range of topics, while others remained firmly taboo. This holds true in particular for information about the grandparents' support for Hitler and National Socialist ideology, the grandfathers' involvement in active combat and war crimes, and experiences of sexual violence against the women in the family. Vesper and Weber (1991, 68) noticed that family stories tended to be gendered and that what was passed on were often the grandmothers' tales of wartime hardship and everyday survival. The male experience, on the other hand, generally remained patchy. The interviewees (who were of the parent generation) knew a few facts about their fathers' time with the Wehrmacht. Yet what they had witnessed, how they had felt, and what they had participated in remained taboo. The thread was only picked up again once they found themselves in POW camps, where the tales of survival suddenly became more colorful and detailed. This is largely in line with my research, but with a few exceptions. In the case of my interviewees whose fathers had been drafted into the Wehrmacht at a very young age, they tended to be much more forthcoming about their experiences. One of the possible reasons for their openness could be that because of their age they felt less guilt and shame about their participation. In addition, while grandmothers might have told their stories more freely, this openness categorically excluded all accounts of sexual violence. The topic of rape was raised in almost half (43%) of my interviews, but rarely as a known fact and mostly only hinted at, as in Karoline's grandmother's case, or suspected by the descendants but vehemently denied by the family. A grandmother's story could suddenly be cut short without an explanation or could drift into general statements such as "everyone knew what happened to the women in the area" without any specifics as to who, what, where, or when.

When it came to war crimes, the wall of familial silence was insurmountable. Ludwig (born in 1978) remembered a photo of his great-grandfather in uniform on the mantelpiece at home. His great-grandfather had not returned from the war, and his official status was still "missing in action." Ludwig knew that he had been part of a police battalion and had been sent east, but no one in the family was willing to give him more information. Ludwig had learned from history books that police battalions followed the advancing Wehrmacht and were often responsible for the execution of Jews, a potential connection that he found deeply troubling but for which he could not get any confirmation.

Not knowing what role a family member had played in the war was a common source of anguish, as people filled in the gaps in their knowledge with fantasies about the crimes their forebears committed. A pervasive sense of guilt and shame lingered, affecting a person's sense of self and identity. For example, Thomas (born in 1968) knew that his grandfather had worked for the railway in Poland from 1943 to 1945, but nothing more. As a teenager he painfully imagined—again and again and in every detail—how his granddad steered the trains to the extermination camps. He never found out whether that had really been the case.

Repression, Denial, Trauma, and Shame: Suspected Reasons behind the Silences

The exact reasons that the parents and grandparents did not want to share more about their pasts remained unsaid, and the Kriegsenkel could only guess what lay behind their families' silences. One reason that I heard almost every time was that they had decided to put all their energy into securing a better economic future. "The war was terrible, but it is over; let's move on" was their leitmotif. The unwillingness to talk was perceived as a rejection of the responsibility that many of the grandparent generation carried for participating in the German aggression but also equally as a denial of the traumatic impact of the war experiences itself. In the eyes of many Kriegsenkel, their families simply refused to confront and work through the past.

A few of my interviewees felt that their families were too traumatized by what they had witnessed and had no choice but to repress their memories. Anna said her parents needed all their strength to get up in the morning, go to work, and raise their kids. In her opinion, there was so much pain buried inside them that they had to keep the past locked away in order to not get swept away by it. After school, Anna had to pick up a few bottles of vodka from the local store to help her mother get through the day. Her father often lost control when some small detail set him off. He brutally beat Anna and her younger sister, Ruth. At the end of the war, he had been separated from his family as they fled from their home in Poland. He was put in an orphanage and was regularly beaten by his Polish schoolmates. That was all Anna knew about his past to help her explain his violent behavior.

The decision to remain silent was sometimes viewed as a way of shielding the younger generation from the pain that their loved ones felt. "I don't want to burden you kids with these things," Karoline's mother used to say. A final yet significant driver for silence was a sense of shame and guilt for participating in the war or for believing in the National Socialist ideology. Marta (born in 1958) told me in 2012 that her mother had only recently confessed to her under a flood of tears that as a fourteen-year-old she had joined the League of German Girls (Bund Deutscher Mädel), the Nazi youth organization, out of her free will and was not forced by her parents as previously claimed. She was so ashamed of the fact that she had enjoyed the organized activities, the singing, and the camaraderie that she had kept it a secret for more than sixty years. I suspect that, when it comes to witnessing the deportation of Jewish neighbors or the acquisition of their houses and belongings, the sense of shame and the awareness that the younger generation would view their actions as morally reproachable provided an equally strong motivation to remain silent. My own grandfather Jupp never denied that he and my grandmother had supported the National Socialist movement, but he always maintained that the Nazis were "uneducated thugs" with whom he had not wanted any closer involvement. In 2012, I found his National Socialist German Workers' Party (NSDAP) membership card in the German National Archive. I wish I could ask him about that now.

"There Were No Taboos in Our Family": Open Sharing

While the vast majority of my interviewees were dissatisfied with the way their parents and grandparents communicated about the past, 20 percent of them recounted mostly positive experiences. I describe "open sharing," positioned in the middle of the spectrum, as a style of communication where there was the perception that the family talked freely about their experiences without taboos blocking the conversation on certain topics. Wajnryb subsumes this under the category of "direct communication," which she defines as "one-on-one interactions in which the spoken text itself was an adequate carrier of meaning" (Wajnryb 2001, 170). In these cases, the times spent sharing stories around the coffee table or in one-on-one conversations were remembered as precious moments of emotional closeness, where the younger generation listened with interest to their parents' and grandparents' life histories. What sets this apart from the previous section on anecdotes is the permission to ask probing questions and initiate or steer a conversation rather than the need to passively listen to a few repetitive anecdotes from the past.

Martina (born in 1967) tells a story that illustrates what so many other Kriegsenkel missed. As a little girl Martina used to sit with her maternal grandmother and listen to her reminisce about the delicatessen she owned in Dresden before the war, about the long and frightening nights she spent in the air-raid shelter with her children, and about the day she cooked a stray cat to provide food for the family. Her grandfather talked about his time with the Wehrmacht in Russia, his inability to understand that German soldiers were looting Russian villages, and his injury and resulting return home before the war ended. Martina listened mesmerized. She wanted to hear the stories again and again, even after she knew every detail by heart. She had the impression that her myriad of questions, including the challenging ones, were being answered honestly. Her grandparents did not hide the fact that they had initially supported Hitler and only changed their minds once the war began. "There were no taboos in our family," she said, summing up her childhood experiences. Her grandparents' vivid descriptions gave her the feeling of being part of the experiences. They allowed for a transfer of historical knowledge that was more memorable and meaningful to her than anything she would later read in history books. Her voice exuded warmth, happiness, and love as she recounted story after story in our interview, treasures she was now passing on to her own ten-year-old daughter.

On her father's side, on the other hand, there were many gaps and missing pieces in the jigsaw puzzle of her family history, including allegations that her paternal grandfather had been commander of a POW camp in Yugoslavia and most likely had been a war criminal. While she would have liked to know more about that, for Martina open sharing did not necessarily have to extend to the whole family. Having just one side of the family, or even one or two family members, available to talk to was sometimes enough to satisfy the younger generation's curiosity, to make them feel part of a family lineage, and to provide a sense of identity, belonging, and connection to the past. However, families like Martina's often said about themselves that they had been the "lucky ones," who had suffered less and were less incriminated than other Germans in the war. It is plausible to think that their memories may have been less painful and consequently easier to share. There may have been less trauma and guilt, which in many other cases obstructed the dialogue between the generations.

"It Was Like Someone Had Taken the Plug Out": Incessant Talking

At the other end of the spectrum, the sharing of war stories was not always experienced as positive but sometimes as excessive, emotionally burdening, and overwhelming. Five of my interviewees (9%) remembered that someone in the family talked about the war incessantly. Lena (born in 1958) used to be proud that she knew much more about her parents' childhood than her school friends did, but the war was also omnipresent in the family home. Every time her parents had dinner with friends and the conversation reached a certain depth after a few glasses of wine, it invariably turned to the war. Her father did most of the talking. In 1941, he had been drafted into the Wehrmacht as a seventeen-year-old. He described the horrors of what he had witnessed again and again, always drawing out the same lesson: "Thank God the war is over, and we need to make sure that it never happens again." On the other side, Andrea (born in 1953) said that her father never spoke about the past—until the day she turned eighteen. Taking the train to another city to celebrate her birthday with her godmother, her father ushered her into a quiet compartment and, without any forewarning, spilled out his entire story. In April 1945, just about to turn sixteen, he had been drafted into the Volkssturm (the German national militia set up in the last months of the war) to defend Berlin against the advancing Soviet Army. He was soon hit by a bullet in the shoulder and was first taken to the hospital and then sent home to his parents. A month later he was arrested and brought to Buchenwald, a former concentration camp converted into a Russian POW camp after the German capitulation. He stayed there for three years and most of his youth. It was a time of hunger, humiliation, and violence. His account was detailed and relentless, conjuring up images of horrible illnesses, brutal beatings, and the smell of decay, filth, and dead bodies. Trapped in the train compartment, Andrea was too shocked to ask any questions. Her father's sudden openness came as a total surprise: "It was like someone had taken the plug out, and everything just started pouring out," she said. After this initial breakthrough, the outpouring did not stop. It happened again and again, always with the same level of pain and desperation.

Kriegsenkel like Andrea and Lena perceived this "incessant talking" as an attempt to alleviate the burden of painful war memories by sharing them with close family members or friends. Lena understood her father's behavior as a form of debriefing for a generation of Germans who were not used to asking for professional help: "It was some sort of therapy-*ersatz* for him, but then I was surprised that this therapy never seemed to end. It just went on and on, always the same stories, from a hundred different angles." As much as she empathized with her father, she still felt his constant sharing as an emotional burden, something that diminished her own childhood and teenage worries as unimportant and laughable compared to the gravity of her father's war trauma. In some cases, the younger generation quietly endured the ordeal, as Lena did, whereas others reached a point where they were no longer willing or able to listen. At some stage, Andrea felt so overwhelmed by the awfulness and sadness of her father's repetitive stories that she asked him to stop. They were too heavy for her to bear, she said. She felt guilty for cutting him off but did not see any other solution.

Among my group of interviewees, those endlessly repeated stories were more commonly shared by male family members with active combat experience, as soldiers, flak helpers, or members of the Volkssturm, and they revolved around memories of endured hardship. Only Cordula (born in 1982), out of all my fifty-four interviewees, said her grandfather talked at length about the heavy burden of guilt he carried since the war:

> He [my grandfather] was difficult. I only knew him as a weird old man. We visited him regularly, but he never really played with us or spent time with us. We had a meal together, and then he would immediately start talking about his war memories. That was the first and only topic ever. He was a soldier, apparently all the way close to Moscow. It was a hard battle, he said, and a lot of friends died next to him, without him being able to do anything about it. They stripped the bodies of dead soldiers of their boots and broke out their gold teeth. I think it was absolutely terrible for him, but he did it to survive. You could exchange the gold teeth for food. He always came back to that; it was an important point for him, these feelings of guilt. He kept saying again and again that you had to rob those people who were lying there, no matter what nationality, of the last little bit they had left. That was very dramatic for him, and he told us again and again, always the same story.

Interestingly, while Cordula's grandfather openly talked about his sense of guilt for participating in the war, this sense of guilt was vis-à-vis his dead comrades rather than the victims of the German aggression. The war generation tended to portray themselves as victims of a war that Hitler had started, rather than the Nazi supporters many of them (at least initially) had been. When talking about their memories, the focus was on their own personal experience of loss and suffering. None of the stories my interviewees recounted extended to the suffering that Germans had inflicted on their victims. These too remained excluded.

The War Is in the House: Communicating without Words

Up to this point, the description of the family communication focused on verbal exchanges about the past, some more direct, others less. Yet around a quarter (24%) of my interviewees described situations where they felt that knowledge about the war was passed to them without words, either in lieu of direct verbal communication or complementing it. While these experiences could be placed at the "silent" end of the communication range, I will reserve the spectrum for verbal communication and treat the nonverbal transmission as a stand-alone communication style in its own right (see also Kidron 2009a, 2009b; Winter 2010; Zerubavel 2010). In her work Carol Kidron shows how, in Holocaust survivor homes, silent knowing about the parents' past was transmitted nonverbally within the family, embedded in everyday life, and communicated through embodied practices and engagement with objects from the past.

In my interviewees' accounts, the war was sometimes perceived as a kind of presence or atmosphere in the family home. Some people described a heaviness, a fog, a cloud, or a dome shrouding the family and creating a sense of isolation, staleness, and disconnection from the outside world. Anna remembered walking home at night as a child looking at the illuminated windows of the neighboring houses and thinking how different they were from her own, because in them "there was peace." Many people complained about a lack of joy in their family homes, where the laughter and lightness of childhood were covered under a thick gray blanket. Elise felt that there was always "something terrible hanging around in the space." This sort of presence could not necessarily be put into words at the time, yet it was clearly perceived and in hindsight attributed to the unresolved emotions and repressed war memories the family was inadvertently and unconsciously exuding.

In one particularly fascinating case, it was the house itself that was seen as holding and transmitting the emotional imprints of the past. When I first met Sanna (born in 1974), she told me that she had inherited a marvelous villa near a lake outside Berlin but that she was struggling to be in the house, where she suspected her grandmother had been raped by Russian soldiers stationed there for a few weeks in 1945. Her mother, a child at the time, was adamant that nothing like that had happened, but Sanna strongly sensed that the house told a different story. She could clearly feel her grandmother's fear, panic, and paranoia oozing out from the walls, tangible and present, in spite of the fact that much time had passed since the actual events. Sanna's grandmother was taken to a psychiatric hospital in 1946 (suffering from "Russian paranoia," the family was told), never to return home. As we were talking about this on a warm and sunny day in 2012, she started to shiver and had to get a blanket before she could continue our conversation. Anthropologist Yael Navaro-Yashin (2009) found in her work in Turkish-Northern Cyprus that the houses and properties appropriated from the Greek community after the civil war were felt to discharge emotive energies, still interacting with their (new) owners today and creating affective spaces of melancholia. Here, as in my example above, the houses themselves constitute nonhuman actors in the dynamic.

Some Kriegsenkel described other experiences, which they believed were nonverbal and unconscious transmissions of their parents' and grandparents' war memories. A few mentioned having nightmares featuring firebombing, burning houses, and charred bodies, some of which were later confirmed to be representations of actual events that had happened to someone in the family. Others had vivid visions of incidents that happened during the war. Udo (born in 1968) kept reliving the same scene over and over again, each time from a different perspective: Russian soldiers shot his grandfather on his farm in 1946 when he refused to relinquish his liquor supplies to the occupying forces. While his family had told him about his grandfather's violent death, he was adamant that these visions were more than just products of his fertile imagination. They happened involuntarily and seemed to be replays of the past with images and other sensations as real as if Udo himself were there. Holger woke up one day in 2005 and suddenly started to cry uncontrollably. A diffuse yet intense feeling of liberation overcame him, a sense of hope, of life starting anew, which he could not relate to anything that was happening for him at the time. A few hours later he realized that the date was May 8, the day World War II had ended sixty years earlier. He believed that the emotions he was feeling were in fact his family's at that very moment in 1945. As an artist, Anja (born in 1965) spent years trying to express an indistinct feeling she carried inside, a *something* that needed to be expressed. She tested different materials, dissatisfied with each attempt, until one day she produced two forty-kilogram concrete models of World War II air-raid shelters. When she started questioning her father about his war childhood—something he had never talked about previously—it all started to make sense. Anja was convinced that she had been unconsciously carrying her father's trauma inside her and that it manifested in the form of these air-raid shelters. Her story will be told in detail in chapter 5.

People who reported these kinds of phenomena had no clear explanation of how they came to have such memories, visions, or images. Yet they sensed very clearly that the images were not their own but that they were related to experiences that happened long before their births and to other people in their immediate families. Asking questions around the processes of transgenerational transmission, Yael Danieli (1998, 5) points out that descendants of Holocaust survivors often reported feeling a "constant psychological presence" of the Holocaust at home and that in some cases the children absorbed the experience of their families' suffering by "osmosis" and without words. Interviewing second-generation Holocaust survivors, Carol Kidron (2009b) hypothesizes that qualities of empathy and closeness among family members create a space in which the boundaries between the generations are relaxed and knowledge about the past is passed nonverbally.

Is There a Perfect Family Communication?

No matter how traumatic, painful, or shameful their families' experiences might have been, the overwhelming majority of my interviewees said that a direct dialogue about the past was (or would have been) preferable to silence.

There was an underlying concept of the "ideal family communication about the war" against which they measured their lived experiences. Deducted from the negative as well as the positive examples, the "ingredients" of an ideal communication could be summarized as follows:

- Willingness to openly talk about the family's war experiences, without taboos or defensiveness.
- Openness and responsiveness to the questions of the younger generation while at the same time respecting their boundaries. This means parents adapting the content of the stories to the children's age and active interest.
- Avoidance of abusing the family as therapy-*ersatz* and overwhelming them with incessant outpouring of pain, which may create a sense that the children are responsible for carrying their family's burden.

Most families fell short of this ideal, resulting in frustration and strained relationships between generations, for two main reasons. Firstly, the lack of open communication and the struggle to obtain information about the family's past had often existed since teenage years, leaving a gap in a person's sense of identity. Family stories told and retold around the kitchen table, which transfer the knowledge and experiences of one's predecessors, were painfully missed. Such stories relay a sense of belonging, a continuity of the family's past. For many of my interviewees, that sense of continuity was missing, leaving a gap in the foundation of the sense of self. "It is like there is nothing that you can stand on," Charlotte concluded. The passing on of stories and life experiences gained during the war was seen as a desirable part of growing up, even though many of those experiences were shameful or traumatic.

Secondly, the expectation of talk was also shaped by the norms of the contemporary therapeutic culture (to which I will come back in chap. 4). Familial silences but also excessive talk around a traumatic past were seen as detrimental to the younger generation's mental health, as they created the psychodynamic environment in which traumatic experiences were passed on. The Kriegsenkel would have welcomed sharing and respectful openness as a sign that their families had been able to confront and work through the past—both in terms of accepting responsibility for the crimes of the Hitler regime and of addressing the repressed trauma the war had left behind. They retrospectively judged familial silence as a proof of failure to achieve this acceptance. This failure, in their view and in the logic of therapeutic discourses, set the younger generation up to inherit their parents' and grandparents' unresolved issues.

Interestingly, however, what my interviewees viewed as a personal decision and a "typically German" way of avoiding the past is a common response to war and violence across cultures. Whenever I mentioned my research to people from around the world, the stories I heard were the same, whether the issue was World War II in Italy, the civil war in Ireland, or the Japanese occupation of Singapore. Parents and grandparents did not talk (a lot) about their memories. My anecdotal observations are underpinned by a wealth of psychological and anthropological case studies. Silences, public and private, in the aftermath of war and violence tend to be the norm rather than the exception. It often takes at least one if not two generations before people start talking about the past. "Silences break down when time passes and needs change. As in personal loss, groups of people need time in order to face collective loss or disaster. In many cultures, the initial stage of mourning demands silence" (Winter 2010, 23). The hesitation to share traumatic memories with children and grandchildren was observed first and foremost among Holocaust survivors in Israel (Kidron 2009a, 2009b), Australia (Wajnryb 2001), and the United States (Stein 2009). Researchers often explained this reticence with the extreme traumatization suffered in the concentration camps or with a wish to protect the children from the overwhelming pain their loved ones had endured. Silences were also reported to dominate in families of World War II survivors from the Dutch East Indies (Aarts 1998), those of Dutch World War II sailors and resistance fighters (Op den Velde 1998), and those of refugees who had fled to Canada to escape the political violence in Southeast Asia and Central America (Rousseau and Drapeau 1998). Children of Japanese Americans who were interned by the US government during World War II said that they had fewer than ten conversations with their parents about their internment over their entire life span, with the average length of each conversation being approximately thirty minutes (Nagata 1998, 132).

In Germany, and in many other cases, the mix of factors of which silences were constructed included an element of shame. The descendants of survivors of the Cambodian genocide of the 1970s said that their parents were ashamed of what had happened to them. They viewed themselves as weak for having endured the political violence (Kidron 2009a). By remaining silent, they regained an element of strength, whereas talking would have implied weakness in this cultural context. As was the case for many Germans, for Dutch collaborators with the Nazi regime, it was a sense of guilt for the crimes they had committed or condoned that prevented them from sharing their stories with their children (Lindt 1998). Some Dutch victims of World War II refrained from talking about their experiences to avoid reliving feelings of powerlessness and humiliation (Op den Velde 1998). Wajnryb (2001) noticed that Holocaust survivors who had fought more actively against the Nazis were more open about their experiences than those who had not. For survivors of the Japanese atomic bombs dropped on Hiroshima and Nagasaki in 1945, it was the shame of passing on sickness and genetic defects to their offspring that motivated their silence (Tatara 1998). Chinese survivors of the Great Famine in the early 1960s avoided talking about the gruesome acts of cannibalism, reported from many rural areas, that took place in a desperate attempt to escape starvation (Feuchtwang 2011). Interestingly, a number of older Chinese whom Stephan Feuchtwang and his team spoke to had tried to share their memories with their children, but in these cases, it was the children who did not want to listen. After the political and economic changes following Mao Zedong's death, the younger generation associated the period of the famine with a past that they felt was not worth dwelling on, and they believed that their parents and grandparents had been foolish to fall for the political enthusiasm that dominated the Maoist era. Conversely, many members of the younger generation, like their German counterparts, did suffer from a lack of knowledge about their families' history, even if they often accepted the silences imposed on them. The absence of knowledge about their parents' camp years, for example, left some children of Japanese who were interned by the United States during World War II to feel sadness and a sense of incompleteness. As one interviewee said, "It felt as if there was a void in my personal history" (Nagata 1998, 132).

Only one person I met, Hubert, born in 1971, believed that trauma simply wears off with time without requiring talk or therapy. Many of my other interviewees were convinced that the ideal family communication about the war would have given them a more secure sense of identity and embeddedness in a family tradition while preventing the passing down of emotional damage related to the war. A double disappointment in these aspects of their upbringing explained much of the lingering anger and judgment against parents and sometimes grandparents that came through in many of my interviews, leading to further deterioration, and sometimes a complete cutting of ties, of often already difficult relationships.

COMPOUNDING LAYERS OF SILENCES

The whole spectrum and the different patterns of family communication around World War II make it clear that the majority of Kriegsenkel were dissatisfied with the extent to which their parents and grandparents shared their war memories. My interviewees tended to portray themselves as the victims of a dynamic imposed on them when their families made the decision of how much they were willing to disclose and what to keep a secret. However, as we delved deeper, a more diverse picture emerged. Silences and taboos were not always created or upheld just by older generations, but in many cases the Kriegsenkel at least respected and sometimes even reinforced them. Many of my interviewees said that they had actively asked questions, trying to challenge and break through the imposed silences—often without much success. Yet, in about a third (34%) of all cases, Kriegsenkel reported that they felt something akin to an "invisible wall" around the taboo topics and had not tried to push beyond it. Explanations ranged from fear and tacit acceptance to the wish to protect the parents and to avoid causing them pain.

Also, not everyone considered the familial silences to be problematic. When I asked Eva-Marie whether she would have liked to have known more about her grandparents' past, she shook her head. She thought that it was preferable for every generation to deal with their difficult memories themselves, rather than burdening their children and grandchildren. "This way, the stories remain with the people they belong to, and it is good like that," she said. Nora admitted that her mother would probably have talked more about her war childhood but that she, Nora, did not encourage her. She simply did not want to listen to her mother lamenting about her lost home in the Czech Republic or feel her bitterness about her experience as a penniless refugee in postwar Germany. These examples support Wajnryb's (2001) findings: the listener plays a vital role in the intergenerational communication about a difficult past. Narratives are constructed in collaboration among all actors, and it is imperative for the process that the listener provide positive feedback and encouragement to enable the sharing. "There needs to be a bonding, the intimate and total presence of an *other*—in the position of the one who hears" (Wajnryb 2001, 190, emphasis in the original). If this feedback is not given, the flow of sharing often will not happen. Similarly, German sociologist Jürgen Zinnecker (2008) found that the younger generation played a key role in the intergenerational dynamic, either by condoning prevailing silences or by stimulating the debate about their parents' and grandparents' past. In spite of the fact that a number of Kriegsenkel did indeed try to push for a more open communication and failed, the younger generation needs to be perceived as active players in the family dynamic. They were not necessarily always the passive victims of their upbringing that they portrayed themselves to be.

This argument is further strengthened by the interesting observation that the siblings of my primary interviewees often recounted different memories of growing up in the same family and held diverging views of what was shared and what was silenced. While Lena complained that her father talked about his time with the Wehrmacht all the time and to an overwhelming extent, her brother Ulrich, born in 1955, remembered that the war was only discussed in passing. He felt that the postwar years were a much more prominent feature in their parents' stories. While Cornelia felt that her father consciously avoided sharing his painful memories and refused to tell her more about his war childhood, her brother Christoph, born in 1963, remembered asking a lot of questions and receiving satisfactory answers from both parents. In some cases, the siblings' accounts of their upbringing resembled one another, while in others I had the impression that they were talking about completely different families. German sociologist Bettina Völter (2008) points out that siblings often interact with different aspects of their familial past and assume different roles in the intergenerational dialogue.

The Seesaw of Denial and Accusations

One important factor blocking the communication in German families was the difference in attitude of each generation toward the Third Reich and World War II. These affected which memories the older family members shared but also the types of questions the Kriegsenkel asked, particularly as teenagers. As mentioned before, the vast majority of German parents and grandparents were uncomfortable with being reminded of a war they tried very hard to forget. In particular in West Germany, the younger generation tended to be judgmental and ask grueling questions about their forebears' support for the Hitler regime or their knowledge of the Holocaust. "What did you do?" and "What did you know?" and "How could you?" the grandchildren would ask with an openly accusing undertone. The response in the majority of cases was a stern denial of any knowledge, let alone any active involvement—either by the grandparents directly or by the parents on their behalf. Silences and denials on the one side, with distrust and suspicion on the other, were, according to Vesper and Weber (1991, 91), so widespread that they almost constitute a cliché of stereotypical "family conversations about National Socialism," ritualistically reenacted over the years in countless German homes. Because of such dynamics, the necessary atmosphere of willingness to share freely and to listen empathically, which Wajnryb (2001) sees as a prerequisite for a dialogue about an emotionally charged past, was simply not given.[2] This conflict within families, and the respective position of each generation, was clearly informed by public debates, TV programs, and history lessons about World War II and National Socialism, as outlined in chapter 1. The attitude relayed in public discourses toward moral responsibility of all Germans—young and old—for the crimes committed by the Nazi regime was internalized by the younger generation and rejected by the older, molding and hardening the family conversations along these fault lines.

Blind Spots

The calcified dynamic that all parties found themselves trapped in not only blocked the exchange of experiences but also led to the creation of blind spots. Certain aspects of the older generations' wartime experiences were played down or overlooked altogether. In both parts of Germany, the younger generation sometimes blocked out parts of their families' stories because their moral lenses prevented them from grasping the full dimensions of their families' war trauma. A number of my interviewees said they were struggling to empathize with the hardship their family had endured, because it seemed like a justified retaliation for the pain Germans had inflicted on the Jews and so many other innocent people. Although the family might have talked about their difficult memories, the information did not really sink in. Udo's mother tried to explain to him how terrifying and upsetting it was for her to have to leave her village in a hurry in 1945 with just a few basic things packed in a suitcase—heading west, never to return home. He dutifully listened but could not get himself to feel any compassion. "I heard what she said, but it was like there was a wall between what she was talking about and myself," he admitted. Sometimes he even said to her, "Look, the Germans started the war, and we really cannot complain about what happened to us as a result."

While Udo's mother had actively tried sharing her painful experiences with her son, in many other cases, the public focus on German perpetratorship led to a situation where the exclusion of wartime suffering from family narratives went all but unnoticed. The older family members did not mention it, and it did not occur to the younger generation to enquire. Quite a few times in my interviews I heard statements such as "I am surprised that I never asked that question before," or "How could I have blocked this aspect out completely?" It was only after the taboo in the public sphere was lifted in the early 2000s and accounts of German wartime suffering flooded the mainstream media that these blind spots were slowly coming to light. Isabelle (born in 1972) was one of the Kriegsenkel who was metaphorically rubbing her eyes, realizing what she had overlooked:

> A while ago, I watched this program on TV about the expulsions from the East. People of my father's age were being interviewed, and they had all been damaged and were traumatized from the experience. That was the very first time—and looking back now I find that really surprising—that I

> thought, "Oh dear, my father had to flee too." I had never thought about that before. I was thirty-five when I thought about it for the very first time! I don't remember how old I was when I first heard about my father's flight. I did know about it, but I did not let it sink in. I never thought it through. That is what now surprises me the most.

My conversations with the German Kriegsenkel clearly showed how the public culture of World War II commemoration reached into the private sphere, creating a strong moral lens through which family experiences were viewed, judged, and filtered. It shaped how stories were shared (or not) and how they were listened to. Historian Peter Novick (1999) concurs that taboos in the public discourse strongly influence private narratives, as discussions in private tend to reflect the topics raised in the public domain. Even more so, as I have argued above, because they are often coupled with the general tendency of the eyewitness generation to remain silent about their memories. In Germany, this dynamic created a layer of gaps, silences, and blind spots in the dialogue between the generations and prevented a more comprehensive picture of a family's war experience from being transmitted and received. Both Udo and Isabelle, whose examples stand for many others, only realized what they had blocked out when the focus of the public discussion shifted. While they both still held on to their conviction that what their families endured was a justified consequence of the crimes that Germans had committed, they started to listen with more compassion to what their parents had to share.

Silences Surrounding the Family

There is a third layer of silence that plays a role in the creation of blind spots regarding German war trauma: the silences surrounding German families. Something that struck me about all my interviewees was that no matter how much or how little they knew about their family history, virtually none of them talked about any of it outside the family home as they were growing up. People did not tend to share with friends their quests to get answers from parents and grandparents, nor did they talk about the experiences and anecdotes that they had heard. In this regard there is no difference between families who talked about the war at home and those who did not. In both cases the Kriegsenkel remained equally silent. Very often, it simply did not occur to them to discuss this part of their family history with their classmates and friends.

As outlined in chapter 1, many Kriegsenkel remembered that Hitler's rise to power, the war, and the Holocaust were talked about at school in varying degrees of detail. Yet those facts about the past remained abstract and impersonal, and very few felt that their family history had any place in the larger national narrative (see also Welzer, Moller, and Tschuggnall 2002). Teachers did not encourage students to make the connection, and personal stories were not part of the history lessons, in either East or West German schools. The only exception was Martina, who said that when World War II was discussed in school, she actively contributed vignettes about her grandmother's delicatessen and the time she cooked the stray cat. In one other case, the sharing of personal experiences happened by accident, as Elise (born in 1961) recounted: "Once our teacher talked to us about the topic of expellees in history class, and she said, 'Well, this surely does not concern any of you!' But lo and behold! About half of the class immediately put up their hands, and we all said from where our parents had fled. That was the first time that I realized how broadly we were affected and how many of us there were. I must have been about twelve at the time."

German historian Dorothee Wierling (2010) claims that neither schools nor institutions like churches were able to pick up on this disconnect and that they failed to provide a context in which family stories could have been shared and elaborated. I believe that, as a consequence, blind spots regarding wartime suffering were fixed further, as there was no broader discussion to help put the family history into a larger context.

I found no major difference between East and West German families regarding the mix of communication styles. Families in both parts of the country tended to talk about their war experience in similar ways, through obscure remarks, life lessons, or anecdotes, and both equally excluded topics evoking guilt, shame, or trauma. Some differences revolved around memories of flight and expulsion and the violence of the Soviet occupying forces, which were hinted at more reluctantly in East German families. The younger generation's focus on and intergenerational tensions around perpetratorship were much more widespread in the West, at least until the collapse of the GDR. But when it came to sharing personal experiences with people outside the home, the wall of silence in East Germany had one thick additional layer. In the West, without an external stimulus, it often simply did not occur to members of the younger generation to talk about their family history with friends or colleagues. In East Germany the rule that what happens in the family stays in the family was strictly enforced to avoid conflicts between the officially sanctioned version of World War II history and divergent personal experiences. Kerstin (born in 1962) remembered: "When I met other people outside the family, I could sometimes feel this hatred for the Russians. But it was diffuse and hard to grasp. Sometimes there were a few hints or half a sentence, but that was it. Now things are different of course, and we know what happened. But during the times of the GDR, it was unthinkable to say that out loud."

LIFTING THE VEIL OF SILENCE: THE KRIEGSENKEL AND THEIR EUREKA MOMENT

This chapter described in detail how German families' communication about World War II was structured, particularly around the time when my interviewees were growing up. Only a minority of families was reported to have a culture of communication that the younger generation found satisfactory, where questions could be asked and were answered with perceived sincerity and openness and without overwhelming the listener in the process. In most other families, conversations about the war remained patchy. Taboos, denial, and an unwillingness to share painful or shameful memories created an atmosphere of secrecy and suppression that left the Kriegsenkel generation without a clear sense of the familial past. However, I also showed that they themselves played an active role in this dynamic, often accepting or reinforcing taboos and silences or preventing more sharing by assuming an attitude of moral judgment and self-righteousness vis-à-vis their families' involvement with the Hitler regime.

This chapter furthermore showed that public narratives about National Socialism and World War II also shaped the intergenerational dialogue in the private sphere, influencing what the older generations shared and what the younger members of the family asked. At the same time, the family unit remained disconnected from its immediate social environment, and personal stories did not travel beyond the walls of the family home. The gaps and silences in each of these layers did not necessarily fully overlap, as there was a degree of sharing of wartime suffering in family stories that was largely absent from the public culture of commemoration. However, the interplay of these different spheres, as well as individual psychological factors and family dynamics, created a complex matrix through which World War II experiences were expressed or, more often, silenced. There were layers of silence around both aspects of the war, perpetratorship and wartime suffering. They differed, however, in that, as they were growing up, the Kriegsenkel (particularly in West Germany) had been largely aware of the aspects of perpetratorship and active support for Hitler. However, they had not been conscious of the full impact of their families' traumatic war memories. These blind spots explain the surprise and emotional eureka moments with which the Kriegsenkel generation responded to discovering the topic. After having been blocked from consciousness for most of their lives, the long-term emotional impact of World War II on their families and by extension on themselves suddenly moved into full view. The public focus on wartime suffering in the media inspired my interviewees to ask new questions and to look at their lives from a new perspective. In some cases, the parents were now more inclined to tell stories about their lives during World War II, and the younger generation also exhibited a greater willingness to ask questions with nonjudgmental openness and empathy.

How the Kriegsenkel understand the relationship between their present psychological issues and World War II, and how they constructed an emergent identity as sufferers of transmitted war trauma, is the topic of the next chapter.

NOTES

1. The phenomenon of familial taboos acting like black holes was also observed by Udo Baer and Gabriele Frick-Baer, *Wie Traumata in die nächste Generation wirken-Untersuchungen, Erfahrungen, therapeutische Hilfen* (2010).

2. Historians Vesper and Weber found in their interviews with German families in the late 1980s that the younger generation tended to display a style of questioning and probing that was driven by the intention to provoke and challenge rather than by a genuine interest in their families' experiences. See Ingrid Vesper and Andrea Weber, *Familien-Geschichten: mündliche Überlieferung von Zeitgeschichte in Familien* (1991).

THREE

BETTER "SICK" THAN "STRANGE"

The Kriegsenkel Movement and the Desire to Legitimize Suffering

THE ANONYMOUS POSTING BELOW, shared in the "Life Histories" section on one of the Kriegsenkel websites, captures well what it means for people to reflect for the first time on how World War II affected their families' psychological health and by extension their own:

> I was born in 1956 and for almost 30 years I have tried to find the reasons behind my problems, or rather a way to resolve them. For years and years, I have been asking myself, "What is wrong with me? Why am I not in the least able to manage my life?" I was addicted to drugs. I have suffered from bulimia and severe depression, and I was dependent on prescription medication. I am entirely incapable of having relationships. I can't find a place to settle down and keep moving house, always feeling like an outsider. I can't hold down a job because I can never stay long enough. . . . I have done numerous psychotherapies. While I could get my addictions under control, and the bulimia is also not an issue anymore, I still can't live a normal life. I have issues with intimacy and emotions, I am always running away (I am always fleeing!), and somehow, I don't know who I am.
>
> Last week I came across *We Children of the War Children* at our local library. It hit me like a ton of bricks. On the one hand there was a sense of liberation. Finally, finally, I know what is going on with me. On the other hand, it was a shock. Since I read the book, my whole life is passing in front of my eyes. Again and again situations with my parents come to mind, which I now see in a different light. It is scary, and the pain of my parents' suffering almost knocks me over.
>
> My parents were both "expellees" from the Sudetenland. They were no longer little children when they had to flee, but they still went through so

> much suffering that it impacted on them for the rest of their lives. My mother never talked about it. Only in the final weeks before her death, she told me about her flight, but she only touched on it very briefly. I did not understand anything, and I did not ask any questions. I grew up under a heavy coat of pain and suffering and a longing for the *Heimat* [the homeland]. But no one ever even uttered a single word about it. The pain was enveloping us but was never given a name. . . . We somehow lived a life shielded away from the "normal" world outside. We never had any visitors. Everything outside our family was dangerous. We were indoctrinated never to trust a stranger. My parents did not go out at night, not to the theater, nor to the movies or to visit friends. They did not have any friends. Our life was at home, that is where one was safe. But I did not understand why, and nothing was explained; that was the worst. How could I have known that war and expulsion were the reasons behind their behavior and their rules? I am grateful that I finally found out why I am having such difficulties in my life and why everything was so strange at home. I hope that now I will finally be able to work through all of this. A. W. January 2011[1]

A. W. was severely struggling in most aspects of his or her life, and up until that point the issues could only partly be resolved through therapy. Then A. W. discovered one of the Kriegsenkel books, which opened up a completely new context: World War II and the traumatic imprint the forced migration had left on the parents. A. W. suddenly realized how these difficult experiences shaped his or her family's life to the present day, something unconsidered until that point. This connection came as a big revelation that changed the way A. W. saw his or her psychological illness. The suffering had a new explanation—transmitted war trauma—and the "condition" had a new name around which the symptoms were gathered: being a Kriegsenkel. Reaching this "diagnosis" provided a sense of relief and the hope that the crippling problems could finally be addressed.

I heard many stories like A. W's during my time in Berlin. Finding the Kriegsenkel topic and putting a label on previously indistinct suffering was a life-changing experience, one that restructured a person's entire history. New connections were made between past events and current emotions. The defining elements of a biography were drawn together in a different way—very much in line with Hacking's (1995) notion of "re-writing the past" after a mental health diagnosis. For the Kriegsenkel, the new framework explained their own and their families' emotional struggles in a convincing and meaningful way and put them into the broader context of a collective German history. It also relayed renewed hope for a happier and healthier future, which previous attempts at healing often had not been able to deliver.

Since my time in Berlin, the number of people identifying as Kriegsenkel in Facebook groups and on designated websites has grown steadily. However, when in late March 2015 members of the war grandchildren association uploaded an entry on the term *Kriegsenkel* onto the German Wikipedia site, a submission was made a few days later demanding that the page be deleted.[2] The requesters argued that the term was only sporadically used in the German public and was therefore not relevant: "Just another self-help concept supposed to support people in a midlife crisis, who are given the opportunity to blame others [their grandparents] for their problems. If it helps people, fine, but I cannot detect any trace of scientific reception or serious research in this entry," one person writes.[3] After a week of debate, the proposal was rejected and the page remained, in spite of the fact that not much further scientific proof for the existence of a Kriegsenkel phenomenon could be cited. Nevertheless, the administrators of the site acknowledged that the word had become sufficiently well known in the German public to warrant an entry. While this incident may well have been the initiative of a notorious Wikipedia troublemaker, as some contributors to the exchange suggested, it did point to a larger issue: as an increasing number of Germans were beginning to see the transgenerational impact of World War II as key to understanding their emotional problems, "being a Kriegsenkel" was not associated with a clearly defined psychological diagnosis or a recognized mental health condition. When I was in Berlin, people who identified as such were still struggling to have their suffering recognized. Their claim that the root of their current issues stretched back all the way to World War II was still frequently dismissed as far-fetched or, as mentioned above, as the complaint of middle-class whiners looking for yet another therapeutic concept to allow them to blame their families for their failures. "Euch geht es doch gut," (But you are so lucky/well-off), my interviewees' mothers and fathers often said, implying that they should not have any complaints, as they grew up in times of peace and prosperity. Or they were brushed off like Martin, whose mother ended his attempt at conversation with, "But you were not even there. How could you possibly be affected by the war?"

In this chapter I explain that, in a situation where broad public recognition was still missing and where psychological research and therapeutic practices were still lagging after decades of taboos and silences around German wartime suffering, the Kriegsenkel were de facto diagnosing themselves as sufferers of transmitted war trauma. To explore and further confirm this new identity, they were meeting in self-managed support groups, in workshops, and on the internet to share their personal stories and to compare their own psychological difficulties with those of their peers. Through these practices of sharing and comparing, they were slowly assembling a cluster of symptoms for a new psychological profile. In spite of the critique of the psychological profession and its growing tendency to "pathologize" and "medicalize" everyday life (Furedi 2004; Kutchins and Kirk 1997), there was a strong motivation for the Kriegsenkel to frame their struggles as an emerging mental health condition. Being sick rather than just strange or different transformed their "imagined" problems into a proper syndrome. This transformation not only confered legitimacy on their suffering but also allowed for therapeutic interventions that hold the promise for a better future.

THE KRIEGSENKEL MOVEMENT: ORIGINS, RESOURCES, AND ACTIVITIES

As mentioned in the introduction, the history of the German war grandchildren movement begins with the publication of two nonfiction books: Anne-Ev Ustorf's (2008) *Wir Kinder der Kriegskinder: Die Generation im Schatten des Krieges* (We Children of the War Children: The Generation in the Shadow of the War) and Sabine Bode's (2009) *Kriegsenkel: Die Erben der vergessenen Generation* (War Grandchildren: The Heirs of the Forgotten Generation). For the first time, these books raised the question of a possible transgenerational impact of World War II on the mental health of the German majority population. Since 2010, a small war grandchildren movement has gained momentum. It is worthwhile to map out these different Kriegsenkel resources and activities in more detail, as they lay the ground on which my later analysis of Kriegsenkel life histories and collective practices is built.

Two Foundational Books

Sabine Bode's and Anne-Ev Ustorf's foundational books portray Germans in their forties and fifties who suffer from a broad range of psychological problems, which the authors link to their parents' and grandparents' experiences during World War II—predominantly as victims but in some cases also as perpetrators. Because the older generations had tried to put their painful and shameful memories behind them and had focused on rebuilding the country and their livelihoods rather than on working through the past, those unresolved experiences, according to the argument, were passed on to their offspring.

Anne-Ev Ustorf interviewed twelve people her own age, all of whom had a family history of flight and expulsion, and all of whom were born and raised in West Germany. She recounts their family history during World War II and describes each person's current emotional challenges. She says that her aim is to demonstrate how the war still manifests in the lives of the Kriegsenkel and that she wishes to contribute to greater communication and understanding between the generations. Some of her portraits draw a direct line from the parents' and grandparents' experiences of flight and expulsion to feelings of homelessness and lack of belonging in some grandchildren or to an overly strong attachment to the hometown in others. For example, Andreas's feelings of anxiety and inferiority are linked back to his parents' wartime experiences of material loss and lack, while Nina's and Doris's relationship problems are traced back to the rape of family members during the war. It is not clear how much of the link between the past trauma and current emotional problems is based on Ustorf's own interpretation and how much was provided by her respondents, all of whom seemed to have accessed psychotherapy.

Sabine Bode is slightly more cautious in directly connecting present emotional issues to past family experiences, and she mostly relies on her interviewees to make this association themselves. Her interest in the topic originated from the first groups that she and her husband, Georg, a family and trauma therapist, initiated in late 2007 to discuss how the war affected people across generations. Her book has an objective similar to Ustorf's: to draw attention to the long-term impact of the time of National Socialism and war on German families. The eighteen portraits are structured around a description of the interviewees' family histories, their relationships with their parents, and their current life challenges. The stories paint a diverse picture of how her interviewees experienced growing up with parents and grandparents damaged by World War II, with some of their issues similar to those found in Ustorf's case studies. One of the people portrayed, Robert, is unable to have fulfilling relationships until he realizes that his grandfather had watched Russian soldiers rape his grandmother and great-grandmother in 1945. Another, Jürgen, complains about the lack of emotional nurturing from his mother, who, as a little girl, had witnessed the bombardment and destruction of her hometown. Andrea is convinced that her chronic neck pain is a psychosomatic response to the horrific crimes her grandfather committed as an SS executioner.

Both authors are journalists and not psychologists, but their books were ground-breaking in that they brought the topic of a transgenerational psychological impact of World War II into the public arena for the first time. By 2016, Ustorf's book had been reprinted five times. Bode's book was available in its eleventh hardcover and twentieth paperback edition, having occupied a place on the best-seller list for nonfiction for many months. Bode's book was by far the most popular, and people would often refer to it to relate their own experiences. Most identified more strongly with the label *Kriegsenkel* (war grandchildren) than with Ustorf's more convoluted "*Kinder der Kriegskinder*" (children of the war children). Sabine Bode explained to me that *Kriegsenkel* was coined in the first self-help groups that she organized with her husband. She believed that it stuck because it gave people a clear, short, self-explanatory term to identify with and to rally around.

Two Core Websites

Following the publication of the first Kriegsenkel books, volunteers set up two internet sites offering information and networking opportunities for interested members of the public: the more extensive www.forumkriegsenkel.de (hereafter Forumkriegsenkel.de), founded in late 2009, and www.kriegsenkel.de (hereafter Kriegsenkel.de), which came into life in 2012 as the official website of the Kriegsenkel association (Verein Kriegsenkel e.V.), founded in 2010. A few Kriegsenkel support groups also established their own websites.[4]

Forumkriegsenkel.de explains its purpose as follows: "War-descendents [*sic*] often may suffer from recurrent psychological blocks, diffuse fears, heavy feelings of guilt or feelings of depression, yet without being able to explain the origin of such experiences. We would like to help those who are interested in learning more about themselves and their family pasts in light of both society and history. We hope to provide a point of departure for grasping these negative legacies, for learning to understand them and, ultimately, for freeing oneself from them."[5]

The site invites people to anonymously share their personal stories, poems, or artwork in the "Life Histories" section or to put ads on the "News" page if they wish to network with like-minded people or form support groups in their region. According to Anne Barth, one of the three founding members and now the sole manager of the site, Forumkriegsenkel.de received around 1,700 hits per month in 2012; by May 2015 that number had increased to about 4,000.[6] The other website, Kriegsenkel.de, contains a more limited number of book titles and media articles on the topic, but it also passes on information about Kriegsenkel seminars, courses, and specialized therapists. In mid-2012, Forumkriegsenkel .de published the results of a survey that had invited people to name psychological issues or character traits that they felt were directly connected to their families' war experiences. A list of more than sixty "symptoms" and personal attributes—not all of them negative—was compiled from the fifty to sixty contributions. They included such personal issues or attributes as the following:

- Sense of homelessness and loneliness
- Fear of abandonment

- Feelings of guilt
- Melancholia
- Tendency for depression
- Burnout
- Panic attacks
- Childlessness
- Empathy
- Creativity
- Independence

The contributors also noted issues with their families of origin:

- Assumption of responsibility for parents' needs and emotions
- Excessive loyalty to parents
- Parents' inability to show emotions
- Lack of role models (i.e., fathers)
- Physical abuse
- Position as the black sheep in the family

Many referred to professional and social difficulties or character traits:

- High rates of moving to different houses or changing cities
- Lack of direction in their careers
- Sense of not moving forward, of feeling stuck
- Sense of isolation
- Tendency to withdraw
- Fear of change
- Feelings of uncertainty
- Ability to create networks
- Freedom from ideology[7]

A Number of Facebook Groups

In addition to these websites, Kriegsenkel also use the internet to connect with each other through a number of closed Facebook groups. At the point of writing, I am aware of eight such groups, with memberships ranging from 19 (*Kriegsenkel München*) to 704 (*Kriegsenkel*). People use the space to share their issues and their family stories and to comment on those posted by others. The more active groups post multiple times a day and inspire lively and often controversial discussions. Members exchange information about new research or books, media articles, radio and TV documentaries, films, and exhibitions. Some are directly related to the Kriegsenkel topic or history of World War II, others to broader issues felt to be of interest. Organizers promote upcoming events, support group meetings, workshops, and seminars.

Two Dozen Support Groups

A number of face-to-face support groups have also formed in the last few years. Around thirty were meeting regularly in larger Germany cities (and one in Switzerland) in 2017.[8] One group, made up of German immigrants with French spouses, was even meeting in Paris. The ones I either attended myself or was told about had between ten and twenty participants (the majority of them women) and normally met once a month in a public space like a local community center or a church. Some groups were open, with a different composition at each meeting; others were closed, with a clearly demarcated and stable membership. Some tailored the content of their discussions to their participants' immediate needs and interests, while others had predefined topics.

One of them, the Berlin Erzählcafé, was founded by communication coach Ines Koenen in October 2012. When we discussed her original idea, she said that she wanted to give people the opportunity to tell their stories and to establish links with others. Her group was meeting every month for some time without a fixed membership. The format evolved from ad hoc storytelling to a facilitated discussion around a fixed topic, such as "war and peace," "relationships with parents, grandparents and siblings," "parentification," and "why do I go through life with the hand brake on?" Ines occasionally invited guest speakers or showed TV documentaries, and from 2013 she charged a fee (around eight euros or twelve Australian dollars) for participation. In March 2013 the Erzählcafé went on a weekend trip to Dresden, tracing the history of the city's total destruction in February 1945. Ines said she enjoyed the company of like-minded people and it was not all just doom and gloom for her. "We are a relaxed bunch, and there is a lot of laughter too," she said in an interview with the *Berliner Morgenpost*, "even if many of the topics are very serious" (Keseling 2013).

The main aim of the support groups, which a facilitator often made clear in an opening statement, was to give people the opportunity to freely talk about their family histories and their own emotional struggles with an empathetic audience. Unlike the second-generation Holocaust survivor groups in the United States (Stein 2009) and in Israel (Kidron 2003), the first wave of groups were organized and facilitated by peers and were neither equipped nor intended to replace professional help. Those participants who needed to more thoroughly work through their issues were encouraged to go elsewhere. Individual group members would, however, commonly discuss healing techniques or recommend books that they found helpful. For many Kriegsenkel, it was the first time they discussed their family histories in relationship to the war and its traumatic impact outside their family homes. The experience regularly brought up tears and painful memories but also a sense of connection, mutual understanding, and comfort.

The Kriegsenkel support group landscape is dynamic and somewhat unstable. Groups appear, expand, morph from open to closed groups, and sometimes vanish in a relatively short space of time. The first Munich group, for example, was founded in 2012 and became very active, only to disappear again together with their website in early 2013—without an explanation. In early 2015 Ines disbanded the Erzählcafé after three years of operation, when she got tired of it but could not find anyone to replace her. Pushed by continuing demand, she restarted it again in 2016, before giving it up once more at the end of the year. Yet, overall, I have watched the number of groups grow steadily over the years. Interestingly, as I will discuss further in chapter 4, the vast majority of them are in the territory of the former West Germany. A second observation about the support groups (at least for the ones I attended or was told about) was that significantly more women attended, which also holds true for the Kriegsenkel movement more broadly. However, this is consistent with self-help circles in other Western countries (Illouz 2008). Women are more likely to frame, express, and address emotional suffering in the context of therapeutic and self-help practices. Of course, this does not mean that men are less affected by their upbringing. Around 40 percent of my interviewees were male. The stories of the impact of their families' past did not differ substantially along gender lines.

A Number of Therapists

A growing number of psychoanalysts, psychotherapists, and alternative healers have started to cater explicitly to a clientele from the Kriegsenkel scene. At the point of writing, their services included individual therapy, coaching and psychoanalytical group sessions, family constellations, hypnotherapy, and eye movement desensitization and reprocessing (EMDR).[9] People who are interested in addressing their issues in more depth can also select from a range of evening and weekend workshops conducted across the country. Trauma therapist Ina Lindauer conducts biographical workshops and individual coaching.[10] Psychotherapist Ingrid Meyer-Legrand's KriegsenkelLab helps with career problems stemming from a family history of flight and expulsion.[11] Her colleague Gabriele Baring offers family constellation seminars for the war generation and their children.[12] Monika Weidlich, who works with techniques of deep relaxation and visualization to address psychological blockages, specifically mentions the "Kriegsenkel phenomenon" on the list of treatable conditions on her website.[13] When I asked her how she would define this specific group and the corresponding phenomenon, she responded:

> It is not easy to describe the typical war grandchild, but something that is true for all of them is a feeling (acknowledged or repressed) of somehow not being OK, and to feel like an outcast. Some of them distinguish themselves through hard work and successful careers, fulfilling the dreams and expectations of their parents as the only way to get their love and attention. Others are more rebellious and don't finish their education, they tend to have more "broken" biographies and display their unhappiness in more obvious forms of depression and hopelessness. Both groups have in common that they can't seem to get a handle on the source of their suffering.[14]

WHO IS A KRIEGSENKEL?

In 2014, Kriegsenkel.de defined the term *Kriegsenkel* as follows: "'Grandchildren of War' are people whose parents have witnessed the time of the National Socialist regime and World War II as children or youths and are until now—often in an unrecognized way—standing under the impact of traumatizing experiences. By the so-called 'transgenerational transfer' of the effects of trauma, grandchildren of war are affected by their parents' war experience."[15]

This definition, which is reflected in most other communications about the topic (Kriegsenkel books, media articles, and support group websites, etc.), makes clear that "being a Kriegsenkel" comprises two different parts. Firstly, it simply means belonging to a particular age cohort and biological generation. Technically, the term applies to every German whose parents were children or young teenagers during World War II (born roughly between 1930 and 1945). Age brackets vary slightly, but the most important criterion is that their fathers had not yet been drafted into the *Wehrmacht*. These members of the parent generation are now commonly called *war children* (*Kriegskinder*). Sociologist Harald Welzer (2008) points out that, rather than being a homogenous sociological age group, the generation of the war children covers a range of diverging experiences. It stretches from children who were too young to remember 1945 to those who might recall nights in air-raid shelters with their mothers, while others were already entering puberty at that time and may have been active in the Hitler Youth or as *Flakhelfer* (antiaircraft helpers).

The war grandchildren (Kriegsenkel), born roughly between 1955 and 1975, are the biological children of those war children. These demarcations are applied fairly strictly within the Kriegsenkel community. More than once I heard murmuring in a support group meeting that a person was "not a real Kriegsenkel" because his or her father had already been a soldier during World War II or because one or both parents were born after 1945.

Secondly, and more importantly, the term also implies a shared psychological burden: being a Kriegsenkel means being (predominantly negatively) affected by the parents' and grandparents' war experiences. Psychological concepts of transgenerational transmission of trauma are a priori enshrined in the self-understanding. This assumption pushes the term away from a particular sociological generation with a shared historical experience (see Mannheim 1928) toward a collective illness identity and psychopathology. Anthropologist Kristin Barker (2002, 284) defines a shared illness identity as "an understanding of self, and affiliation with others, on the basis of a shared experience of symptoms and suffering." Although she worked with sufferers of fibromyalgia syndrome, a controversial pain disorder, this definition is transferable to the German Kriegsenkel. Only people who suffered emotionally and who understood the war to be the causal agent of their pain would call themselves Kriegsenkel, while others of the same age and family background (or even the same family) would not.

Yet, while concepts of transgenerational transmission of trauma are at the core of the Kriegsenkel identity construction, the interesting fact is that there is only limited psychological research to back this claim for the German case. Most of the research was not available when the first war grandchildren books were published and the first self-help groups started to meet. Both Ustorf (2008) and Bode (2009) point out that the body of research on which their presentation of Kriegsenkel life histories is built originated from other contexts—in particular (and controversially, as I pointed out) from Holocaust survivors and their families.

DO TRAUMATIC EXPERIENCES TRAVEL ACROSS GENERATIONS?: A BRIEF OVERVIEW OF PSYCHOLOGICAL RESEARCH ON TRANSGENERATIONAL TRANSMISSION

Transmission of Trauma and the Phenomenon of the "Second Generation"

As mentioned in the introduction, questions about the transgenerational impact of trauma were first raised in relation to families of Holocaust survivors. Over the past decades, a substantial body of research was put together, examining from many different perspectives whether and how the pain endured during the Holocaust affected the children and grandchildren of survivors. Overall the findings remained inconclusive. Some research found that children of Holocaust survivors were in general not more prone to psychopathology than the rest of the population of their respective countries (Felsen 1998; Solomon 1998; Kellermann 2008). Yet they were also said to be more vulnerable to mental health issues, and those who were adversely affected by their emotional legacy were found to suffer more deeply than their peers (Danieli 2007). Reviewing the population-based (as opposed to clinical) studies on children of North American Holocaust survivors, Irit Felsen (1998, 57) concluded that while most of them were functioning within a "normal range," their typical characteristics included a higher tendency for depression and anxiety; more difficulty in expressing emotions; and more intense feelings of guilt, self-criticism, and psychosomatic complaints. Comparing the mental health of Israeli Holocaust descendants with that of the general population, empirical studies reviewed by Zahava Solomon (1998) found no difference in levels of anxiety, depression, and neurosis at the time of the study (although many reported past symptoms) but did find evidence of higher levels of guilt and self-criticism, lower ego strength, and more difficulties in managing aggression. In both countries, the younger generation was reported to have difficulties separating from their parents and becoming independent. Parents were often described as enmeshed and overly involved in their children's lives, while other descendants complained about parental disengagement, emotional inaccessibility, and lack of support (Felsen 1998; Solomon 1998).

Based on data from the 2007 Israel National Health Survey, Natan Kellermann (2008, 263) identified a group of descendants who suffered from severe "Second Generation Syndrome." They saw Holocaust experiences of their parents as the source of their issues, either through a direct transmission of parental symptoms associated with the "Survivor Syndrome" (Niederland 1968) or an indirect result of growing up with parents whose parenting skills were impaired because of their extreme traumatization (Felsen 1998). On the other hand, in their nonclinical study of ninety-eight families of Holocaust survivors and their (female) descendants, Abraham Sagi-Schwartz and his colleagues found that in spite of the fact that the survivors were still suffering from the trauma of the Holocaust fifty years on, there was no evidence that their suffering had been transmitted to their daughters (Sagi-Schwartz et al. 2003). They concluded that the survivors had successfully protected their family relationships from the influence of their Holocaust experiences.

Research about families of Holocaust survivors provided the foundation for subsequent investigations into the transgenerational effects of trauma in other contexts, such as the Vietnam War (Ancharoff, Munroe, and Fisher 1998; Rosenheck and Nathan 1985, 1994); the genocides in Turkey (Altounian 1999; Kupelian, Sanentz Kalayjian, and Kassabian 1998) and in Cambodia (Kidron 2009a, 2012; Kinzie, Boehnlein, and Sack 1998; Münyas 2008); repressive regimes in the Soviet Union (Baker and Gippenreiter 1998) and in South America (Becker and Diaz 1998; Dickson-Gómez 2002; Edelman, Kordon, and Lagos 1998); and the repression of indigenous populations (Brave Heart and DeBruyn 1998; Cross 1998; Raphael, Swan, and Martinek 1998). Clinical studies and empirical research based on accounts by mental health practitioners from different countries reported a range of symptoms observed in patients from families who had lived through war and violence. For example, Dutch psychologists, psychiatrists, and social workers who treated children of World War II war sailors and civilian resistance fighters noticed that their clients' complaints commonly included feelings of isolation and authority conflicts, problems with work and with relationships, and delinquent behaviors and psychosis, as well as separation and identification problems and a reversal of the parent-child role (Op den Velde 1998). Drawing on qualitative research on children of Dutch collaborators with the Nazi regime during World War II—until the 1980s a taboo topic in Dutch society and families—Martijn Lindt (1998) found shared feelings of anxiety, social insecurity, and hyperalertness, as well as struggles with guilt and a lack of belonging. Petra Aarts (1998) interviewed psychotherapists about their experiences with sons and daughters of World War II survivors from the Dutch East Indies. Many of these patients had sought help to alleviate problems with separation from their parents, individuation, and autonomy. They were perceived to lack basic trust and to have difficulties in regulating or expressing strong emotions. While they often displayed high levels of occupational functioning, their therapists found these patients more difficult to treat than other clients, in terms of both the intensity and the duration of the treatment (Aarts 1998). Lastly, Rosenheck and Nathan (1985; cited in Ancharoff, Munroe, and Fisher 1998) described typical children of Vietnam veterans suffering from PTSD as prone to a range of symptoms from insomnia, headaches, tearfulness, and feelings of helplessness to attention problems at school, fears of being kidnapped or killed, and fantasies that resembled their fathers' flashbacks of traumatic situations. While these studies do not claim to present an authoritative list of common psychological symptoms, they do point to the existence of a second-generation profile—a similarity in how descendants in their respective countries were seen to struggle as a result of their parents' trauma. This profile may also—as in the case of the Dutch collaborators—include difficulties resulting from a family history of perpetratorship.

German War Trauma: A Blind Spot in Psychotherapy and Psychological Research

Comparable research for the German majority population has only started to emerge in the last few years. Bettina Alberti (2010), for example, reported from her psychotherapeutic practice that children of parents who lived through World War II often carried a deep-seated sense of loneliness, a depressed worldview, and negative attitudes toward life. She found that they lacked confidence and had problems with self-worth and emotional expression. Psychoanalyst Andreas Bachofen (2012) observed that his patients of this age group tended to have difficulties with separation and individuation from their parents. Lamparter and Holstein (2013) paint a picture of descendants of families who lived through the firebombing of Hamburg in 1943 as a group with an insecure sense of identity and higher rates of anxiety. Psychotherapists Udo Baer and Gabriele Frick-Baer (2015) seek to help people with diffuse fears, inexplicable feelings of loneliness and unworthiness, or an excessive high-achievement orientation to address these issues in light of their families' World War II trauma. While they suggest something akin to a second-generation profile also for the German case, these studies are recent and still relatively few in number.

The reason that German research is at least two decades behind that of many other countries can be found, again, in the taboos and silences around German wartime suffering explored in the previous chapters. There is a general consensus among practitioners that until around 2000 psychologists did not commonly talk about the war with their patients (Ermann 2007; Jerouschek 2004; Radebold, Bohleber, and Zinnecker 2008). Hartmut Radebold believes that therapists, many of whom were of the Kriegskinder generation themselves, did not acknowledge the damage the war had left in their patients because they had no awareness of it in themselves. "That part of our biography was ignored by an entire analytical generation," he said in an unpublished interview with Andrea Frey in 2012. "Of course we were also highly identified with the German guilt, so that what we had experienced ourselves took a step back and was not allowed to play a role." None of the therapists I talked to in Berlin had previously paid any attention to World War II when treating Germans of any generation, in spite of the fact that the war constituted a constant presence in the public sphere. Taboos, gaps, and blind spots also clearly dominated the realm of psychotherapy.

Since 2000, a number of psychological studies on the occurrence of PTSD in German seniors have appeared (for example, Brähler et al. 2011; Eichhorn and Kuwert 2011; Glaesmer et al. 2010, 2011; Kuwert, Klauer, and Eichhorn 2010;

Spitzer et al. 2011; Teegen and Meister 2000). Post-traumatic stress disorder, with clearly defined symptoms and ways to capture them, became available as a psychiatric diagnosis for the Kriegskinder generation (although none of my interviewees' parents had been diagnosed with it). However, there was no equivalent when it came to their children. Being a Kriegsenkel was not linked to a recognized psychological disorder, and those who identified as such had no way of proving that their suffering had its "causal agent" (Swoboda 2006, 234) in the war.

As a consequence, the Kriegsenkel were taking it into their own hands to validate and legitimize their suffering and to underscore that they were experiencing not just individual problems but a psychological burden shared by many across their generation. As has been observed for cases of contested or emerging illnesses where the status as a legitimate condition is still controversial, a self-help community gathered around a shared illness identity to confer legitimacy and to offer mutual support (Swoboda 2006). The German Kriegsenkel engaged with the self-help community's resources to diagnose themselves as sufferers of transmitted war trauma, and they affirmed their emergent identity in face-to-face and Facebook groups. Through their practices, they were also negotiating the "symptoms" belonging to an emerging Kriegsenkel "condition." In the process something akin to a psychological profile as a German "second generation" was (and still is) being assembled.[16]

KRIEGSENKEL PRACTICES: TRANSFORMING "MIDDLE-CLASS COMPLAINERS" INTO SUFFERERS OF TRANSMITTED WAR TRAUMA

Diagnosis: Kriegsenkel

I was often puzzled that when I asked my interviewees in Berlin, "How do you know that you are a Kriegsenkel?" they consistently responded with statements like "You know, my mother is one of these 'cold mothers' that Sabine Bode mentions in her book," or "Sabine Bode says that Kriegsenkel often feel homeless; I also have this sense that I don't belong," or "Do you remember so-and-so in Ustorf's war grandchildren book? They constantly moved house—that is just like me; I also cannot settle anywhere!" Like A. W. quoted at the beginning of this chapter, people found their own issues reflected in the published Kriegsenkel life histories, triggering a big eureka moment and a complete reassessment of their individual and family histories. The fact that people of similar age were struggling in similar ways was understood as a clear indication that this was not just personal but part of a wider phenomenon affecting an entire generation. Anthropologists and sociologists have described the process of narrative reconstruction of a person's identity as "codependent" (Irvine 1999), as a "non-drinking alcoholic" (Cain 1991), or as a "second generation Holocaust survivor" (Kidron 2003) in the context of the self-help groups. The facilitator and other group members instruct participants to narrate their lives in accordance with a particular "narrative formula" (Irvine 1999, 3). For the German Kriegsenkel, on the other hand, the "identity acquisition" (Cain 1991, 6) and subsequent rewriting of their life history happened through individual interactions with the Kriegsenkel books.

In particular, Bode's (2009) book seemed to have the status of something akin to an unofficial diagnostic manual that many of my interviewees used to identify themselves as sufferers of transmitted World War II trauma. Any problems described there were accepted as belonging to a collective Kriegsenkel profile. This role of the books is similar to what Barker (2002) describes for the fibromyalgia (FMS) self-help movement. There, a substantial number of self-help guides define FMS and the range of possible symptoms (not necessarily the same ones in each book) attached to it. Some have questionnaires to help people ascertain whether they are indeed suffering from FMS. In the absence of a medical diagnosis, the purpose of the books is to enable sufferers to confirm that they have the condition (as well as offer advice on how to manage pain). The Kriegsenkel books, on the other hand, make no such claims, and the informal diagnostic role attributed to them may well have been accidental rather than intended by the authors.

Some Kriegsenkel also made reference to the life histories shared on Forumkriegsenkel.de to underscore that they were suffering from the same predicament. Or they pointed to the list of "symptoms" collected and published on the same site following the online survey mentioned above. This happened in spite of the fact that the list was a simple compilation of all contributions received and was never intended to be representative or scientific (Barth 2012). Still, one person said that she would print the list and keep it in her wallet as a daily reminder that whenever she felt a certain emotion, it was because she was a Kriegsenkel and not because she was "strange" or "different," as she had always assumed before. The Wikipedia entry states that the term *Kriegsenkel* is a "*Selbstbezeichnung*" (self-identification or self-labeling), but it is more than that. Identifying as Kriegsenkel is a self-diagnosis, and it has clear connotations of a mental health condition. In the absence of official psychiatric or psychological assessments, building on international research embedded in the Kriegsenkel books, the war grandchildren were de facto diagnosing their families as sufferers of war trauma, and they were diagnosing themselves as victims of transmitted trauma.

Assembling a New Psychological Profile

While the Kriegsenkel books allowed their readers to assume a new identity as sufferers of transmitted war trauma, other self-help resources such as the websites and the support groups provided an affirmation of the diagnosis and further validation. In particular the groups that met in person but also the Facebook communities helped their members break through social isolation and offer empathy, peer-to-peer advice, and emotional support. Yet I believe the practices performed in these contexts also serve another, more implicit, function: the collection and negotiation of symptoms seen as belonging to an emerging Kriegsenkel profile.

In support group meetings I attended in 2012–13 and in the Facebook group discussions I observed later on, participants were comparing their own issues with those of others to affirm that their difficulties were part of a common Kriegsenkel experience. The face-to-face group meetings tended to follow a certain pattern. After a first round of introductions that provided key information to confirm a person's "credentials" as a "true" Kriegsenkel ("Hello, my name is Lina. I was born in 1966, my parents were born in 1933 and 1940, and my father's family had to leave their home in Poland after the war"), participants either picked up on some of the issues raised (such as the impact of flight and expulsion) or focused on a preselected topic. The largest part of the evening was always filled with storytelling and comments about the participants' experiences. People would describe their past and current difficulties and explain these problems with their parents' war childhoods. They would talk about their own issues and set them in relation to their upbringing in these families affected and impaired by war and violence. Other participants would contribute their own similar experiences, validating the person's sharing and confirming that the problems were of wider concern.

In the Facebook groups, a member could start a discussion with a statement like "It is hard for me to be happy and look forward to things, because I am always worried that suddenly everything is going to end and that I will have to start all over again," sometimes followed by the question "Can anyone else relate to this?" Other people would then respond in the affirmative and share their own perceptions. Sometimes they explicitly linked their current emotions back to the war, while in other instances that causal connection was only inferred, simply because the person posted in that particular forum. Again, the responses from other members reassured the person that the emotions were valid and real and that they were more than just individual character traits, oddities, or personal flaws. While it was never explicitly acknowledged, through these practices of "sharing and comparing," the participants were slowly fleshing out a psychological profile. With the case studies in the Kriegsenkel books and on the websites as a starting point, these groups were negotiating and cementing common attributes and typical emotional difficulties attached to a Kriegsenkel diagnosis.

There is an interesting comparison with Carol Kidron's research (2003) among Israeli support groups for the children of Holocaust survivors. There, a psychologically trained group facilitator helped structure the storytelling, carefully pointing to the connection between the group members' current psychological issues and their parents' trauma. Each of the eight group meetings focused on one particular aspect defined by the psychological literature as typical for children of Holocaust survivors (e.g., repression of emotions, difficulties with intimacy, fear of separation, an overly enmeshed childhood and adult relationship with parents, and failure to separate and individuate; Kidron 2003). The facilitator, Kidron argues, therefore instructed the participants to understand themselves as a "second generation" and supplied them with a predefined list of symptoms belonging to this profile.

In Germany a similar structure did not (yet) exist. The portraits in the war grandchildren books and the list collated on *Forumkriegsenkel.de* offered a significant number of emotional problems and character traits viewed to be the result of transmitted unresolved war experiences. However, while some traits are mentioned more often than others (a sense of homelessness, for example), the list was long, broad, and general, and there was no final, authorized version. What I observed was an organic rather than a deliberate process of collecting symptoms, driven by the Kriegsenkel desire to understand and validate their emotional struggles rather than by trained professionals. In both cases, that of the Kriegsenkel and the second-generation Holocaust survivors, the identity construction was based on psychological concepts of transmitted trauma. Yet in many ways the Kriegsenkel practices were closer to other "intentional communities of suffering" (Goldstein 2004, 125) formed in the context of emerging or controversial illnesses such as fibromyalgia or chronic fatigue syndrome (CFS). While the psychological issues of second-generation Holocaust survivors are widely recognized, the Kriegsenkel were still looking for validation of their pain and of the realness of their condition. Debra Swoboda (2006, 242) points out that self-help communities allow sufferers to understand their contested illness as a particular collection of symptoms or a syndrome, even if the cause of the condition remains unclear. The exchanges with like-minded people help participants identify symptoms and experiences they have in common and therefore corroborate the idea of a shared illness identity. Through their interactions, group members can also expand the diagnostic frame of the condition by attributing a broader range of symptoms to the disorder (Koski 2014). Lastly, they engage with others to discuss potential healing approaches, including alternative cures, while official treatments are still lacking (Swoboda 2006). All these characteristics also describe the Kriegsenkel self-help community.

BETTER "SICK" THAN "STRANGE": FROM THE DESIRE TO LEGITIMIZE SUFFERING TO CONSUMER-DRIVEN MEDICALIZATION

"Finally, I Am No Longer 'Crazy' by Myself. It Is a Phenomenon."

Medical sociologist Phil Brown (1995) explains that a diagnosis serves an important psychological function: it helps the person find meaning in confusion, gives credence to a condition, and legitimizes suffering. Many Kriegsenkel had always felt that there was "something wrong" with them; that they were different and strange and were not coping as well with life as expected. A. W. stands for many others in that, while finding some help in psychotherapy, they could not get a handle on their whole suite of psychological symptoms until reading Anne-Ev Ustorf's book. "Now I finally know what is going on with me," A. W. sighed with relief. Through the Kriegsenkel self-diagnosis, the indistinct malaise of seemingly disparate and unconnected symptoms was transformed into a "real" condition. A condition with a name, associated symptoms, and a clearly defined cause—transmitted World War II trauma.

According to sociologist Frank Furedi (2004, 180) having a name for one's illness is an important step toward legitimization and public recognition. Being relabeled as sick rather than strange is also seen to shed a new light on past failures and current struggles, as it allows victims to account for their problems in life. Furedi suspects that this is one of the reasons behind the steadily increasing demand for official diagnoses of emerging conditions. "Disease explains an individual's behavior and even helps confer a sense of identity. The medicalization of everyday life allows individuals to make sense of their predicament and gain moral sympathy" (Furedi 2004, 183). He furthermore picks up on the growing tendency to make disease into an ongoing aspect of one's sense of self, with labels like "cancer survivor" or "recovering alcoholic" (97).

Some of my interviewees were quite aware of these implications and were carefully weighing the consequence of taking on or retaining the Kriegsenkel label. Sitting in her garden during our second meeting in May 2012, Nora deliberated: "Saying about myself that I am a Kriegsenkel means I am *gestört* [damaged or crazy]; it has something pathological. At times, when I was a bit more into the topic, I did use the term. Now I would probably rather say, 'I am the daughter of a war child.' That my mother is a war child is certain. But to put myself in a position of saying, 'I am a war grandchild and the war belongs to me,' I would not say that at the moment, but that might very well change again in the future."

Paula was also cautious: "*War grandchildren* is too narrow for me; it has so much heaviness. *Children of war children* means the word *war* is not part of me. But with *war grandchildren*, all the cruelty and heaviness of the war ends up with me. *Children of war children* means the war is where it belongs, with my parents' generation. Eventually, you will pass the parcel back to your parents and they will then pass it back to theirs, and at some point, things will get easier. *War grandchildren* for me has something so . . . hopeless."

When Ines gave up the Erzählcafé again at the end of 2016, she wrote an email to all past participants. She thanked them for their trust and openness and all the valuable discussions, enriching encounters, and shared moments. However, her decision to quit, she declared, was final: "Although this topic will forever be part of me, I do not want to be a Kriegsenkel for life!" Nora, Paula, and Ines refused to permanently enshrine the word *Kriegsenkel* in their identities, which in their view would turn them into victims of their families' emotional legacy for good. They were exceptions, though. Also, while they rejected the label, they still had no doubt that processes of transgenerational transmission were real and that the war had influenced their lives in a major way. Most of my other interviewees who shared this belief wholeheartedly embraced their Kriegsenkel identity.

I admit that there is something infinitely more powerful in presenting oneself as a sufferer of transmitted war trauma than in being dismissed as a middle-class whiner complaining that life did not quite turn out the way one had hoped. However, hearing stories like A. W.'s brings to mind Leslie Irvine's comment that while narratives of suffering are socially constructed, suffering itself is always real for the person experiencing it (Irvine 1999). How much of it has its indirect cause in the war is a second question, one for which there will probably not be a definitive answer. It needs to be said, though, that while around two-thirds of my interviewees believed that World War II had an impact on their families' and their own mental health, very few of them insisted that this was the only factor that caused their emotional problems, even if it was often an important one.

One cannot help but notice, though, as Barker (2002) also observed for the fibromyalgia self-help movement, that through the groups' resources and practices a broad range of disparate symptoms were drawn together under the Kriegsenkel label. This lack of clear boundaries could be attributed to the recency of the topic. Not enough time has passed for a body of research to emerge and allow for the formalization of symptoms. However, more importantly, this openness was also due to the permissiveness of the illness narrative (Barker 2002, 285). The broad and rather vague definition of the Kriegsenkel "condition" (being affected by one's family's war experience) allows for the attribution of a vast number of issues. Many of them are quite generic (depression, burnout, anxiety, etc.) and some even contradictory. In Anne-Ev Ustorf's (2008) book, for example, the impact of flight and expulsion on the person's life was seen as the need to constantly move to a new house in one case study and as an overattachment to home and reluctance to move in another. This raises the question of what would be considered "normal" (i.e., not influenced by the war). In the Facebook and support group exchanges, a special effort was often made to reassure people that whatever they felt to be the consequences of the war on their lives were legitimate concerns.

In fact, occurrences of transmitted trauma are not easy to diagnose, even with psychological assessment techniques. Von Issendorff (2013) points out that while there clearly is something quite distinct about growing up with parents and grandparents who had a difficult past, two levels of assessment are needed to substantiate the claim that a transmission of traumatic experiences has happened. Firstly, it needs to be established that the older generation was indeed traumatized. Yet not every person who witnesses or experiences war, loss, or violence responds in the same way. Some people are more resilient, while others suffer more intensely and more lastingly, depending on a broad range of psychological and environmental factors. In many cases, the original incident lies far back in the past, without the eyewitness generation ever having sought psychological help (and when diagnoses such as PTSD did not yet exist). This makes a retroactive assessment difficult, as Kitano (1985, cited in Nagata 1998, 135) explains in the context of Japanese Americans interned by the US government during World War II: "The problem of measuring the results of an event that occurred over 40 years ago is complicated by intervening years, a lack of relevant material, a complexity of many interacting variables that affect behavior, the vagaries of memory, and the near impossibility of reconstructing an event not designed for evaluative purposes." Even if a person is diagnosed with PTSD later in life, it is difficult to ascertain that the current symptoms are related to a specific event (Wierling 2013) and that these manifested during the crucial time when the person was raising children (Von Issendorff 2013). Secondly, the mental health problems reported by the children need to have a clear causal relationship with the parents' trauma. However, the transmission of traumatic experiences can be influenced and overlaid by a great number of other biographical and psychological factors, and symptoms cannot be cleanly observed and attributed in isolation (Von Issendorff 2013).

Some allies that helped strengthen the Kriegsenkel claim come from the field of epigenetics. Recent research that was reported in the media (for example, Hurley 2013) showed that parental trauma is transmitted to the offspring at the level of the genes. This was quoted a few times during my interviews to underscore the point that transmission of trauma is not only real but also inevitable because it "even changes the genes." In that sense, being a Kriegsenkel is not unlike other forms of biological or "genetic citizenship" where sufferers define their identity and selfhood around an inherited biological illness (Lemke, Casper, and Moore 2011, 98).

In spite of the fact that there may not be final proof to underpin their perceptions, it remains that for the Kriegsenkel their new illness identity provided a coherent framework and a name that they intuitively felt to be a true representation of their suffering. The unofficial diagnosis provided by the books and fleshed out and cemented in the support groups and the internet forum offered an acknowledgment of their pain and a level of comfort they had been missing. This is how Sabine S. expressed this sentiment: "I had no idea that there are so many other people who feel like I do, who are also struggling with diffuse fears and depression, which 'somehow do not belong to them.' It is a relief and a shock at the same time. Disconcerting and comforting. One would like to meet them all and call out: 'Hey guys and girls, I am just like you!' And to laugh and cry about it together. Finally, I am not alone anymore. Finally, I am no longer 'crazy' by myself. It is a phenomenon."[17]

The Medicalization of Growing Up in Families Affected by World War II

Furedi (2004) points out that increasingly it is not professional bodies that are pushing for the introduction of a new medical or psychological disorder but the sufferers themselves who demand recognition of their condition. Social movements and interest groups have been pivotal in raising public awareness and in championing the acknowledgment of new conditions by the medical profession. Peter Conrad (2005) cites the introduction of alcoholism as a disease as an example, where Alcoholics Anonymous and the "alcoholism movement" were driving the process while physicians were reluctant or resistant. Another well-known case is the inclusion of post-traumatic stress disorder (PTSD) in the third edition of the American Psychiatric Association's Diagnostic and

Statistical Manual in 1980, which was the result of intense lobbying by Vietnam veteran groups and lay activists. Their coordinated effort made trauma into an officially recognized disorder and opened the door for veterans to gain access to specialized treatment (Cotten and Ridings 2011; Kutchins and Kirk 1997).

In the twenty-first century, sufferers who define their problems as medical have come to function as one of the main "engines of medicalization" (Conrad 2005). The construction of shared illness identities as it happens through participation in health-related self-help communities are key to this process (Barker 2008). The rise of the internet in particular has transformed suffering into more of a public experience and has created increased demand for medical goods and services. Participants in electronic FMS support groups, for example, not only affirm the medical character of their problem but also empower one another to search for physicians who will recognize and treat their condition (Barker 2008). Debra Swoboda (2006) found that sufferers of chronic fatigue syndrome, multiple chemical sensitivities, and Gulf War syndrome who were active in support groups, internet chat boards, and mailing lists played a significant role in developing case definitions and a social consensus of their conditions that would then feed into further scientific research. Chronic fatigue sufferers also demanded the provision of funding for medical research to systematize diagnostic markers for their illness, which, it was hoped, would legitimize their symptoms and allow for better treatment (Furedi 2004).

When I left Germany in late 2013, the German Kriegsenkel were only in the early stages of this process. The participants in most of the activities were still first and foremost focused on exploring and affirming their newly found identity for themselves and with one another, as well as on trying to communicate this identity to their families (not always successfully). There was, however, clearly an emerging demand for specialized therapeutic interventions, which was initially predominantly satisfied by alternative healers (as we will see in chap. 4). In spite of that, it was obvious that the Kriegsenkel definition, their resources, and their practices were all pushing toward a pathologization of growing up in families who survived World War II.

This is not uncontroversial. For many years, the continuous broadening of categories of mental illness and the constant creation of new disorders and syndromes have been criticized as pathologizing and medicalizing the problems of everyday life (Furedi 2004, 99). Allan Horwitz (2003) argues that most conditions currently regarded as mental illness could be viewed as normal reactions to stressful social circumstances or forms of deviant behavior. Thomas Szasz (2007) adds that it was modern psychiatry's desire to explain the human condition that led to the treatment of life's difficulties and oddities as clinical illnesses. Kutchins and Kirk (1997) bemoan the "growing tendency in our society to medicalize problems that are not medical, to find pathology where there is only pathos and to pretend to understand phenomena by merely giving them a label and a code number." Lastly, authors such as Atwood Gaines (1992) and Eva Illouz (2008) are critical of the rapid expansion of the categories of mental illness, which they see as driven by the financial interests of mental health professionals and pharmaceutical companies keen to sell more and more drugs for ever new disorders.

In the case of the Kriegsenkel, their interests were clearly pushing in the direction these authors criticize. Charlotte (born in 1966) suspected that many Kriegsenkel would be glad to be categorized, labeled, and diagnosed and to be told by a psychologist that their predicament was a (new) mental health condition, rather than understanding themselves as victims of an overreaching mental health system. However, the main driving force behind the Kriegsenkel's push toward medicalization was more than just the need to give meaning and legitimation to suffering or to be granted an exemption from personal responsibility vis-à-vis one's failures and shortcomings in life. It relates to the fact that with a shared illness identity also comes a promise for treatment and healing. Unlike a diffuse sense of malaise and disparate symptoms, which are hard to address, a clear diagnosis is the first step on a path toward targeted therapeutic interventions to lessen distress. It seems that in order to go from being "strange" and "different" to being "normal" and "happy," one has to go through being "sick" first.

The next chapter looks more closely at the construction of Kriegsenkel identities and the way this generation tries to overcome the emotional legacy of World War II within the framework of contemporary therapy culture.

NOTES

1. Shared on Forumkriegsenkel. n.d. "Lebengeschichten." Accessed November 9, 2019. http://www.forumkriegsenkel.de/Lebensgeschichten.htm.

2. See Wikipedia, The Free Encyclopedia. "Löschkandidaten," March 30, 2015. http://de.wikipedia.org/wiki/Wikipedia:Löschkandidaten/30._März_2015. As per Wikipedia's policies, members of the public can request the deletion of a particular entry. The request is open for discussion for seven days, after which a Wikipedia administrator decides to delete or retain the entry on the basis of the arguments brought forward by both sides.

3. Wikipedia, The Free Encyclopedia. "Löschkandidaten", March 30, 2015. Accessed November 9, 2019. http://de.wikipedia.org/wiki/Wikipedia:Löschkandidaten/30._März_2015.

4. See, for example, Kriegsenkel EU. 2019. Accessed November 9, 2019. http://www.uni-forst.gwdg.de/~wkurth/psh/k_links.htm; Kriegsenkel Dortmund. 2014. Accessed November 9, 2019. http://www.kriegsenkel-dortmund.de; Integrative Psychotherapie in Leipzig. 2019. Accessed November 9, 2019. https://www.psychotherapie-und-beratung-in-leipzig.de/bewusstsein-le/leipziger-kriegsenkel-gruppe/.

5. See Forum Kriegsenkel. n.d. Accessed November 9, 2019. www.forumkriegsenkel.de (English translation as per website.)

6. Interview with Anne Barth on September 17, 2012, and email correspondence in May 2015.

7. For the complete list, see Forumkriegsenkel. n.d. "Studie." Accessed November 9, 2019. http://www.forumkriegsenkel.de/Studie.htm.

8. Kriegsenkel e.V. n.d. "Gesprächsgruppen." Accessed November 9, 2019. http://www.kriegsenkel.de/gespraechsgruppen/.

9. Family Constellations. n.d. Hellinger sciencia. Accessed November 9, 2019. http://www2.hellinger.com/en/home/; See EMDR International Association. n.d. Accessed November 9, 2019. http://www.emdria.org.

10. Back2Future. n.d. "Emotionales Gefühlserbe." Accessed November 9, 2019. https://www.back2future-kriegsenkel.com/angebote/seminare/.

11. KriegsenkelLab. n.d. Accessed January 9, 2019. https://www.meyer-legrand.eu/portfolio/kriegsenkellab.

12. Baring's family constellations were portrayed for an English-speaking audience in the *New Yorker*, September 12, 2016. http://www.newyorker.com/magazine/2016/09/12/familienaufstellung-germanys-group-therapy.

13. See SynergetikPraxis Monika Weidlich. n.d. "Anwendungsgebiete der Synergetik." Accessed November 9, 2019. http://www.synergetik-hannover.de/anwendung.htm.

14. Interview with Monika Weidlich on June 11, 2012, and personal email correspondence.

15. Kriegsenkel e.V. n.d. Accessed August 9, 2015. http://www.Kriegsenkel.de (English translation as per website). The website was redesigned in late 2015, and the text was replaced by a longer explanation.

16. The German Kriegsenkel do not tend to call themselves "second generation" because they want to avoid all inappropriate comparison with Holocaust survivor families, yet in terms of psychological research the term is equivalent: they are the children of the eyewitness generation.

17. Forumkriegsenkel. n.d. "Lebensgeschichten." Accessed November 9, 2019. http://www.forumkriegsenkel.de/Lebensgeschichten.htm.

FOUR

"HOORAY, I AM A KRIEGSENKEL!"

Suffering and Liberation in the Age of Therapy

THIS IS HOW SOME MEMBERS of the war grandchildren generation described the moment when they came across the term *Kriegsenkel* for the first time: "When I read Sabine Bode's book it was as if a veil was suddenly lifted from my eyes"; "When I heard about the 'project war grandchildren' from the local newspaper, I immediately felt caught out"; or "'Kriegsenkel'! YES! Finally! That is me!" It often came as a big revelation, as an eye-opener. It stopped people in their tracks. Something clicked in, rewired the brain, and kick-started a powerful psychological process. It was the beginning of a journey, during which people transformed themselves from middle-aged Germans with emotional problems into Kriegsenkel. They rewrote their life histories, established new senses of identity and belonging, and treaded new ways to liberate themselves from the burden of the past.

The last chapter described the Kriegsenkel movement more generally: its history, self-understanding, and activities as well as the processes and practices that led people to an informal diagnosis as victims of transmitted war trauma in their search for legitimization of suffering. This chapter investigates how the group constructs, explores, performs, and manages this newly found identity in the cultural framework of contemporary self-help and "therapy culture" (Furedi 2004).

A shorter version of this chapter was published as "Suffering and Liberation in the Age of Therapy: Germany's 'Grandchildren of the Second World War'" in *Ethnography* 18, no. 4 (December 1, 2017): 450–70. The article was first published online on October 20, 2016.

There is a broad consensus that what has been subsumed under such labels as "therapeutics" (Rose 1998), "therapeutic ethos," "therapeutic culture," "therapeutic worldview" (Furedi 2004), "therapeutic gospel" (Moskowitz 2001), or "therapeutic persuasion" (Illouz 2008) has exerted an unparalleled influence on modern Western (and increasingly global) societies. Psychological thinking has transcended the relationship between an individual and a therapist, spilling over into almost every aspect of private and public life. The therapeutic discourse "has come to constitute one of the major codes with which to express, shape, and guide selfhood" (Illouz 2008, 7). This chapter shows how this discourse plays out in the lives of Germans who have come to identify as Kriegsenkel. The reader will be invited to follow Kerstin's Kriegsenkel journey from her first contact in early 2012 until the end of 2013. Using her story as an example, I draw out and discuss common features core to constituting a Kriegsenkel identity. Later, I will question how pervasive this new "collective identity" (Stein 2009) is and why some people identify so strongly with the topic while others—including those who grew up in the same families—do not. At the end of the chapter, I will discuss some of the controversial aspects of the contemporary therapy culture. Sociologists have long critiqued therapy culture as cultivating vulnerability and victimhood and as promoting political disengagement and narcissistic self-concern. Looking from the subjective experiences of "consumers" of therapy and self-help culture, I suggest a more nuanced view. Therapeutic discourses also create meaning for emotional problems, help break through social isolation, and offer therapeutic interventions, often seen as the only hope for a better and healthier future.

Now, please meet Kerstin from East Berlin.

BECOMING A KRIEGSENKEL

Kerstin's Story

Kerstin was a lively fifty-year-old woman with short brown hair, a broad smile, and an even broader Berlin accent. During our first meeting in a popular coffee shop buzzing with tourists and mothers with prams keen to enjoy some rays of rare afternoon sun, she kept jumping up to have a quick chat with friends who happened to walk past. Kerstin seemed happy and extroverted; her face lit up when she talked about herself. It was easy to relate to her, and we laughed a lot, but every now and then hints of sadness shone through her outward display of joviality. Kerstin was born in East Berlin in 1962, a year after the building of the wall that divided the city for almost thirty years. Her family history was different from most others I heard, because Kerstin came from one of the few families of genuine "antifascist heroes" of which the GDR was so proud. Her maternal grandparents were committed communists and had fled to the Soviet Union in the 1930s when Hitler's helpers started to lock up people with diverging political views. She explained: "When she was twenty or twenty-one, my grandmother emigrated in quite an adventurous fashion through Scandinavia to Moscow because my grandfather was a member of the Communist Party. He followed her later, and they both spent most of their youth in the Soviet Union. Both were working and had quite a good life. Then the war started, and Stalin ordered all foreigners to leave Moscow, including all Germans. They could not go back to Germany and only had the choice between Siberia and Kazakhstan. My grandmother decided to move to Siberia."

Kerstin's mother was born in the Siberian winter of 1942. Her grandfather continued to work for the international communist movement. As member of a partisan group, he parachuted into East Prussia in 1941. He made it all the way west to Berlin, where he was betrayed and captured by the Gestapo—the Nazis' secret police. After that his trace was lost. The rest of the family returned to Germany in 1947, and Kerstin's grandmother married another German communist resistance fighter.

Growing up in the GDR, Kerstin led a privileged life. As a "victim of fascism," her grandmother received a generous state pension, and the family had no material worries. Unlike many others, East or West, Kerstin's family did in fact talk about the war. However, the stories around the dinner table were tales of male heroism, of clever strategizing, and of fierce battles against the Hitler regime. They were the stories read to children in schools, archived in GDR history books, and converted into TV programs. What was omitted, publicly and privately, were accounts of the fear her grandparents felt during the years of Stalinist persecution, the hardship they endured during the cold winters in their Siberian exile, or the fact that her grandmother was struggling with depression after her grandfather's death. Kerstin's mother also suffered from depression, and the relationship with her daughter was tense and often interrupted. "She is one of these 'cold mothers' that are often mentioned in Sabine Bode's book," Kerstin explained to me over pumpkin soup, "someone who keeps her distance, not letting anyone come close. And that has affected my life too, that is also my leitmotif, to be alone all the time."

On the surface Kerstin seemed to be managing her life: she was in a stable relationship, and she worked in her own business. Yet underneath, she admitted, she always felt lost and lonely, and although she had friends, she did not feel as if she belonged. She changed careers a few times without ever having the sense that she was using her full potential. Life was simmering, somewhat muffled and low-key. Nothing was terribly wrong, but it was not quite right either. Over the years, Kerstin had sought help from different therapists, but things did not really change. She never related her issues back to the war, until one day in 2012, when she came across a local newspaper article about the transgenerational impact of World War II. There she read the word *Kriegsenkel* for the first time, and the sudden realization that they could be talking about *her* hit her like a ton of bricks. There were other people who were struggling with similar issues, and they all came from families who had lived through the war. Kerstin immediately caught fire. She bought Sabine Bode's books and passed them on to people around her. She discovered the Kriegsenkel websites. She said of the experience: "I found so much of myself in the internet forum and in the war grandchildren books, and I thought, they don't know me at all, how come they are writing about me? That was a wonderful realization, and it helped explain so much about me. I wrote a few things down that characterize me, and that now has a name. I gave myself this label: Kriegsenkel—great!"

Kerstin looked back over her life with fresh eyes and came to new conclusions about her own and her family's emotional difficulties. "I now know that my mother could not behave in any other way because she was traumatized," she said. Kerstin's previously indistinct sense of malaise had become tangible. It now had a name and a concept behind it: transgenerational transmission of trauma. She wholeheartedly embraced the Kriegsenkel label. She started going to support group meetings and for the first time felt part of something bigger: a group with a shared fate.

I saw Kerstin often in the months following our first meeting. We went to Kriegsenkel workshops and meetings together and spent many afternoons in coffee shops exploring her issues with her family. What I found striking in our conversations was the fact that she was adamant that World War II had traumatized her family and that they had passed this burden on to her. Yet she found it hard to pin this intuitive knowing onto something specific. What exactly was passed to her or how, she could not say: "Being a Kriegsenkel means to me that there was a transgenerational transmission of trauma. Well, I for myself am not traumatized, but I am sure that my mother gave some of it to me. And so did my grandmother . . . probably. At least that is what it seems like, but I am not entirely sure," she admitted. However, it simply *felt* right, and she found so many of her own issues reflected in the life histories of other Kriegsenkel: her feelings of not belonging, of not being loved and accepted; her fear of rejection; her job changes; and her childlessness.

When I met Kerstin again almost a year later in 2013, she was still extremely active in the Kriegsenkel scene, attending support group meetings, going to talks and lectures, and giving interviews for newspapers. She was doing sessions with a homeopath, who used hypnosis to help her work through some of her family issues. She was also booked in for a family constellations workshop to look more closely at the theme of betrayal that seemed to be lingering in her life, which she suspected might go back to her grandfather. Since I had last seen her, she had found out that he had been taken to Buchenwald concentration camp after his capture, where he was shot in February 1945. The fact that she had managed to find his official death certificate in a historical archive had given her a sense of calm and closure. It also provided her with an explanation for the strange depression that befell her in early February every year, which coincided with the time of her grandfather's violent death.

Kerstin was definite that becoming a Kriegsenkel and looking at her life and family through that lens had helped her more than any other previous therapies. "I gained so much clarity about myself. Now I know why I often feel like I am drifting, without firm ground beneath my feet. I have since become a lot calmer. I now know why my family is like it is, so disjointed and with those frequent interruptions in contact. I can now accept that. I also have a good network in the support groups to talk to other people who help and understand each other." Kerstin kept repeating how much of a liberation the entire process had been for her and said that she no longer felt the "heavy backpack" that she used to carry around. "*Hurra, ich bin ein Kriegsenkel*" ("Hooray, I am a Kriegsenkel"), she proclaimed, summing up her experience. When I asked her what that entailed, she said "a new sense of identity and a new *Lebensgefühl*"—a new feeling about life in general.

Kerstin, like all the people I met, was unique. Yet many elements of her Kriegsenkel journey also appeared in many other accounts. In her story, it is uncanny how much therapeutic thinking and analysis winds through her narrative: diagnosing her mother and grandmother as traumatized; accepting that trauma was transmitted to her and was responsible for many of her present struggles; addressing her issues with different kinds of therapy; and achieving a sense of acceptance or closure in the end. Kriegsenkel identities are firmly grounded in contemporary therapeutic culture. Its rules, logic, and practices provide the framework in which members of this generation understand, explore, perform, and address their emotional suffering. Therapeutic culture is the fabric that weaves and holds Kriegsenkel narratives together. It provides meaning, offers tools to overcome suffering, and relays hope for a better life.

Therapy in Germany and Therapeutic Culture More Broadly

The majority of my German interviewees were experienced in therapy. They had accessed counseling at one or more stages in their lives and were well versed in psychological ideas and language that had percolated into mainstream society. Expressions such as "this problem was delegated to me to work through" or "my grandparents were not able to properly mourn their losses" would flow into our conversations without an assumed need for an explanation.

Compared to countries like Australia, Germany allows broad and comprehensive access to psychotherapy. Since the late 1960s treatment by psychotherapists and psychiatrists has been included in the statutory health insurance, and since the 1990s the number of psychotherapists has grown exponentially in many German cities (Radebold 2012). The health insurance covers the costs for three psychotherapeutic methods: analytical psychotherapy, psychodynamic psychotherapy, and behavior therapy. Other forms, such as client-centered therapy and systemic therapy, are recognized but not currently covered. People are able to choose from a range of mental health professionals, from psychiatric and psychosomatic treatment in hospitals for more serious cases, to psychiatrists and psychotherapists in private practice, to psychosocial counseling centers that are usually specialized to focus on particular issues, such as pregnancy, parenting, addiction, or trauma.[1]

In many cases, the demand for counseling exceeds the offer, and waiting times of four or more months are common (Walendzik et al. 2010). However, once a request is approved, the insurance will cover the cost for the entire treatment up to 160 hours for analytical psychotherapy (in special cases up to 300 hours); up to 50 hours of psychodynamic psychotherapy (in special cases up to 100 hours); and up to 45 hours of behavior therapy (in special cases up to 80 hours). In 2011, the average therapy took forty-six sessions stretched over twenty months (Best 2012). These numbers refer to one distinct phase of therapy from start to finish. A new contingent of sessions is approved for each new phase. It is difficult to have a comprehensive overview of the use of these services because of the fragmentation of Germany's mental health care system (European Commission 2013), but this availability shows that people who access therapy have a long and deep exposure to therapeutic thinking and techniques. Germans who are interested in less traditional approaches and are able to cover the costs themselves can also choose from a vast range of therapies offered by alternative health practitioners (*Heilpraktiker für Psychotherapie*), such as hypnotherapy, reincarnation therapy, and breath and body work.

However, therapeutic culture is much broader than the relationship between a therapist and a patient. Sociologist Eva Illouz (2008) explains that today, not only has a large portion of the entire US population consulted a therapist at some stage in life, but psychological thinking has been institutionalized in many different social spheres, including corporations, the mass media, schools, and the army. Nikolas Rose (1998, 34–35) observed that the "psy sciences" have been eager to lend their vocabulary, explanations, and judgments to other professions and that the "translatability" of their ideas helped their rapid dissemination into most other areas of society. Psychological thinking is now relayed in confessional talk shows and self-help books, magazine advice columns and school curricula, professional development and social welfare programs, prisoner rehabilitation, and hospitals (Illouz 2008; Rose 1998). It is woven into every aspect of life, shaping the ways people think about their relationships, how they rate and improve their sense of professional competency, how they conduct social relations, and how they understand their emotional problems. Psychology, Eva Illouz (2008) summarizes, offers tools and technologies to help people deal with the challenges and complexities of modern life. It has even found its way into animated children's movies. In *Frozen* (Buck and Lee 2013) Princess Elsa withdraws into a solitary ice palace, unable to embrace her special powers and open up to her sister's love. Po, the hero of *Kung Fu Panda 2* (Yuh 2011), is searching for inner peace while being tormented by traumatic flashbacks of his parents' violent death. "He's got daddy issues," the praying mantis says, mocking him when he is yet again unable to control his rage. Illouz argues that the therapeutic narrative has emerged as the basic schema to construct stories about the self and to assemble the autobiographical discourse. It has come to organize "contemporary narratives of selfhood and identity" (Illouz 2008, 155), prescribing the ways people tell their life histories and explain others' behaviors. With this in mind, I will now draw out the common elements from Kerstin's and other Kriegsenkel life histories to explore them in the broader context of the current therapeutic discourses and self-help culture.

FROM INDISTINCT SUFFERING TO VICTIMS OF WAR: THE KRIEGSENKEL JOURNEY IN THE CONTEXT OF THERAPEUTIC CULTURE

The Malaise

A significant number of the people I met in Berlin were surrounded by an aura of loneliness, depression, and frustration. Some, like A. W. from chapter 3, struggled with more severe mental and physical symptoms; others were more generally unhappy and unfulfilled. Many talked about their depression, anxiety, and hopelessness, often finding it hard to establish fulfilling careers and committed relationships. Half of my interviewees did not have children, which was repeatedly pointed to with regret and a feeling of loss (although the reasons were varied). Others did not feel at home in Germany, in spite of being born there. They felt as if they were drifting, never quite arriving anywhere, and at the same time stuck, unable to loosen the hand brake and get started. In spite of having already hit middle age, like Kerstin, they were still waiting for life to begin. Initially, these Germans found it difficult to articulate their unhappiness, the more so because they did not feel entitled to it. Most had grown up in middle-class families without material worries. In their own accounts, they had not experienced any major hardship.

The Yoke of the Family: "It Always Turns Out to Be Your Mother's Fault Anyway"

In this situation of indistinct malaise, the Kriegsenkel could potentially have considered a number of external causes as explanations for their discontent: the job market, lack of suitable life partners, government policies, destiny, karma, or God, among others. Yet all of the people I spoke to, Kerstin being no exception, looked inside themselves to find the answers to their problems and then—as a second step—turned invariably to their families.

Anthropologist Allan Young (1996, 246) explains that while states of suffering "variously described as psychological, existential or spiritual" belonged in the realms of philosophy and religion in the past, today psychobiology and psychiatry have provided a new rhetoric to express these forms of internalized suffering. It was Freud who created a new language to describe, understand, and manage the psyche, and he moved the nuclear family into the center of attention. Parental influences and early childhood traumas are attributed vital importance for emotional issues in a person's later life. This explains why my interviewees looked to their families to identify the source of their anguish. While consideration of her father's war trauma was new to Anja, whose story will be told in the next chapter, previous attempts to pinpoint the reasons for her depression had always stayed within the confines of the family system—her mother's sickness and early death, maybe sexual abuse somewhere in the female family line, etc. Nora confessed that, before picking up the Kriegsenkel topic, she had already churned through "legions of therapists." "It was all a bit of the same, because in the end it always turns out to be your mother's fault anyway," she half-jokingly concluded.

Concepts of Transmission of Trauma as Scaffolding for Kriegsenkel Narratives

Many of the issues mentioned above could be viewed as quite generic psychological problems pervasive in many Western societies.[2] However, at some point my interviewees had come across the Kriegsenkel books and found their own issues and family histories reflected. Binding the collected stories together is the fact that they all belong to the same generation—a generation that grew up in families who lived through World War II. As was the case for Kerstin, considering a possible connection between their own problems and the war for the first time always came as a big revelation. Something *clicked*, and a process was initiated during which people rethought, reevaluated, and ultimately rewrote their life histories. While this *click* often came with an intuitive certainty and embodied knowing, one needs a degree of familiarity with psychological concepts of trauma and its transgenerational transmission to facilitate this link to the past. As shown in chapter 3, the assumption that the war generation had handed down difficult or traumatic war experiences is a priori embedded in the very definition of what it means to be a Kriegsenkel. The overwhelming majority of my interviewees, even those who did not feel affected by the war to the same extent, accepted this premise without questioning. No one I met had actually read the psychological literature on transmission of trauma, but as anthropologists Fassin and Rechtman (2009, 2) noted, ideas of trauma have become mainstream knowledge in many Western societies, a "shared truth."

Looking back on their childhoods, the Kriegsenkel reinterpreted their parents' and grandparents' character traits and behaviors in the light of their war experiences, as Kerstin did with her family. The sense of lacking they experienced when growing up, feeling that their parents were emotionally withdrawn, cold, violent, depressed, or fearful, was now understood to be the result of their war trauma. Trauma that their families would have needed to acknowledge and work through—preferably in therapy. However, because it was extremely rare for Germans of those generations to seek professional help (Ermann 2007), the unresolved emotional damage, so the logic went, was passed on to them and had become their burden to resolve. Psychological concepts of transgenerational transmission provide the narrative backbone around which Kriegsenkel life histories are structured, often acting as a kind of crutch *in lieu* of factual information. Because parents and grandparents rarely talked about their experiences with sufficient openness, the Kriegsenkel could only infer what they may have lived through. While often supported by an embodied certainty, the "truth rule" (Irvine 1999, 85), that unresolved trauma invariable gets passed on to the next generation, helped bridge the gap in factual knowledge about the family history.

Carol Kidron (2003) observed a similar narrative structure in support groups of children of Holocaust survivors in Israel. The causal sequence (historical trauma—damaged parents—descendants' emotional problems) served as a template that enabled group members to renarrate their life histories as having been constituted by the Holocaust and to fill in the holes in the knowledge they had about their parents' past. At the same time, psychological concepts of transgenerational transmission of trauma provided the scaffolding holding the template together (Kidron 2003).

The logic and rationale of the therapeutic discourse enabled the German Kriegsenkel to consolidate their diffuse sense of suffering into a coherent narrative, which provided meaning and a cohesive structure to past life events and current struggles. This narrative transformed the seemingly unjustified middle-class "complainer" into a legitimate sufferer of transmitted trauma and, ultimately, into a victim of war. However, according to the norms of the therapeutic culture, individuals are responsible not only for understanding their problems but also for transforming themselves and constantly striving toward emotional health (Illouz 2008). For the Kriegsenkel the question was consequently never *whether* they needed to work through their emotional inheritance but only *how*.

Exerting Agency and Working Through the Emotional Legacy of World War II

The strategies people chose to address their problems could be subsumed under four categories: emotional support, working through, creative expression, and filling the gaps. People made selections (often more than one) based on their personal preferences and needs, as well as the availability of support structures in their hometowns. Not long after Kerstin diagnosed herself as a Kriegsenkel, she started to look around for emotional support. Realizing that there were others who shared a similar fate, she consulted the designated websites and joined two of the self-help groups in Berlin, longing to connect with her peers. In addition to helping contextualize and legitimize suffering, these groups offer mutual support and emotional comfort. After having felt different and isolated all her life, Kerstin found in them a new sense of belonging and community. When it came to working through on a deeper level, my interviewees mostly chose from the large range of alternative approaches rather than the traditional talk therapy (Illouz 2008). In 2012–13 psychotherapists were still seen as lacking in understanding of the specific issues and concerns and therefore as unable to offer the appropriate strategies for help. Kerstin chose a homeopath to help her alleviate her symptoms with natural remedies and hypnosis. She also took sessions with a hypnotherapist to access and release unconsciously transmitted memories related to the war. Other techniques that were mentioned in my interviews included psychokinesiology, bodywork, dancing, physiotherapy, and, in particular, the extremely popular family constellations workshops, dozens of which are offered in Berlin on any given weekend. Founded by German psychotherapist and former priest Bert Hellinger in the 1990s, family constellations are a kind of psychodrama claiming to reveal and heal the hidden dynamics that span multiple generations in a given family by reenacting the family system with a group of unrelated volunteers. Many Kriegsenkel, Kerstin included, mentioned that they had participated in these workshops and found them helpful. Paula told me that during one of these workshops she had been able trace her asthma attacks back to her grandmother's experience of nearly suffocating in an air-raid shelter in 1944. Paula said that after the weekend, she was able to reduce her medication by half. Other Kriegsenkel expressed and helped themselves through their artwork, music, or writing. In his song "Auf der Flucht" (here best translated as "On the run"), comedian Rainald Grebe humorously attributes his restlessness and inability to put down roots to his mother's flight from Eastern Europe in 1944,[3] and Anke Jablinski (2012) wrote a book about how rock climbing helped her liberate herself from the war trauma her family had passed on to her. There was also Martin, whom I met in 2012; he wrote convoluted stories that all talked about some kind of war, and he illustrated them with beautiful sketches. "These books are my salvation," he said to me one night as we were waiting for the tram home, "particularly when I feel down." He had filled twenty-seven of them in the previous years.

A last approach in dealing with the past is the attempt to fill in the informational gaps in the family history. Some Kriegsenkel consulted historical archives, which provide family members with copies of the files from the time of the Third Reich. These can be membership cards of the Nazi Party, court documents about trials for war crimes, or information about movements with the German Wehrmacht.[4] Others turned to the extended family as a last resort to get more information about the family history or traveled to their family's country of origin to look for a sense of connection with the "lost home" in the East. (I will come back to this in detail in chap. 6.) The lack of information about the trajectories of one's forebears because of the family's silence was one of the cited reasons that the Kriegsenkel found it hard to let go of the past. Attempting to fill in the gaps was one of the key strategies to put the past to rest. Kerstin described in vivid detail how a clerk led her into the dusty basement of the city archive and helped her find her grandfather's death certificate. She spoke of the sense of relief, calm, and closure she felt when she finally held a copy of it in her hand, even though the piece of paper confirmed that the Nazis had shot her grandfather as a traitor in Buchenwald in 1945: "I had no appreciation what it can do to you to suddenly have an official document like this. I took it home and I thought, 'OK, this is it.' It was strange."

In one way or another, everyone I met in Berlin who was active in the Kriegsenkel scene was trying to work through the past. For some, just reading about the topic or talking to others was enough to reach a degree of understanding and acceptance. Others tried a number of different therapeutic techniques, including the ones mentioned above, or extended weekends to explore individual trajectories, such as creative writing workshops to find and express the underlying themes in their lives. What always struck me when we talked was the hope for a happier future. At the same time this was often coupled with a sense of heaviness and burden. According to the norms of the therapeutic culture, individuals are responsible not only for understanding their problems but also for transforming themselves and constantly striving toward emotional health (Illouz 2008, in particular 183–86). It was obvious that many of my interviewees felt it to be their duty to resolve the issues from the past because "no one else in the family was going to do it" and they wanted to protect their children from a similar fate. They often repeated the idea that the chain of transgenerational transmission can only be broken if the person is able to work through the traumatic influences and remove them from the psyche. Most mothers and fathers felt a painful sense of guilt for the damage they had already unconsciously done to their children before finding the Kriegsenkel topic. I sometimes asked myself whether therapeutic thinking was not actually adding to their depression in this regard. However, in spite of these aspects (which no one ever questioned or complained about), actively dealing with the issue of the emotional inheritance was always portrayed as positive and transformative.

Hooray, I Am a Kriegsenkel!: Creating Meaning and Making Peace with the Past

Based on her fieldwork among support groups of codependents in the United States, Leslie Irvine (1999, 3) describes how the "narrative formula" of codependency allows the sufferers to make sense of their lives by providing a clear and coherent sequence to order life events: the dysfunctional childhood family that set them up for codependency, the unhealthy relationships, the crises when things fell apart, and then the road to recovery. "They [the support group members she interviewed] put events and situations together to give their experience meaning—for themselves as well as for me. Indeed, narratives are the primary form by which human experience is made meaningful" (Irvine 1999, 5). For people identifying as codependent, this discourse provides an opportunity to integrate their entire life into a "more or less coherent assemblage" or "narrative strategy." This assemblage is transferable to Kriegsenkel narratives. They allow members of this generation to reorganize their life histories and trace current emotional issues through the family history, all the way back to World War II. For most of my interviewees, this narrative strategy, as a subset of the broader therapeutic discourse, was extremely meaningful. On the one hand, it intuitively just felt right; there was often an embodied certainty that the link to the war was real. On the other hand, this feeling was also due to the strategy's convincing logic and the coherence of the elements it is constructed with, in particular the "truth rule" (Irvine 1999, 85) that unresolved war trauma is passed on in the family. World War II is still seen as the defining time in Germany's modern history, a time that is constantly referred to and recapitulated in public discourses, reminding Germans of its paramount significance and catastrophic impact. It is not a difficult stretch to understand World War II as equally crucial for one's family history and, through processes of transgenerational transmission, one's own.

When I visited my key informants again in August 2013 and asked them what their Kriegsenkel journey had changed for them, this was what they mentioned most often: Their own and their family's stories had been rewritten and were now making more sense, something they experienced as reassuring and calming. The war and its emotional legacy had become an integral part of their sense of identity. "If I had to tell somebody about myself now," Charlotte said, "I would mention that I am a Kriegsenkel and explain how that plays out in my life and where it all came from. I would include that in the introduction of myself. It is now part of my understanding of who I am; it is part of my biography." Martin, who had a cheeky sense of humor that gets a bit lost in translation, added, "Being a Kriegsenkel means being the child of parents who suffered plenty of damage, a bit more damage than other people maybe. But at least you get a rough idea of where it all came from and—who knows—maybe you will even learn how to deal with it." Most of my core interviewees said they were more understanding and accepting of themselves and their parents as a result of intensively thinking about the topic, even though the family relationships did not tend to improve. For example, although Kerstin now had an explanation for her mother's coldness, she still did not want to see her and be exposed to it.

A second outcome of the Kriegsenkel journey was that it offered a new sense of community and belonging. Many had felt isolated and lonely before, the black sheep in their families. Now, like Kerstin, they found themselves part of a larger collective. Anne Barth (2012), organizer of *Forumkriegsenkel.de*, called it "black sheep finding each other." Breaking through social isolation and providing connection and mutual support are some of the core features of self-help movements more broadly, from groups for children of Holocaust survivors (Stein 2009; Kidron 2003) to those formed around a psychological or medical issue, such as codependency (Irvine 1999), bipolar disorder (Martin 2009) or fibromyalgia (Barker 2002). "If I had to sum it all up, I would say, 'I do belong after all!'" Charlotte said. "I was always different from other people, always felt different, like an outcast, never part of mainstream society. Now, after dealing with this topic, I feel like I do belong after all. I belong to Germany, to my family." Martin viewed his newly found identity as a kind of secret handshake that immediately connected him to other people who were also into the topic. "At least I stopped feeling like an alien now," he said with the broadest grin. The last time I heard from him in early 2017, he was dating a woman he had met through the *Forumkriegsenkel.de* website.

Did the therapeutic culture's promise to liberate the individual from the burden of the past and to enable a happier future hold true for the Kriegsenkel?

While not everyone said it explicitly, it can be deduced from their complaints that the prime aspirations of the therapeutic and self-help culture of contemporary middle-class US society also apply to the Kriegsenkel: "emotional health" (for Kriegsenkel that means overcoming depression, anxiety, panic attacks, hopelessness, etc.) and "self-realization" (loosening the hand brake and living up to one's potential, achieving more fulfilling relationships and careers, etc.) (Illouz 2008, 172). I could not say with conviction whether my interviewees were happier and more self-realized in 2013 than they were in 2012, but eighteen months may be too short a time to come to firm conclusions. Kerstin did say that she felt a sense of liberation from the "heavy backpack" she used to carry around, and most others confirmed they were more at peace with themselves as a result of becoming Kriegsenkel and all that it entailed. Anja noticed that something that had been blocking her all her life was finally starting to move, and many others expressed a renewed sense of hope for the future.

However, it needs to be said that for many who now identified as Kriegsenkel, this was not the first nor will it most likely be the last therapeutic narrative they connected with. There seem to be "narrative fashions" (Illouz 2008, 172) that people go through. Alice Miller's (1979) *Drama of the Gifted Child* and Elaine Aron's (1996) *The Highly Sensitive Person* were only two of the many previous subjects of interest mentioned during my interviews. Each of these topics had a certain shelf life; their concepts were each intensely used for a while. Then, at some point, they had exhausted their potential to identify causes of suffering and suggest solutions, and they consequently receded into the background. Following a number of people over eighteen months, I saw that this progression was uncanny for the Kriegsenkel issue. Although at the moment of writing new streams of people still share their eureka moments and the start of the Kriegsenkel journey on a daily basis in the Facebook groups, the more senior members of the scene were already starting to put the topic to rest by the time I returned to Berlin in August 2013. They still firmly believed in and identified with the Kriegsenkel narrative, but they felt they had fully explored its parameters. The topic had lost some of its urgency. As Charlotte mentioned, it had been "digested," and the result had become part of the person's biography. Yet, while it may not be the only one, the Kriegsenkel narrative was nevertheless felt to be particularly powerful. It enabled members of this generation to find plausible reasons for their own and their families' emotional problems. It offered community and a sense of belonging, and it propelled people on a particular path to overcome their suffering. All of these benefits combined are encapsulated in Kerstin's exclamation, "Hooray, I am a Kriegsenkel!"

A THERAPEUTIC SUBCULTURE OR A NEW COLLECTIVE IDENTITY?

The analysis of the Kriegsenkel movement in chapter 3 and of the Kriegsenkel narratives in this chapter raises the question of how pervasive this new collective identity is. According to the Federal German Statistical Office, at the end of 2015 there were around twenty million people in Germany who had been born between 1960 and 1975.[5] Even if one deducts those from migrant backgrounds and others whose parents were not children during World War II, this still leaves millions of people who could potentially identify as Kriegsenkel. Yet during my stay in Berlin it was very obvious that while some people related very strongly with the topic (often the reason they chose to talk to me), others I met did not, or not to the same degree. In one of our conversations, I asked Kerstin whether her brother felt the same way about their family history, but she shook her head. "I can't imagine that he would be at all interested in this," she responded, although they hadn't talked to each other for a while. All except two Kriegsenkel I met were disappointed that their siblings did not share their views. A number of brothers and sisters denied my request for an interview, saying that nothing had been passed on to them or that they had "no idea what this is about." Charlotte's brother initially agreed to talk to me but said up front that he had a very different view of their upbringing. He postponed the meeting several times, and in the end it never happened. My interviewees tended to pass judgment on their siblings, saying that they were "in denial" (another therapeutic concept) and "just didn't get it." It was clear, though, that not everyone of this generation felt affected by the war.

Also, while most Kriegsenkel I met had keen interest in family history, not all of them felt affected by the past to the same degree. Thirty-five of my fifty-four interviewees identified very strongly with the topic, while nineteen acknowledged that the war had left some imprint in their parents and grandparents but did not feel that much damage had been passed on to them. Maybe, as the result of their upbringing, they needed to have a full fridge or to choose a stable job to feel secure, but these were perceived as minor aspects of their lives. Some with more open family communication even felt a positive influence from the life lessons their family had passed on. None of the above talked about the war in the same defining and all-encompassing way as did Kerstin and the other Kriegsenkel portrayed in my previous and next chapters. A substantial number of Germans I spoke to casually during my stay felt that the war had happened a long time ago and had nothing to do with them whatsoever.

Another interesting observation about this emergent identity was that it seemed to have found a much stronger resonance among people who grew up in West Germany. Looking at the list of Kriegsenkel support groups, one cannot help but notice that until 2015, with the exception of the groups regularly meeting in Berlin, they were all located in the *Alten Bundesländer*, the old states, which prior to the reunification in 1990 were part of West Germany. The first East German groups were only formed in Leipzig in July 2015 and Dresden in 2016—lagging behind by more than five years. None of the thirty portraits in the two war grandchildren books were of people who grew up in the GDR, and psychologist Bettina Alberti shared with me that she was struggling to find a volunteer for an East German case study for her book. Even if one takes into consideration that the East German population is only around one-third of that of the West, this is still striking. This is not to say, of course, that there are no Kriegsenkel in East Germany. Kerstin, and some of the most active members of the Berlin scene, were *Ossies* (Easterners). Also, while they were a bit more difficult to find, in the end quite a number of East Germans were happy to meet me for an interview. Still, overall there seemed to be a difference in how strongly people responded (or maybe responded publicly) to the ideas of the war grandchildren movement.

So why do some people "become" Kriegsenkel while others do not? The first logical explanation is of course exposure. Not every member of this age group is aware of the topic. The Kriegsenkel movement is a relatively recent phenomenon. While the topic is more widely known at the point of writing in 2017, it is still evolving, and its full breadth and penetration is yet to be determined.

Second, research shows that even in extremely traumatized families like those of Holocaust survivors, not all offspring are equally affected. While some seem to suffer from their families' inherited problems, others do not seem to require (or access) psychological treatment. Danieli (2007) claims that a number of different factors affect the process of transgenerational transmission—for example, the extent, time, and duration of the trauma itself; the survivors' survival and adaptation strategies; the extent of the "conspiracy of silence" surrounding the trauma and its aftermath; the way the child relates to the parents' trauma; and the parents' ability to adapt to life postwar. Natan Kellermann (2008, 263–64) adds other influences found to aggravate or mitigate the risk for psychological damage in descendants of Holocaust survivors: how close after World War II the children were born; whether they were the firstborn or the only child; whether one or both parents were survivors; how enmeshed the relations between parents and children were; and whether the Holocaust was talked about too much or too little. In addition, some children had developed coping skills that enabled them to withstand the damaging influence of their upbringing. Kellermann (2008, 269) suspects that not only trauma was passed on in these cases but certain survival skills were also handed down, making some members of the second generation more resilient than their peers. Some of these factors could also help explain the different responses in non-Jewish German families who lived through World War II.

Where Are the East German Kriegsenkel?

When it comes to the particular question of why there seem to be fewer East German Kriegsenkel, different explanations are possible. A number of East Germans explained to me that many were still in the process of working through their more immediate (and often also traumatic) memories of the communist regime to be concerned with the more distant topic of World War II. The contributions to Christoph Seidler and Michael Froese's (2009) edited volume *Traumatisierungen in (Ost)-Deutschland* (Traumatizations in [East] Germany) provide examples from private psychotherapeutic and psychoanalytical practices. They show that even in cases where people look back as far as the war to identify the source of their present emotional problems, these memories are often intermingled and overlaid with traumatic experiences incurred during the time of the GDR. This intermingling was also very clear in my interviews.

My impression was also that East Germans still tended to be less confident about speaking up in public and were extremely reluctant to join organized activities, which had dominated their childhoods in the socialist society. Marta, born in 1958 in Dresden (ex-GDR), went to one of the support group meetings in the West German city where she now lived, but she felt uncomfortable. Everyone else around her was a *Wessie* (Westerner), she told me, and "they were much more confident and more articulate than me. They did all the talking." She never went again. East German Kriegsenkel may consequently have been less visible than their West German counterparts because they did not participate to the same extent in the support groups and other organized activities.

Interestingly, historian Dorothee Wierling (2010) made a similar observation about the Kriegskinder, the war children movement. She traced the biographies of people actively publishing in the scene but found only three East Germans in this diverse group of around fifty historians, psychologists, physicians, journalists, educators, and literary scholars. Wierling (2010, 112) concluded that "apparently no 'generation of war children' exists in East Germany in the empathetic sense of self-conscious generation building." She explains this with the fact that concepts of generation played no significant role in the official discourse of the GDR, as categories of class were more important in communist terminology. Also, certain aspects of wartime childhood memories were taboo and could not be discussed in public.

I believe that a key reason that some people identify as Kriegsenkel again comes back to therapy culture. It is clear that some parts of the population have had more exposure to therapeutic culture than others. The laws of the GDR prevented private psychotherapists from practicing, and clinical psychologists were scarce. From the 1970s until the fall of the Berlin Wall in 1989, there were on average 130 psychology students enrolled each year across four universities. While numbers have steadily increased since the 1990s, in 2011 there were still only about half the therapists per capita compared to their Western counterparts (Peikert et al. 2011). This means that East Germans were less likely to access therapy, and they also spent the first half of their lives with less exposure to the "therapeutic worldview" (Furedi 2004). It always struck me that when I asked, "How do you think the war affected yourself and your family?" East Germans tended to talk about the impact of the war on society more generally, rather than the impact on their personal situations. I attribute this to their upbringing in a socialist education system.

When it comes to Kriegsenkel profiles more broadly, a study by the University of Duisburg-Essen (Walendzik et al. 2010) provides some interesting insights:

- More than 70 percent of all Germans accessing therapy are female (except in the group of very young patients of twenty-one years or younger).
- Almost a third of all patients accessing therapy in 2010 were between forty-one and fifty years old. They are by far the largest client group, in spite of the fact that this age bracket only constitutes around 17 percent of the overall population.
- People who access therapy tend to be better educated, with almost twice as many as in the population average having completed at least a year twelve or a tertiary education.
- 40 percent of all patients were recorded as *Angestellte* (salaried employees) and only about 7 percent as *Arbeiter* (working class), although the latter constitute around 20 percent of the overall population.

These points match exactly the profile of my Kriegsenkel interviewees: predominantly middle class, well educated, and more likely to be female. Across Western countries, this segment of the population is found to be the core clientele of counseling practices, consumers of self-help literature, and participants of support groups (Illouz 2008; Irvine 1999; McLeod and Wright 2009). The Kriegsenkel identity is strongly embedded in the therapeutic culture and its discourses with their specific logic, vocabulary, and truth rules. Outside this framework, the narrative does not hold together (remember Martin's mother, who said, "But you were not even there. How could you possibly be affected by the war?"). Although access to therapy and self-help culture is extremely broad in Germany, it is clear that some people have (or choose to have) more exposure to it than others. This does not mean, of course, that in other segments of the population, or in East Germany more generally, transgenerational transmission of trauma did not occur. It does mean, however, that those among them who were emotionally suffering were less inclined to explain their issues in this way.

A CALL FOR A NUANCED ASSESSMENT OF THERAPEUTIC CULTURE

Authors have long critiqued the rise of counseling and therapy culture as fostering moral collapse (Furedi 2004; Lasch 1991; Rieff 1966), as encouraging extreme individualism and a "narcissistic over occupation with the self" (Lasch 1991, xv), or as creating a "new faith" (Moskowitz 2001) to fill a need that was once addressed by religion. They have labeled the modern, individualized self as empty and severed from tradition and communal relationships (Cushman 1990; Furedi 2004), as socially disengaged and withdrawing into the private sphere, losing sight of the larger public good (Moskowitz 2001). Many authors claim that, rather than alleviating emotional suffering, therapeutic culture ends up creating or perpetuating the pain it is trying to cure, by promoting an attitude of victimhood vis-à-vis the challenges of modern life (Furedi 2004); by insisting on a self-contained individualism that cuts the individual off from others (Cushman 1990); or by setting vague benchmarks of emotional health and happiness against which people invariably find themselves falling short (Illouz 2008). "Continental and conical, right- and left-wing critics agree that therapeutic culture formalizes and exacerbates unhappiness. It encourages individuals to discover and label every possible symptom of mental disquiet, produces additional anxiety on top of the anxiety it purports to cure, and makes people neurotic about their own neuroses" (Aubry and Travis 2015, 12). Lastly, Michel Foucault (1995) and those inspired by his work expose the therapeutic discourse as a technology of government and an insidious form of social control (for example, Chriss 1999; Lasch 1991; Rose 1990, 1997, 1998). Power is exerted not only by authoritarian suppression but also through an alignment between government interests and the desires of the individual for autonomy and emancipation, which makes them susceptible to being managed and disciplined (Rose 1998).

These authors tend to focus on the broader social and cultural impact of therapeutic culture rather than the lived experiences of people engaged with self-help techniques and counseling. Aubry and Travis's (2015) edited volume aims to "rethink therapeutic culture." While its contributors indeed present a more positive analysis of its multifaceted influence, their assessments also neglect the perspective of the therapeutic subject. Julie McLeod and Katie Wright (2009) point out that the impact of therapeutic culture on the everyday life of individuals is more complex than critical voices account for. Drawing on their research of marginalized women in Australia, they demand closer attention to the different ways in which therapeutic narratives and practices are mobilized and performed by certain social groups and which effects they are felt to have.

What can the German case study and an anthropological perspective contribute to this debate? Extrapolating from the subjective experiences of the German Kriegsenkel and their engagement with the therapeutic culture in which they grew up, I here focus on two of the phenomena seen as resulting from the influence of therapeutic culture: "narcissistic self-concern" and the perceived lack of social and political engagement (Illouz 2008, 2), and the enshrining of an all-encompassing sense of vulnerability and victimhood into the understanding of the modern self and its life challenges (Furedi 2004).

Narcissistic Self-Concern or Safe Haven?

One part of the debate revolves around the perceived narcissistic self-absorption of the modern therapeutic subject and its lack of social engagement (Chriss 1999; Cushman 1990; Furedi 2004; Lasch 1991; Moskowitz 2001). Christopher Lasch (1991) laments that since the radical political activities of the 1960s, Americans have withdrawn to purely personal preoccupations. Eva Moskowitz (2001) believes that with most of the attention now on private life and the family, people ignore the larger public good. From the 1970s on, therapeutic discourses are largely seen to discourage social and political action, stifle dissent, and disguise structural and systematic issues by stressing individual responsibility and alleviation of problems through therapeutic interventions. Moskowitz (2001) and Furedi (2004) are both concerned that because the focus has turned inward, problems that used to be perceived as political, economic, or educational are today considered emotional and personal, and are addressed as such rather than through social or political change. Against this critique, Eva Illouz (2008) points to the influence of therapeutic culture on more recent collective actions in the United States. Once "psychologized" (170), social problems are funneled into the public sphere by social actors promoting narratives of disease and victimhood. Although feminist groups fighting for the rights of victims of child abuse or Vietnam War veterans requesting official acknowledgment as sufferers of war trauma may not have been advocating for radical political change, they did nevertheless push for public recognition of issues affecting larger groups of people.

When this discussion is applied to the German Kriegsenkel, the first position seems more fitting. One of the features of the Kriegsenkel movement is its lack of any broader social and political goals. As Kerstin's journey showed, being a victim of transmitted World War II trauma is very much seen as a personal psychological issue, to be traced back to the childhood family and to be addressed in private therapy or explored and performed in self-help groups of peers, carefully cordoned off from outsiders. All my interviewees who were active in the scene, as well as the two authors of the Kriegsenkel books, confirmed that there were no organized attempts to achieve social change, not even, as in the case of the Vietnam veterans, coordinated lobbying for recognition of their own interests. On the contrary, being "ideology-free" and apolitical is one of the character traits listed as typical for the war grandchildren generation.[6] Quite a number of people pointed this out to me with a certain pride. This trait could be viewed as social disengagement and focus on private concerns, and at least in some interviews and in quite a few support groups meetings, that was definitely also my impression. For Kriegsenkel, who were raised in and strongly internalized the logic, discourses, and practices of the "therapeutic mode" (Stein 2009, 48), the aspiration, drive, and strategies for change focused on the individual and personal rather than the social and political.

However, one consideration that may have been overlooked so far is that framing issues as psychological may also be a way of addressing problems in a political environment where the topics in question are still considered sensitive. Although individual Kriegsenkel now occasionally share their personal stories in newspapers and TV programs, none of my interviewees felt comfortable advocating for public recognition as second-generation victims of a war, in which their grandparents had participated and which had resulted in the death of millions of people. Nora explained why: "The Neo-Nazis are marching through my hometown every year to commemorate the war. You have to be really careful when you portray Germans as victims; it has to remain strictly personal, among family and friends. What the Germans did was much worse. I believe that German victimhood should never be a collective public matter. It is just not appropriate."

Therapeutic culture and frameworks, on the other hand, provide a protected space where emotional suffering can be voiced without fear of repercussions or embarrassment.

Fostering Victimhood or Promoting Agency?

My findings also dent the claim that, rather than increasing resilience, therapeutic culture promotes vulnerability, erodes self-reliance (Furedi 2004; Sommers and Satel 2005), and encourages narratives of suffering, victimhood, and disease (Furedi 2004; Illouz 2008). Both Sommers and Satel's and Furedi's books argue that therapeutic approaches are propagating concepts of the modern self as vulnerable, diminished, weak, and constantly at risk of being traumatized or otherwise emotionally damaged. In their view, difficulties that were once accepted as a normal part of life are now being pathologized and medicalized and seen as in need of therapeutic intervention. Furedi (2004) shows that mentions of the word *trauma* have skyrocketed in the British media since the 1980s. Counseling is now offered for every aspect of life seen as potentially damaging to people's emotions—from changing from primary to secondary schools to unemployment, natural disasters, and bereavement. Rather than alleviating emotional suffering, Furedi argues, therapy culture encourages people to feel traumatized and depressed. As early childhood experiences are understood as defining for a person's biography, people are instructed to see themselves as victims of their families and upbringing rather than as self-determined agents in control of their lives. Illouz (2008, 184) concludes that, "far from actually helping manage the contradictions and predicaments of modern identity, the psychological discourse may only deepen them." Because therapeutic discourses are "contagious," the victim status is not confined to those individuals who have directly suffered from a particular event but also extends to their children and grandchildren.

Because of my observations among my German interviewees, I agree that having been socialized to understand one's problems in therapeutic categories reinforces a sense of victimhood rather than highlighting resilience and agency. Many Kriegsenkel indeed portrayed themselves as emotional casualties of their dysfunctional families, and they would wholeheartedly subscribe to concepts of the self as vulnerable and constantly at risk of being traumatized. Juliane, born in 1967, whose story will be told in the next chapter, offered this laconic statement, which sums up the sentiment: "I have problems with sex and relationships because my family's trauma was passed on to me. How could I possibly be any different?" Anger, resentment, and judgment against parents dominated many of our interviews, as well as support group meetings and Facebook exchanges.

Yet the argument about the ability of past generations to master life's challenges better than the current ones (Furedi 2004; Sommers and Satel 2005) does not hold up in my view. I heard many stories about grandfathers who came home from the war and quietly rebuilt their lives without complaint. Yet they had lost their joie de vivre; they spent their evenings drinking or beat their wives and children, unable to control their bottled-up rage, pain, and frustration. I sincerely doubt that they were coping as well as these authors may like us to believe. While critical of the construction of PTSD as a psychopathology, Allan Young (1995) stresses that the suffering related to traumatic experiences has always existed. Leslie Irvine (1999) points out that therapists did not create the problems people are experiencing but merely provided a framework and vocabulary for expressing them. Using the case of the introduction of telephone counseling in Australia as an example, Katie Wright (2008) argues that therapeutic strategies have enabled the recognition of pain and suffering previously hidden away in the private domain. Therapeutic culture offered my interviewees the tools to explore and address psychological distress, and these tools were subjectively experienced as effective and empowering. While some people I met in Berlin seemed to be stuck in their victim role, others were feeling more hopeful and more at peace with themselves as a result of their engagement with their Kriegsenkel identity.

McLeod and Wright (2009) conclude that pessimistic assessments of therapy culture ignore the sense of capacity and competence that therapeutic models can provide. I agree with that. The discovery of the topic and the ensuing journey many Kriegsenkel went on were experienced as unequivocally positive, providing resources, tools, and strategies and instilling a sense of optimism for the future. Therapeutic culture was perceived to offer a complete system to actively conceptualize, safely explore, and successfully alleviate emotional suffering. "In transcending despair through counseling or therapy the self can be restored to its conviction that it is the master of its own existence," Nikolas Rose (1998, 159) writes, and while he would see this belief as an illusion of autonomy, as people are not aware of the powers that influence their desires, this is nevertheless very much how the German Kriegsenkel experienced it. It was clear in my interviews that conceiving of and talking about the self using therapeutic language has become a way of life, so deeply internalized and taken for granted that it almost defies articulation (Illouz 2008). Nobody ever questioned its validity or weighed its positive and negative influences. There simply was no known alternative framework in which to understand and address emotional problems. Therapeutic culture is "just how you do things."

However, are there other ways to conceptualize the relationship to a difficult familial past? The next chapter asks this question.

NOTES

1. For more detailed information, see the *Paths to Psychotherapy* brochure at https://www.bptk.de/wp-content/uploads/2019/09/2019-09_bptk_patientenbroschuere_englisch_web.pdf. Accessed November 9, 2019.

2. Interestingly, the level of depression in the overall population (not just the Kriegsenkel age cohort) is not higher in Germany than in other European countries. It is lower, for example, than in Switzerland, which was only peripherally affected by World War II. See Ferrari et al. 2013. "Burden of Depressive Disorders by Country, Sex, Age, and Year: Findings from the Global Burden of Disease Study 2010."

3. See Rainald Grebe. 2012. "Auf der Flucht." *YouTube* video. April 12, 2012. https://www.youtube.com/watch?v=MELex2djA6E.

4. The most frequently accessed archives are the *Bundesarchiv* (http://www.bundesarchiv.de) and the *Deutsche Dienststelle* (WASt) *für die Benachrichtigung*

der nächsten Angehörigen von Gefallenen der ehemaligen Deutschen Wehrmacht (http://www.dd-wast.de).

5. Statistica. n.d. Accessed December 1, 2016. http://de.statista.com/statistik/daten/studie/1351/umfrage/altersstruktur-der-bevoelkerung-deutschlands/.

6. Forumkriegsenkel. n.d. "Studie." Accessed November 9, 2019. http://www.forumkriegsenkel.de/Studie.htm.

FIVE

THE INVISIBLE WOUNDS OF WAR

Kriegsenkel Accounts of Transgenerational Transmission

WHILE CHAPTERS 3 AND 4 were concerned with the broader social characteristics of an emergent Kriegsenkel identity, chapters 5 and 6 now delve more deeply into individual life histories. They explore in greater detail how my interviewees understood their biographies to be influenced by events of World War II. I will introduce you to four women and one man: Anja and Juliane in this chapter and Charlotte, Rainer, and Paula in the following. I chose those five people because their stories demonstrate particularly well the points I am trying to make. This chapter is built around Anja and Juliane, who had recently found out (or had started to suspect) that their families were suffering from war trauma. As a child, Anja's father had to witness terrible scenes of death and destruction when his hometown was heavily bombarded toward the end of the war. Juliane, on the other hand, was certain that some of the women in her family were raped when the Russians occupied their village in 1945. Both women felt that those events, which happened long before their births, had a crippling effect on their own lives and emotions because their families passed much of their trauma on to them. I will pause my telling of their stories from time to time to show where and how they represent Kriegsenkel life histories more broadly and provide background on topics such as war childhoods, National Socialist child-rearing practices, and sexual violence during World War II. This information has now become more widely available in the German public and was implicitly or explicitly woven into Kriegsenkel narratives.

Later in the chapter I look at how common models of transgenerational transmission underpinned my interviewees' understanding of their emotional problems. How well do these approaches actually capture the lived experiences of descendants? What side effects do they have? And are there other ways to explain the long-term impact of war and violence?

ANJA: THE ABYSS WITHOUT A NAME

Born and raised in a medium-sized town in southwest Germany, Anja was forty-six when I first met her in a Russian café in Berlin in September 2012. She looked like an open and confident woman with long blond hair; a deep, raspy voice; and a dark sense of humor. As a trained journalist, she had a great way with words, able to articulate her perceptions to the finest detail and nuance. Her life seemed settled. She was married, both partners worked, and they lived with their six-year-old son in their own house with a garden. Yet behind the facade of this middle-class family life, Anja had had severe psychological problems for more than twenty years. Over coffee and Russian pancakes, she gave me snapshots of her ongoing battles with depression, agoraphobia, and panic attacks. She told me about the breakdown she had before moving into her current home from another part of town, when her legs gave way in the shower and she was unable to walk or eat for three days, crying incessantly. Then there was the heaviness that often caught her first thing in the morning, turning even mundane life tasks into insurmountable feats and leaving her clueless as to how to get through the day. Anja was struggling in every aspect of her life: her career, her relationship, and her role as a mother. Just the day before our meeting, she had been sitting at home, staring at the wall for three hours, desperately struggling to ramp up the courage to get dressed, pack a bag, and take her son to the swimming pool—just down the road. "I feel I can't breathe," Anja said when I ask her to describe the feeling. "My whole being is compressed into a tiny ball, as small as a marble but as heavy as lead on my chest. When I get to feel the pain itself, it is just a sense of infinite sadness, but I never found any correlation with anything that I experienced in my life." She had been in therapy and on antidepressants and antianxiety medications for most of her adult life, without much improvement in her condition.

The Heaviness Inside

For a number of years, Anja was searching for an artistic expression of this indistinct sense of leaden heaviness she carried inside. She played around with different materials, but nothing seemed to work quite right. Only when she began to experiment with concrete did things start to fall into place. In the end, Anja produced two forty-kilogram models of above-ground air-raid shelters. She described the experience: "I remember this feeling when I unpacked the first shelter from its mold. I immediately knew that that was it. I started to cry because I knew that was exactly the form that matches my feeling. I tried lifting it up and realized that I couldn't really carry it."

She had no idea where the models came from, but suddenly there they were, in front of her on the table. "Oh, how very Freudian," her therapist said, and they both laughed.

The next time Anja visited her hometown in southern Germany, she realized that one of the models was an exact replica of an above-ground air-raid shelter right next to her family home, a relic from World War II. She was stunned that, in spite of its impressive size, she had never noticed it before. It had just been part of the landscape of her everyday childhood life.

Both of Anja's parents had been children during World War II; her mother later died of bowel cancer when Anja was fourteen. Anja was peripherally aware of the family history but had never given it much thought. Her father did not talk about his war memories, nor did anyone else in the family. She remembered a few of his odd throwaway lines ("It smells like death here") that she later interpreted in the context of the war. Otherwise the topic was a taboo, upheld by mutual agreement; her father did not volunteer any stories about the war, and Anja in turn did not ask. Father and daughter had a difficult relationship, she explained. She was his only child, and he adored and spoiled her, but he was never the strong and protective father she had longed for. Instead of showing her the ropes in life, he always seemed to be the one in need of emotional care. His daughter was his confidant, the only one he talked to, even after he remarried. Anja admitted that she enjoyed this privileged status, but it also felt suffocating. The walls in the family home seemed to have hands, grabbing, strangling, and smothering her.

When Anja told her father about the air-raid shelters and her discovery, he just looked at her. "*Beredtes Schweigen*" (loaded silence), she called this typical reaction of his. He did not respond, but she knew that he had registered what she told him. It took another three years until one day, over coffee and Black Forest cake, she finally said to him, "Why don't you tell me a bit about the war?" After he first stressed that "it really wasn't so bad," fragments of a story started to trickle out, a story with screaming farm animals, with stables engulfed in flames and dripping with burning fat. "There was nothing I could do," her father suddenly sobbed before breaking down and crying uncontrollably. "It was like he was back in 1943 or 1944. There was no more distance; he was a child again," Anja recalled. "He was trembling and crying. I had never seen him like that before. . . . There were twenty people around us in the café, staring, but he did not care." Over the next couple of months, her father shared his worst memories from the war with her, his "top ten," as Anja called them with her special kind of humor. Each episode was more horrific than the previous one. There was the story about their hometown being heavily bombarded toward the end of the war because it produced chemicals that were vital to Hitler's war machinery. The children had to help clean up after every air raid, clearing the streets of debris and dead bodies. Or another one, in which her father was trying to find his way home through enemy lines all by himself at the end of the war. He made it across the river with the last ferry before the German captain sank the boat; the water was dense with the floating bodies of dead soldiers and civilians. His worst account, however, was from winter 1944–45. Anja's father had gone ice skating with his school friends on a frozen lake near his home when the group was attacked by low-flying Allied warplanes. Everyone ducked for cover to escape the machine-gun fire. When the planes finally left and Anja's father looked out from behind the bush where he was hiding, the ice was soaked with blood. All eleven of his classmates were dead. He was the only survivor.

Although he had never consulted a psychologist, Anja had no doubt that what her father experienced during World War II had severely traumatized him. These stories finally explained to her why he could never be the dad she had yearned for. "His emotional development stopped at the age of eleven," she said. "He really never grew up. He could not be the responsible father to take me by the hand and protect me. He just couldn't." She now also understood his constant tension and his desperate need for set routines. Her father was trying to keep his fears under control. He always took the same road home, always needed to eat at the exact same time. She explained that she had been aware of these behaviors before but had never seen them in relation to the war: "I knew that there was something very wrong with him, but it was just never a topic, it was always so suppressed. Now I understand why my father is scared when he is in unfamiliar environments and why he always looks around for an escape route. Before I just noticed that he was very tense, but those symptoms were so removed from anything concrete that I could not place them anywhere."

Growing Up with Damaged Parents

Anja's family had enough money, and they were doing well. Even though her mother's death was a terrible shock, Anja went to school, had friends, and enjoyed the material safety and pleasures of the comfortable life her father built for her. The majority of my interviewees grew up in families that in the 1960s and 1970s put an enormous effort into creating *Heile Welten* (idyllic worlds) with picture-perfect houses and picket fences, carefully mown lawns, and cars washed every Saturday. Appearances were paramount and being judged by the neighbors a major concern. The children were expected to fit into the mold set for them without complaint: doing well at school, being quiet and well behaved, and not causing any trouble. "Do not make waves" was the rule. Andrea's family is another such example: After coming home from a Russian POW camp, her father found a job, got married, and had children. "Everything is fine now" was the motto; "no more war, and no more violence—just working and rebuilding." Austerity, conscientiousness, order, and discipline ruled at home, she explained, "even a bit more than in other postwar families." Like many of his generation, Andrea's father worked hard: he left early in the morning and returned home late at night. Her mother, like many West German women in the 1960s, raised the children mostly on her own.

While it sounds like a cliché, many Kriegsenkel described their upbringing along similar lines. Yet, behind closed doors, something felt off in these idyllic homes. There was an inconspicuous yet inexplicable lack of happiness and laughter. Depression was frequently named as the dominant mood, a lack of levity and happiness that seemed to jar with the outward display of ordinariness and stability. As a child Elise thought of this heaviness as normal, "but somehow it was also burdensome and troubling. Something was hanging in the air, but I could never really grab hold of it." Many described an acute sense that there was something not quite right with their families as they were growing up, yet they were not able to put a name to this perception. Their parents (and often grandparents) seemed to be carrying an emotional burden; they showed behaviors and had reactions that the children could not understand or contextualize. When I asked people to describe their parents, *cold* was used many times—a complaint made more frequently about the mothers. They were seen as *functioning*, providing for the family as expected of them, but incapable of feeling and expressing emotions. A deeper connection to their children, as well as emotional support and empathy, were missing. With sadness written all over her face, Karoline said: "My mother was somehow so far away from me. I could never reach her emotionally. Not as a child and not now. When I split up with my partner last year, she complained that I never call her and never visit. I told her that I was feeling really bad, but she just stayed silent and did not want to know about it. When it comes to emotions, she just freezes. She disappears and is just gone."

Like Anja's father, parents would often stick to strict daily routines, mainly around work and meals. Some would get upset or even lose control when these habits were interrupted. Robert remembers getting his most severe beating from his father one day after school because he had not paid enough attention when walking up the stairs and a squeaking floorboard had woken his father up from his "sacred" lunchtime nap. When Sabina first got married, her husband would regularly find her hiding behind the couch when he returned home at night. It took months before she found the courage to tell him that "coming home from work time" was the occasion when her father had routinely beaten her if anything had set him off—an untidy room, a toy carelessly left lying around, a less than perfect mark at school.

The roles were sometimes reversed, as between Anja and her dad, and the children said they had to assume the parenting role, mainly in terms of providing comfort and emotional care. "I think I felt that it was my duty to make the world safe for my parents," Andrea explained. This emotional enmeshment and sense of responsibility made it difficult to separate from their families and to build independent lives. Some children had to be in charge also in practical terms. Paula told me that as a little girl she once had to call the neighbors when there was a fire in the kitchen, because her mother just stood there screaming, incapable of moving or responding.

Since the early 2000s, these parental behaviors and character traits have been subsumed under the label *war childhoods*. A wealth of information is now available on this topic in the academic realm (for example, Ermann 2007; Grundmann, Hoffmeister, and Knoth 2009; Hondrich 2011; Janus 2006; Radebold 2000, 2004, 2005; Seegers and Reulecke 2009). Even more can now be found in mainstream literature: entering *Kriegskinder* (war children) on www.Amazon.de brings up around four hundred book titles, including many autobiographies and family memoirs. The overarching finding is that, largely unnoticed until that time, the events the Kriegskinder experienced during World War II often had a defining impact on their entire lives.

Many Germans born between 1930 and 1945 were confronted with violence, loss, death, and destruction at a very young age. In a survey conducted by the Allensbach Institute in 1952 among young men, 51 percent had lost family members; 41 percent had experienced air raids; 36 percent had a father or brother who was in a POW camp; 21 percent had their houses destroyed by bombs; 21 percent had been forced to flee or were deported after the war; and 19 percent had a family member who was disabled (Förster and Beck 2003). Not every child was affected in the same way. A range of personal circumstances played a role in how they coped, first and foremost the presence of close family members who were able to provide a sense of protection in life-threatening situations (Drost and Lamparter 2013; Möller and Lamparter 2013). Psychoanalyst Hartmut Radebold believes that about a third of all Germans who were children or teenagers during World War II would be classified as traumatized according to present psychological standards. In the case of another third, he believes the war had a significant and lifelong impact on the person's biography, while about 40 percent are said to have survived the time more or less unharmed (Radebold 2012). Although they provide solid ground to represent the discussion that has taken place, these statistics need to be understood as personal estimates only. As explained in chapter 3, diagnoses such as PTSD were not available until the 1980s, and because of the long passage of time, it is difficult to ascertain whether or not a person suffered any lasting damage. According to my interviews, families who lived in (or were evacuated to) the countryside, with fewer air raids and better food supplies, tended to describe themselves as the "lucky ones" who got through this difficult period with fewer losses and less ongoing damage than others.

A number of studies have been conducted on the current prevalence of World War II–related post-traumatic stress symptoms in the German war children generation. The results vary substantially from study to study, ranging from 3.4 percent (Maercker et al. 2008) to 7.2 percent (Glaesmer et al. 2010); 10.8 percent (Kuwert et al. 2007); and 25 percent (Teegen and Meister 2000). Again, such studies need to be read with caution. Firstly, their results do not easily lend themselves to being generalized or compared with one another, as different sample sizes and methods of participant selection are used and different PTSD symptoms (full or partial PSTD) are captured, all of which may explain the variance in results. Also, they only capture a narrowly defined range of clinical symptoms and do not necessarily present a full picture of how the war affected a person's life, memories, attitudes, and behaviors. For example, while only a smaller proportion of German seniors actually displayed PTSD symptoms sixty-five years on, between 20 percent and 66 percent of participants (increasing with age) in the representative survey conducted by Heide Glaesmer and her colleagues recalled war-related memories, often reported as the most difficult in the person's life (Glaesmer et al. 2010). An interdisciplinary project focuses on survivors of the *Hamburger Feuersturm*, the firebombing of Hamburg in July 1943, during which up to 35,000 people perished and about 250,000 homes were destroyed (Lamparter 2013).[1] While about 50 percent of all interviewees said the firebombing was the worst experience of their lives, most described their current state of mental and physical health as stable (Möller and Lamparter 2013). However, they showed slightly elevated scores for anxiety and depression, and 14 percent reported current PTSD symptoms (Lamparter et al. 2013). Around a quarter said that they still had nightmares; another quarter reported getting anxious when they smelled smoke, and about half when they heard the sound of an alarm (Drost and Lamparter 2013).

Behind the psychological profile of a hardworking generation, psychologists now see repressed trauma and loss, as well as a defense against feelings of guilt for the crimes committed during the war (Brähler, Decker, and Radebold 2004). "Pathological normalcy" ("*Pathologische Normalität*"; Radebold 2000) and the creation of idyllic homes are today interpreted as coping mechanisms aimed at keeping the demons of the past at bay. Set routines and well-behaved children were to provide emotional stability to a traumatized parent (Bachofen 2012). The act of children taking on the parenting role is now called *parentification* (Radebold 2012), and the emotional neediness of the parents is seen as one of the main causes for the Kriegsenkel's struggles to become independent (Bachofen 2012). Underneath the emotional numbness that many Kriegsenkel observed, strong but unresolved emotions such as sadness, desperation, helplessness, grief, and shame, as well as anger and aggression, are suspected (Radebold 2008, 2012). Because of a lack of empathy and support that they themselves suffered in their childhood, many never developed the ability to relate to their children's needs and concerns, and they often could not provide emotional closeness and stability that they themselves had never experienced, psychologist Bettina Alberti concluded (2010).

None of my interviewees mentioned that they had read the academic literature on war childhoods, but they did pick up on the topic in the mainstream media, and a few had read Sabine Bode's earlier book on war children (Bode 2004). Like Anja, they subsequently looked at their parents' emotions, attitudes, and behaviors in this light. A third of my interviewees explicitly said that they believed that the war had traumatized one or both of their parents (and sometimes grandparents), and most others explained at least some of their family's character traits and behaviors to be the result of World War II.

Getting Unstuck and Moving Forward

During her conversations with her father about his horrific memories, things also started to click for Anja regarding her own psychological problems. It was difficult to pinpoint exactly where the link was because her own symptoms differed from her father's. However, when she heard his stories, she felt a bottomless pit of pain behind his words, an abyss that opened up and swallowed him, which was similar to something she felt somewhere deep down in herself. It was inside her, but it did not feel as if it belonged to her. It was pain, panic, and sadness beyond words, to a degree that she could not relate to anything that had happened in her own life. She said: "I could only imagine feeling like this if my child died. It is a level of embodied pain as a result of something happening to you that cuts into you so deeply, where you have to go through such a dark hole, that you cannot come out on the other side as the same person. You just cannot come out whole."

She admitted that she found it hard to distinguish this from the pain she felt watching her mother die of bowel cancer. Yet, after years of therapy, there was the clear sense of having discovered the core of her issues, of having found the missing link to explain her constant psychological struggles. Anja felt the same sense of clicking, the big eureka moment, that I also heard described by many other people: "Looking back now, I find the thought that only eighteen months ago I did not know about this connection completely absurd. I could not see the wood for the trees. It really was the elephant in the room, so much so that I now find myself standing there and thinking, 'How could I not have seen this before? How could I have ignored that so completely?' That I was missing this tiny yet all-important bit of information? That I only needed this one key to be able to understand everything?"

The second time we talked, on a beautiful Berlin autumn day, Anja was still frustrated. Frustrated that in spite of the fact that she felt she finally had all the pieces of the jigsaw puzzle she needed, the same emotional pain that had been coming and going for the past twenty years was still there and had all but immobilized her. Anja still felt the leaden heaviness, her body exhausted, and she found it almost impossible to make decisions and realize her professional ambitions. She was also afraid she would pass her problems on to her son. Yet, when we caught up again almost a year later, she immediately struck me as different. She was feeling better, she confirmed, smiling cautiously. Finally, things were starting to move. There had been so many psychological issues in her life: her fears and her depression, her mother's death, and also difficulties with her husband and her career. "It was all so overwhelming. I never knew where to start. There was always this one huge issue blocking me right at the base, and everything else was piled on top of that. Now that I have finally been able to tackle this, everything else has become manageable." She was still seeing a therapist, but her mood swings and panic attacks had diminished, and she had been able to stop taking her antianxiety medication for the first time in fifteen years. She had not talked to her father about the war again, although he had made a few attempts. She found his ritualistic retelling of the same terrible stories, the crying, and the outpouring of emotional pain now too overwhelming to handle. Anja was trying to distance herself from him and the symbiotic relationship they had always had. She now wanted a more independent life. Anja was reluctant to put down all of her problems to her father's war trauma, yet it was obvious to her that something major had changed in her, that "a knot was untied" (*"ein Knoten ist geplatzt"*), and that she was finally able to move forward with her life. "I am quite content at the moment, and this is really the first time ever," she said, summing up her situation before we said good-bye.

I have told Anja's story in detail here to give you deeper insight into the way a person of the German Kriegsenkel generation understands her life and emotional problems. Anja had access to the general findings of the war children literature to explain her father's previously inexplicable behaviors, and through the Kriegsenkel books, she had become aware of concepts of transgenerational transmission, which helped her make the link between her own problems and her father's past. As for Kerstin from chapter 4 and many others of her generation, this provided a new meaning for her emotional suffering and enabled her to "get unstuck." Yet Anja's story was also different from most others I heard, in two ways. Firstly, she was able to hear directly from her father about the events he had lived through as a little boy. This, as previous chapters showed, is far from common. She was therefore able to better pinpoint the damage his war childhood had left behind and explain his odd behaviors and psychological problems. Secondly, because of her sophisticated perception of how her own emotional struggles were connected to her father's—as a physical heaviness felt in her body, which she expressed through the air-raid shelter sculptures, and as an emotional link to the abyss of sadness in her that resonated with something inside him. No one else I spoke to was able to describe the connection between their own pain and their family's wartime damage so clearly, deeply, and precisely.

Occurrences of transgenerational transmission are by their very nature elusive and hard to grasp, as they happened not only in the past but also outside a person's conscious perception. In a moment I will discuss the different approaches with which researchers, mainly from the "psy sciences" (Rose 1998), have tried to explain these mysterious processes. But before doing that, I would first like to tell you a second Kriegsenkel life history: that of Juliane and her family secret.

JULIANE: "MEN ARE PIGS"

At the age of forty-six, Juliane was a single mother who lived with her four-year-old daughter, Mona, in a small two-bedroom government-provided apartment in one of the poorer neighborhoods of Berlin. She was twice divorced, currently unemployed, and struggling to manage her life after a long history of depression, panic attacks, and a series of abusive relationships. Juliane was waiting for me in her apartment for our first meeting on a cold, gray Berlin winter day. She made coffee and arranged the pastries I had brought on a plate. She seemed happy to see me, pleased that someone was taking an interest in her. Yet, in spite of her soft features, her curly dark hair, and her round face, Juliane was a challenging person to interview. Before we even sat down in her cozy lounge room decorated with children's paintings and a colorful couch, she unleashed a tirade of words, an incessant stream of frustration, anger, and bitterness about almost everything in her life: her husbands, her unsuccessful job hunting, her friends, her neighbors, and her family—first and foremost her mother. She crafted her story mostly by herself, without questions or prompts from me—not just that first time we met, but also the three other times that followed over the course of 2012 and 2013. After each meeting a painful atmosphere of loneliness and depression followed me home and lingered around in my apartment for a few days, leaving me feeling helpless and wishing I could do more for her than just sit and listen.

Juliane grew up in a small country town in southern Germany, surrounded mainly by women: her mother, grandmother, and two aunts. Her mother had not married her biological father, and Juliane had never met him or the grandparents on that side. Her maternal grandfather had died when she was little. Her family were not *Alteingessessene,* not old locals in the region like most of their neighbors, who had long roots in the small community stretching back over centuries. Her family had come as refugees from the East after the war, from a region that now belongs to Poland. With her mother working to support herself and her daughter, Juliane spent a lot of time growing up with her grandmother. She depicted both women as hard, cold, and relentless. They raised the girl with frequent beatings and verbal degradation. She remembered a home devoid of warmth, touch, or praise. "Old school," Juliane said laconically. The last time she was beaten up, she was already nineteen. Traces of National Socialist ideology clearly came through when the grandmother ranted against the *Polacken* (a derogatory term for Polish people) or yelled "Hitler would have sorted you lot out" when she was angry with the girl. "Keep your trap shut and stop whining; you don't know how lucky you are" was a sentence Juliane heard throughout her childhood.

Relics of National Socialist Child-Rearing Practices

What Juliane referred to as "old school" points to the harsh style of raising children still commonly found in the older generation at the time. The coldness many parents, and in her case also grandparents, displayed may not only be due to experiences of war. Prussian values of discipline, obedience, and duty, as well as National Socialist ideology, still shaped parenting styles. First published in 1934, Johanna Haarer's child-rearing bible, *Die Deutsche Mutter und ihr erstes Kind* (The German mother and her first child), promoted National Socialist practices for caring for babies and young children. It was widely distributed and consulted during the Third Reich—and after. The book gave clear instructions to German mothers on how to raise the proponents of the future "master race," tempered and hardened for the demands to be made on them in later years. Which basically meant preparing them for war. To prevent attachment, children were separated from their mothers after birth and kept in isolation for the first twenty-four hours of their lives. Women were encouraged to avoid all "unnecessary" touching, talking to, or making eye contact with their babies. According to Haarer, a medical doctor, "The child should be fed, bathed and diapered, but beyond this left alone" (Chamberlain 2004, 374). The enforcement of cleanliness and obedience and the drill of order and discipline were paramount. Corporal punishment and the withdrawal of affection were encouraged to break the child's will. Mothers were instructed not to comfort their children when they were crying. They were to remain "hard and relentless" at all times, and not "sin" because of an "excess of love or foolishness" (374). Unbelievably, the book was reprinted with only minor changes after the war. It remained a standard item in most German households until the 1970s and was last published in 1996! While child-rearing practices started to become more respectful of children after the movement of 1968, physical and psychological violence (including verbal abuse or degrading punishments) were still quite common at the time when the Kriegsenkel were growing up, and they were only declared to be punishable offenses by law in 2000 (Alberti 2010, 122). Germany may stand out as a particularly harsh example. However, other Western countries also only shifted away from more authoritarian parenting practices around a similar time. For example, a fifth of all participants in a Swedish study, born in the 1950s and 1960s, still remembered being frequently slapped at home (Trifan, Stattin, and Tilton-Weaver 2014). An interesting counterexample is the United States. Historian Paula Fass (2016) notes that "in the United States, much earlier and more emphatically than elsewhere in the West, authoritarian controls over children gave way to a more relaxed relationship between the generations." There, the most popular parenting book since 1946 has been Benjamin Spock's *The Common Sense Book of Baby and Child Care*, which has sold more than fifty million copies to date. Along with offering practical tips about nutrition, illness, and physical growth, the book also provides advice on the psychological development of children. Its gentle approach to caring for babies and its encouragement of parents to have a "natural, easy confidence in themselves" came to define parenting of the baby-boom generation (Fass 2016, 184).

"Männer sind Schweine" *(Men are pigs)*

While Juliane mostly remembered her grandmother's beatings and verbal degradation, she also sometimes told the little girl stories from the war. Her grandmother talked about the air raids, about having to share their food with the pigs, and about her journey west with her three daughters: Juliane's two aunts, twelve and eight at the time, and her mother, who was just four. Her graphic descriptions of fear, threat, hunger, and death scared the little girl, but they were also precious moments when the grandmother gave her the attention she so desperately craved. Juliane listened attentively, just wishing that those stories had a happier ending.

When I asked Juliane whether she thought some of her family's war experiences had been passed on to her, she nodded and gave me a number of examples: her fear of planes, tanks, and sirens, which her grandmother had instilled with her vivid stories; her compulsive need to have a full fridge; and her fear of another war or a catastrophe like the nuclear accident in Fukushima in the previous year. However, the one aspect of her life that she felt had been most negatively affected by the past was her relations to men. Juliane had been struggling with relationships all her life. In her teens she looked for love and affection from the Turkish boys in the neighborhood, saying with a derogatory undertone that "they were the only ones she could score with." She often experienced those encounters as violent and abusive. Juliane described herself as a lonely and insecure teenager. She smoked, drank, and took her grandmother's sleeping pills because they made her feel so "blissfully high." She started skipping school and had to repeat year eight. All in all, however, she said looking back, she was not as useless a student as her mother was trying to make her believe. When she later moved to Berlin to go to college, loneliness and depression hit her harder, and anxiety and panic attacks were added to her list of difficulties.

At some point Juliane got married. Twice. Both men were foreigners she met when traveling overseas. She said she did not love either of them and agreed more out of a sense of obligation than affection. "*Wer A sagt muss auch B sagen*" (you must finish what you started), her grandmother had taught her. Juliane talked about the panic attack she had at the registry office while waiting to sign the papers for her second wedding, "because it just felt so wrong deep down." She went through with it regardless. Both times she was unhappy but unable to stand up for herself. She had three abortions before she got pregnant with Mona. Her second husband pressured her for sex after the birth of their daughter and was routinely verbally abusive when she did not comply. After one particularly distressing argument with him, Juliane took Mona and moved to a women's shelter. The counselor at the center for victims of domestic violence listened to her entire story. At one point, out of the blue, she asked Juliane whether someone in her family—maybe her mother or grandmother?—may have been raped at the end of World War II and whether that trauma may have been passed on to her and could explain her problems with men. Juliane had never considered this before, and nothing along those lines had ever been mentioned at home. "I always knew that there was something wrong with my family, but I could not put my finger on it. Sure, there was the war, but that was so long ago, we talked about it at school, and it was all very terrible, but you kind of block that out when it comes to your own family," she explained during my first visit. Yet as soon as Juliane heard those words, she immediately knew that the psychologist was right, and the realization shot through her body like an electric shock. She interrogated her mother and the one aunt who was still alive, but both categorically denied that anything had happened to them or the grandmother.

Nevertheless, after this session with the counselor, Juliane started to look back at her life and her family history with completely different eyes. Different bits of information stood out from the fabric of the past, and she connected the dots in a new way. The fact that one aunt never got married, never wanted a relationship or children. She did have occasional affairs, she told Juliane, but she never wanted to have a man in her house or let anyone come emotionally close to her. The other aunt had lost two children and was incapable of relating to the two she eventually had, and she later developed cervical cancer. Lastly, her mother's and grandmother's coldness and inability to feel emotions struck her. Her mother got pregnant with Juliane from a man she did not love, because "she could not say no," and she openly displayed her physical aversion to the man she later married when Juliane was ten. The girl picked up strong verbal messages like "*Männer sind Schweine*" (men are pigs); "men are disgusting"; "sex is disgusting"; "it is something you have to do, so just shut up, don't move, and let it happen." That was also the motto she lived by in her own relationships. "Keep still, endure, keep your mouth shut, play dead," she said, summarizing her approach to sex and intimacy.

Suddenly her own and her family's attitudes, behaviors, and life choices took on a new meaning as she linked them back to an experience of rape that may have happened more than sixty years earlier. She had no proof to support this new explanation of her own difficulties, but intuitively it made total sense to her. Deep down, it simply felt right.

The Grandmothers' Secrets: Sexual Violence at the End of World War II

Juliane is not alone in this. The topic of rape was mentioned in half of all my interviews. Like a specter, it haunts many family histories, mostly as a rumor, a hunch, or a secret—as in Juliane's family—almost never as a known fact.[2] Ludwig was the only one among my fifty-four interviewees who heard directly from his grandmother that she had been raped when fleeing from Silesia in

1945. He was already in his midtwenties when she told him about her ordeal, under a flood of tears and with a lot of distressing details. She admitted that she developed a strong aversion to Russians and Czechs as a consequence but said she also understood that it was the Germans who had started the aggression. "No more war" was the lesson she strongly imparted to her grandson.

It is estimated that around 1.9 million German girls and women were victims of sexual violence at the end of World War II, 1.4 million of them in the former German territories in the East and during flight and forced migration, and at least 100,000 in Berlin alone (Radebold 2008). Most of the perpetrators were soldiers of the Red Army. Rapes by US and French soldiers are also documented but were far less common (Sander and Johr 2008). Approximately 300,000 children were born as a consequence; the number of abortions is unknown. Around 200,000 women are said to have committed suicide (Messerschmidt 2006). Many women kept their experiences to themselves after the war; being a victim of rape was felt to be particularly humiliating and shameful, even more so than being a victim of other forms of war trauma (Eichhorn and Kuwert 2011). Talking about sexual violence was, and still is, off limits in most German families. When they returned home, the fathers and husbands often did not want to know about what had happened to their loved ones. Many may have been ashamed of not being able to protect their wives and daughters or of having committed similar crimes when rampaging through Russian villages with the Wehrmacht (Sander and Johr 2008).

The topic was taboo also in the public domain until 2003, when *Eine Frau in Berlin (A Woman in Berlin)* was published. The anonymous diary, written between April and June 1945, is a gruelingly detailed depiction of the serial rapes of German women by Soviet occupying forces in Berlin in spring 1945. The book first came out in the United States in 1954 and was not available in German until 1959, when it was published by a small publishing house in Switzerland. It was met with an outcry of protest. Critics lamented that the author was "besmirching the honor of German women" (Kanon 2005), who consequently decreed that her book should not be published again until after her death. It was thus only reprinted in 2003, bringing the topic into the center of public attention. Many of my interviewees had read the book or had watched the movie that came out in 2008 with the same title (Färberböck 2008). A psychological study conducted by Svenja Eichhorn and Philipp Kuwert (2011) concluded that every second woman who was a victim of sexual violence in World War II still showed symptoms of post-traumatic stress disorder sixty-five years later, affecting in particular relationships with family (26%) and friends (15%) and most of all the realm of intimacy and sexuality (81%). Among the twenty-seven women who volunteered to participate in the study, three said that they were raped more than ten times, two more than twenty times, and five more than thirty times. One woman counted an inconceivable seventy-one times, a horrific fact that the authors leave inexplicably uncommented (Eichhorn and Kuwert 2011).

As was the case for the topic of the war children, information about sexual violence at the end of World War II is now more widely available in the public domain, and this knowledge was woven into the Kriegsenkel life histories. It was a frequent consideration in our interviews that someone in the family may have been a victim or witness of rape. Twelve of my interviewees (nine women, three men) were certain that they could feel traces of sexual violence running through the family—showing in their parents' and grandparents' as well as in their own lives. As in Juliane's family, the most common thread was the prevalence of extremely negative and hostile attitudes toward men. Men were said to be "worthless," "useless," and "incapable of controlling themselves," and daughters were often instructed "to be very careful" when dating. Karoline said her grandmother was incredibly bitter and only referred to men as *Kerle* (thugs)—including when talking about her own husband and her son-in-law. Karoline herself also had problems with relationships, and in 2012, after a recent separation, she suddenly found herself "almost hating all men." Given the experiences of her own life, the intensity of these emotions did not seem appropriate to her, but she did not have more than a vague suspicion to rely on. "This issue catches up with me again and again," she said, "and I can't move forward. It is a feeling of heaviness and fog, and there is no one I could ask." Sabine's mother always warned her three daughters not to be too trusting with men, and she rejected each boyfriend and later the husbands they brought home. Unlike others, though, Sabine did not take her mother's advice. She remembered being a rebellious teenager who quite enjoyed hanging out with the boys, and she "really did not understand what Mum was going on about." Martin and Robert both told me that their grandmothers committed suicide by hanging themselves "like the women who were raped by the Russians did" (Martin). While neither of them had details about their grandmothers' fates, both men said they had past relationships with women who were rape victims.

Sitting at her kitchen table, Sanna traced the topic through her own biography: As part of her training to become a psychologist, she did several internships. The first one was with an institution that provided psychiatric support for Bosnian women, many of whom had been victims of rape during the civil war in Yugoslavia in the 1990s. Confronted with the victims' stoic silence, their profound sense of shame and deep pain, Sanna started to feel an intuitive connection with her own grandmother, who she had never met but whom she knew had been admitted to a psychiatric ward in 1947 with a diagnosed "Russian paranoia" after Russian soldiers had occupied the family home for a time after the war (the story of the villa was told in chap. 2). Without it being a conscious decision, Sanna opted to do her next internship in a men's prison, working with a group of convicted rapists. It was an extreme time in her life, she reflected, with intense feelings of hatred up to the point where she started to see a rapist in every man she came across in the street. Although she was somewhat aware of her family history at the time, it was only in 2012 that she felt she could clearly see how all these dots connected and linked back to events that she suspected happened in her grandmother's house. Sanna's sister Bettina, born in 1976, did not feel the same kind of impact of the past on her own life. However, she admitted that until she was in her midtwenties, she experienced sexual encounters often with a "certain degree of violence." During one of my visits to the family villa, Sanna's mother showed me the room where the grandmother "had gone mad" in 1947 and had been found screaming and sitting in a pool of her own urine. Her daughter still fiercely denied that anything had happened to her.

Coming to Terms with the Past

In July 2012 Juliane sent me an excited email saying that she had managed to catch her aunt off guard when she accidentally dropped the words "what the Russians did to us" into a telephone conversation. That time Juliane was not willing to let it go. She insisted, and her aunt finally told her most of the story. Russian soldiers had come into their village in eastern Prussia in 1945, storming into a house where only women and children were hiding. They had grabbed Juliane's four-year-old mother and had taken her with them, knowing that the grandmother would follow to protect her daughter. The aunt did not want to give the exact details, but it was made clear to Juliane that the soldiers had raped her grandmother and that her mother, as a little girl, had been forced to watch.

The next time we met, I asked what her aunt's disclosure meant to her. "I now know why I am so twisted" ("*krumm und schief*"), she responded without hesitation. "I have problems with sex and relationships because my family's trauma was passed on to me. How could I possibly be any different?" She said the knowledge about the past had helped her to make peace with herself and to accept the "defects" ("*Macken*") that she carried inside. She was also somewhat proud of herself for surviving her upbringing and turning out "OK overall."

Relationships with men were off the table at that point. She was still battling with Mona's father, who did not want to accept the separation, and she shared many stories of his aggressive behavior. She was certain that she did not want another man to ever touch her again and that she was now at peace with that decision. Juliane considered that her mother was also a victim, incapable of giving love and affection because of her own experience of violence, but their relationship remained strained. Eventually, Juliane cut all ties after one final attempt to get her mother to understand how abusive and neglectful she had been. She could not get through. Mona was in the room and overheard the heated telephone conversation, in which her mum cut her off from her grandmother. The little girl was utterly distressed. Like Anja, Juliane was worried that she could be passing her own damage on to her daughter. She admitted that she was struggling to cope with being a single mother and that she herself still had yet to learn how to be affectionate. She had been seeing a counselor for some time to help with her parenting skills, hoping to get rid of what she called her "negative programming." Yet under stress she still tended to lose control, and the messages that she had heard when growing up now resurfaced and hit Mona. "Stop whining; you don't know how lucky you are," Juliane heard herself say in times like that.

MODELS OF TRANSGENERATIONAL TRANSMISSION OF TRAUMA: OVERVIEW AND DISCUSSION

Both Anja and Juliane felt a strong connection between their own experiences and their families' World War II past. In Anja's case it was the heaviness, fear, and sadness related to her father's war memories that she also felt inside herself. For Juliane it was a secret history of sexual violence that she believed had left her incapable of having fulfilling relations with men. The two women, like many of my other interviewees, had an intuitive and embodied knowing that there was indeed a causal link between their own pain and the events of the past. However, they also implicitly relied on common models of transgenerational transmission to frame their perception, most of them from the "psy sciences". The following section borrows from Natan Kellermann's (2001b) summary to describe the most prevalent approaches that informed Kriegsenkel life histories: psychoanalytical, sociocultural, family-system, and biological models of transgenerational transmission. They play a role in my analysis not as diagnostic tools but as narrative frameworks that inform and shape how each person made sense of the familial legacy. These discourses—mainstreamed, condensed, and simplified—provide the concepts and the vocabulary with which Kriegsenkel conceptualize their emotional suffering.

Psychoanalytical Approach to Transmission

The longest-standing and most influential model of transgenerational transmission has its roots in the psychoanalytical tradition. Psychoanalytical theory claims that traumatic memories that could not be consciously experienced and worked through by the eyewitness generation are passed on to the next for resolution (Kellermann 2001b). In relation to offspring of Holocaust survivors, Abraham and Torok (1994) introduced the metaphor of the crypt, a psychic space created to wall in unbearable experiences, memories, and secrets. The crypt, Derrida (1976, cited in Argenti and Schramm 2010) explains further, is formed in violence but also in silence, buried deep down in oneself. Defying narrative memory, it turns into a space of incorporation rather than introjection, the root of somatic embodiment. Offspring can inherit these psychic secrets, reified as a presence or an object, "a sort of psychic cyst" (Argenti and Schramm 2010, Kindle location 315), passed down from generation to generation. They can manifest symptoms that stem from their forebears' trauma. Psychiatrist Vamik Volkan believes that because of the fluidity of "psychic borders" between parents and children during the formative years, parents' unresolved emotions such as anxiety and depression, as well as their unconscious perceptions, images, and expectations of the external world, are passed from one generation to another (Volkan, Ast, and Greer 2002; Volkan 1997). It is understood that the chain of transgenerational transmission can only be broken once the person to whom trauma has been passed on gains an understanding of these influences and is able to work through and to remove them from the psyche (Volkan, Ast, and Greer 2002).

Although in the case of the Kriegsenkel no one would argue that their parents' trauma is in any way comparable with that of Holocaust survivors, psychoanalytical thinking still strongly comes through in their life histories. They often imagined that, unbeknownst to them, a distinct parcel of unresolved war memories was deposited into their psyches as they were growing up. It had now become their duty to work through and extract these memories as the only way to prevent further transmission to future generations. According to Gabriele Schwab (2010), psychoanalysis is the only theory able to trace the effects of an unconscious transmission of experiences through the generations. In this case, it allows people to explain their issues in relation to World War II even when they have no active knowledge of the family history. The past trauma can be inferred through current symptoms, life choices, and dreams. With the help of her psychiatrist, Anja interpreted the creation of her air-raid shelters as a physical manifestation of the heavy burden she had unconsciously inherited from her father. Sanna understood her attraction to the theme of rape, which came through in her professional choices, as a replay of her grandmother's trauma, even though she had never met her. A handful of people reported dreaming of scenes of war and destruction, which they took as representations of their family's war memories they had unknowingly absorbed as children. In one of our conversations, Anja pondered:

> Now I understand the nightmares that I used to have as a little girl. How often did I dream that I was getting shot, I don't know . . . countless times. Or how many times did I dream that I was walking through a cemetery at night and I knew I would walk through the gate and the place would suddenly become alive? The tombstones all came to life, and they closed in on me. That was the worst nightmare. . . . I know that is pretty abstract in some ways, but I really wouldn't know why else a five- or eight-year-old should have dreams like that.

Sociocultural and Socialization Models

While the psychoanalytic approach focuses more on unconscious aspects of transgenerational transmission, sociocultural and socialization models emphasize the conscious influence parents have on their children. Experiences of (Holocaust) trauma were sometimes found to negatively affect survivors' child-rearing and parenting skills, creating problems with attachment and detachment as well as exaggerated worries and anxieties. Traumatized parents were also seen to damage their children by being emotionally distant or overprotective, overly permissive or too harsh (Kellermann 2001b). Furthermore, as children take their parents as their role models and learn by observation and imitation, they may take on parental behaviors, attitudes, and emotional responses to certain situations. Working with Vietnam veterans, Ancharoff, Munroe, and Fisher (1998, 262) speak of a "traumatized world view" that is passed on to the offspring. They found that the fathers' experience of the Vietnam War permanently shaped their beliefs about themselves and the world, with which they in turn raised their children. When a three-year-old boy asked his dad to catch him at the bottom of the slide at the playground because he was scared, the father promised but then deliberately did not catch his son. Asked to explain his behavior, the father said that the boy needed to learn "never to trust what people told him" (265).

While she also described aspects of embodied and unconsciously transmitted traces of rape, much of how Juliane told her story follows the logic of the socialization models. She picked up the "traumatized worldview" ("men are pigs") from the women around her in the way they spoke about or behaved around men, and she internalized their attitudes regarding sex, love, and relationships. This was mirrored in many other stories I heard, coming through in parental life lessons (as explored in chap. 2) about food, financial security, and the ability to trust men (or people more generally).

Family Systems Models

Family systems models of transmission account for the fact that both conscious and unconscious transmission of trauma always takes place in a particular family setting. Holocaust survivor families, for example, are often described as "tight little islands" (Kellermann 2001b, 260), focused in on themselves and disconnected from their social environments. Parents are said to live vicariously through their children, while children strongly identify with their parents' difficult past. Children of survivor families also tend to have problems with individuation and separation and find it hard to build independent lives.

Descriptions of social isolation and of difficulties with separating from emotionally needy parents were also typical features in Kriegsenkel life histories, including in Anja's. Although already in her midforties, she still found it challenging to focus on her own family. After she learned about her father's war experiences, Anja came to the conclusion that, because of his trauma, he "really never grew up" to be the responsible father she had longed for. She still felt she needed to take care of him, in spite of the fact that he had remarried and she now lived hundreds of kilometers away.

Biological and Genetic Models

Lastly, biological and genetic models of transmission explore how vulnerability to post-traumatic stress can also be passed down physically from one generation to the next. Levels of cortisol, a hormone that helps with the management of stress, were found to be lower than average not only in traumatized mothers but also in their children. As a result, the children are more predisposed to being overwhelmed by feelings of anxiety, fear, and stress. If confronted with a stressful event, they have a significantly higher likelihood of also developing PTSD (Yehuda 2006; Yehuda and Bierer 2007; Yehuda et al., "*Vulnerability to Posttraumatic Stress Disorder,*" 1998). Studies in the field of epigenetics show that times of starvation, persecution, and mass violence can leave molecular scars on a person's DNA. These become part of the genetic scaffolding and are passed on to offspring. A child may, for example, inherit a grandmother's predisposition toward depression caused by the neglect she suffered in early childhood

(Hurley 2013). These kinds of findings were distributed in the German mainstream media and were often shared in Kriegsenkel Facebook groups. They played a role in validating and underpinning subjective experiences of suffering: "Of course transmission of trauma is real," several of my interviewees said emphatically. "We know now that it even changes your genes!"

The approaches outlined above belonged to the repertoire of psychological theories into which my interviewees tapped to explain how their parents' and grandparents' war experiences affected them. Relayed directly in counseling sessions and introduced into mainstream German society by the therapeutic culture more broadly, these psychological models provided the basic narrative structure and logic for how people talked about themselves and their families. This basic structure was populated further with recently publicized knowledge of sexual violence during World War II and the psychological impact of war childhoods. While concepts of transmitted trauma were variously critiqued in the academic realm as overly deterministic (Summerfield 1996), as too mechanistic and unidirectional (Völter 2008), or as pathologizing descendants of trauma survivors as victims of a past that they did not actually experience themselves (Kidron 2012), the Kriegsenkel I interviewed explained their lives quite narrowly within their boundaries. As detailed in the last chapter, having the analytical tools and models to describe one's previously inexplicable emotional problems helped many to find meaning in their predicament, feel more at peace with themselves, and, at least in some cases, get better. When Anja was able to make the connection between her depression and panic attacks and her father's war trauma, something became "unstuck," and, supported by her therapist, her life started to move forward.

However, as I listened to my German interviewees, it struck me that these models did not completely fit, and they also came with certain side effects. In particular, the psychoanalytical model is highly abstract and mechanical. It creates images of distinct parcels of traumatic experience handed down from generation to generation, imprinted by one or both parents on their children during their formative years. The lived experiences of growing up in families that survived World War II seemed messier than this. Anja's relationship with her father, for example, suggests that the past has a lifelong impact on family life and relationships rather than being limited to distinct instances of passing on an emotional burden in childhood.

Secondly, transgenerational transmission may not always be a linear process. Juliane pointed to the many signs of sexual violence in the female family members she was in contact with as a child: her mother, her grandmother, and her two aunts. Rather than depicting a neat handing down from generation to generation, Juliane described how the negative attitude toward men (and the trauma of rape) were all around her as she was growing up. She could have absorbed them from any one of these women—or from all of them. As for Juliane, and for many other Kriegsenkel, the grandparents played an important role in their lives. It is plausible that some traumatic memories had been passed directly on from grandparents to grandchildren without going through the parents first.[3]

Juliane's case also underpins a third observation: that the effects of past trauma in descendants cannot necessarily be clearly demarcated. Anja admitted that she found it hard to distinguish between the depression and fear she took on from her father and the pain she felt as she watched her mother die in the hospital. She found herself "hanging upside down in life" after that time—a state, as she said, from which she also never really recovered. Other stories similarly pointed to a mix of traumatic experiences that affected the same family. While Gabriele (born in 1961) was certain that her parents' war childhoods and the loss of both grandfathers had a big impact on her upbringing, her parents had also lost two children to a rare genetic disease. Neither trauma was talked about at home, creating compounding layers of pain and silence that Gabriele felt she absorbed organically and without being able to tell where exactly her depression came from.

Fourthly, from my interviewees' stories, I also question an (often repeated) assumption that psychological models infer: only unresolved traumatic experiences are passed on. However, my research showed that even parents who were described as having adjusted well after the war raised their children on the basis of the experiences formed during that defining time and passed on their attitudes and worldviews.

The last observation that struck me as I was listening to how my German interviewees framed their suffering was that they came with certain side effects. They pathologize not only, as Kidron (2010, 2012) critiques, the descendants' emotional states (labeling them as sufferers of transmitted PTSD) but child rearing more broadly. The task of these approaches is specifically to define and diagnose mental illness. As a consequence, they lead to imaginations of transgenerational transmission as a compartmentalized process. They artificially and abstractly cordon off undesirable, unwanted, and ultimately "sick" aspects from the overall transfer that happens as an integral part of raising children. Many of my interviewees believed that only unresolved emotional problems are passed on to the next generation and that there would not and should not have been such a transmission had their family been capable of adequately addressing their emotional issues. This belief exacerbated anger and judgment vis-à-vis the parents and sometimes led to the breaking off of relationships altogether. Therapeutic interventions were described almost like surgical procedures to extract the burdensome familial inheritance, aimed at leaving only the "healthy" parts behind. Juliane used the even more technical term of getting rid of her *negative programming*, which imagines the psyche as a computer system from which unwanted content can be successfully deleted. Anja and Juliane, and many others, felt it was their duty to free their psyche of the traumatic remnants as the only possible avenue to a better life and as a moral duty to their children.

These were the models of transmission that the German Kriegsenkel had access to because of the pervasiveness of therapeutic thinking in mainstream society. But are they the only ways to conceptualize a possible link between past events, difficult family relationships, and current emotional issues? What other approaches might capture and explain descendants' experiences, and could they counterbalance some of those side effects?

IS THERE ANOTHER WAY?

While the "psy sciences" clearly dominate the field, researchers from other disciplines have also explored the phenomenon of transgenerational transmission. Memory studies, for example, offer the concept of *postmemory* (Hirsch 1996, 2001, 2008; Hirsch and Spitzer 2006). Marianne Hirsch explains that descendants of people who experienced or witnessed cultural or collective trauma remember the past only through the stories, images, and behaviors among which they grew up. However, these experiences are transmitted so deeply that they almost become memories in their own right. These kinds of internalized memories can also include bodily and affective connections to traumatic events, and they can incorporate images relayed by the media (such as photos of concentration camps) (Hirsch 2008, 106–7). Anthropologists have also provided a number of case studies observing how traces of a violent past were passed on in families in different parts of the world. Stephan Feuchtwang (2009, 2011) conducted interviews in Luku, a Taiwanese village, where the authoritarian Kuomintang government had brutally cracked down on a communist movement in the early 1950s. Memories of past violence haunted families in the form of unquiet ghosts because they had lacked the money to give their ancestors a proper burial. Later, when they conducted formal domestic rituals of remembering the dead, the haunting ceased. Feuchtwang also claims that once the state officially recognized the past violence, and once survivors' traumatic memories were incorporated into official narratives, the transmission of trauma ended. As commemoration took over, victims were allegedly not only able to articulate their pain but also able to forget the past and achieve a sense of closure. Janine Klungel (2009) documented the multiple ways in which a lasting memory and fear of rape spread through families and the community in Guadeloupe—from the time of the French colonial occupation until today. Here, women openly shared stories of rape and of visits from spirits of the dead that solicited sex while the women were asleep. Sexual violence was also perpetuated through the embodied practice of virginity testing, which anxious Guadeloupian mothers performed on their daughters, thereby, while seeking to protect them, effectively reenacting the rape. In families of *campesinos* who survived the civil war in El Salvador (1980 to 1992), the past came through in personal stories as well as in parental reactions to everyday situations. As mentioned in the introduction, Julia Dickson-Gómez (2002, 417) found traces of a "traumatized world view" in children as young as six years old, born long after the events. These children displayed a fundamental mistrust of the police, neighbors, and politicians, as well as an exaggerated sense of responsibility for their parents' well-being. The trauma of war was furthermore transmitted in the family through the embodied symptoms of *nervios*—a common form of distress in Latin America. Lastly, Carol Kidron (2009b, 2010) describes how the Holocaust constituted a constant presence in the home of survivor families. Predominantly silent knowing about the past was transmitted from parents to children through embodied everyday practices (such as putting shoes out at night in case one has to leave in a hurry), attitudes (in particular toward food), and engagement with objects from the past.

Each of these studies describes a unique mix of verbally discursive and embodied forms of transgenerational transmission. They do not attempt, however, to extrapolate a more general model, nor do they dwell on the finer details of the processes involved. Carol Kidron's (2009b) work is the exception in that she contemplates how exactly knowledge about the past passes from parents to children in a home environment where the Holocaust is not necessarily openly talked about. Drawing on Josselson's work (1995), Kidron believes that feelings of empathy and love create a space where the individual boundaries between family members are relaxed, enabling the children to gain empathic knowledge of their parents' traumatic experiences without the need for words and explanations.

Could we take this one step further? What if those boundaries between people not only were relaxed in certain situations but did not exist in the first place? This fascinating idea is relayed by the field of affect theory, more specifically in Teresa Brennan's (2004) book *The Transmission of Affect*. According to

Brennan, Western psychology and psychoanalysis assume that an individual is energetically and emotionally bounded and self-contained. Affect theory, on the other hand, understands human beings as fundamentally open systems, constantly interacting with and influenced by other people and the environment around them. "By the transmission of affect, I mean simply that the emotions or affects of one person, and the enhancing or depressing energies these affects entail, can enter into another" (Brennan 2004, 3). Received affects can have either an enriching (for example, affection and warmth) or a depleting impact on a person, "when one carries the affective burden of another, either by straightforward transfer or because the other's anger becomes our depression" (Brennan 2004, 6). The affects that the receiver internalizes are not entirely the same as the original ones but are mediated by the receiver's own thoughts, associations, and experiences. While the transmission of affect is in its origin a social process, its effects can be measured through subtle changes in a person's physiology, for example on the level of hormones.

As a model of transmission outside the sphere of the "psy sciences," this approach has some assets to contribute to Kriegsenkel experiences. Firstly, it offers an extremely simple explanation of how transmission happens. Here, things just pass between people who are in close physical proximity to each other—freely and constantly. Each person senses and picks up on another person's affects. This matches the description that many of my interviewees gave of the atmosphere at home. They effortlessly sensed their parents' and grandparents' emotions even if these were not verbalized. They could feel them "hanging in the air" like a fog or a dome, and they clearly felt them influencing their own mood and happiness. Living with her father, Anja would have simply soaked up his sadness and fears, and some of these emotions stayed in her system. While the way she internalized them made her "symptoms" different from his, they still resonated.

Secondly, thinking this approach through further brings the individual relationship between family members into sharper focus. Whether the other person is a grandparent, a father, or anyone else, a transmission cannot occur without physical and emotional closeness. In Juliane's case, for example, affects around men and relationships would have passed between her mother and her and between her grandmother and her at the same time. Brennan's (2004) model could also account for the different responses among siblings, who may have different degrees of emotional closeness to and distance from their parents (and grandparents).

Most importantly, according to this model, transgenerational transmission would be considered the norm, not the exception. Rather than pathologizing the relationship between parents and children, this model explains that it is natural and unavoidable that all affects (enhancing and depleting) flow between family members. Instead of compartmentalizing and separating traumatized (unhealthy) and normal (healthy) content, proponents of this model would not consider the transmission of affect stemming from the war to be a separate and distinct entity. Instead they would see it as an integral part of the overall transfer of "cultural and psychosocial resources" (Zinnecker 2008, 142) that invariably happens between the generations as part of child rearing.

Processes of transgenerational transmission are mysterious, invisible, and multifaceted. It may ultimately be impossible to adequately capture them in just one comprehensive model. Each of the approaches outlined above has its merits in helping explain the phenomenon, and they are also not mutually exclusive.[4] However, I do believe that Brennan's ideas could suggest a meaningful addition to the suite of models commonly used to conceptualize transgenerational transmission. They may prove helpful to people who grew up in families with difficult pasts and may alleviate some of the side effects of the psychological approaches. Applying Brennan's logic, the German Kriegsenkel would still understand themselves as affected by their parents' traumatic war experiences. People like Anja and Juliane would probably continue to be disappointed that their families were not able to provide them with the necessary positive affects (warmth, care, protection, etc.) to allow them to become happy and well-adjusted adults. However, accepting that "things just pass between people" could take away at least some of the judgment vis-à-vis their parents and the implicit expectation that transmission should have been preventable with the appropriate access to (or uptake of) therapy. It could also offer at least some relief from the heavy task they put on themselves to break the chain of transmission. In place of the mechanistic view that trauma gets handed down indefinitely from generation to generation and needs to be worked through and extracted in therapy, this model would allow for a view that, with the passage of time and with each subsequent generation, influences of traumatic memories that go back to the war would naturally be mixed with and diluted by other emotions related to more recent (positive and negative) biographical experiences.

Lastly, as chapter 3 showed, the Kriegsenkel wanted to prove that their intuitive perception that emotions from the war were transmitted to them was real. From the standpoint of affect theory, however, the issue is simply turned on its head. The question becomes "Why would there not be a transmission of experiences?" It might be naive, but maybe framing and normalizing transgenerational transmission in this way could not only provide validation for the emotional distress of the Kriegsenkel but also encourage more understanding and acceptance between the generations.

While many of my German interviewees portrayed in this chapter, including Juliane and Anja, imagined the intergenerational impact of the war as the handing down of a heavy emotional burden, the last chapter examines these experiences from the perspective of absence. It explores how the Kriegsenkel wrestle with places and people that were not there as the result of World War II or whose relationships were cut off because of a family legacy of perpetratorship and war crimes.

NOTES

1. The scenes of destruction after the *Hamburger Feuersturm* are described in detail in W. G. Sebald's *Luftkrieg und Literatur* (2001).

2. On the topic of transgenerational haunting and sexual violence against women, see Grace M. Cho, *Haunting the Korean Diaspora: Shame, Secrecy, and the Forgotten War* (2008).

3. I suspect that it is a sad fact that many psychological and psychoanalytical models do not include the extended family in their observations of the dynamic because they are based on work with descendants from Holocaust survivor families, where the grandparents had been murdered in the concentration camps.

4. Kellermann suggests that experiences are best captured in an integrative model of trauma transmission, which combines all of the different approaches and which also takes aggravating and mitigating factors into account. See Kellermann, "Transmission of Holocaust Trauma: an Integrative View" (2001b).

SIX

THE LOSSES AND THE SHAME OF WAR

Absence in Kriegsenkel Narratives

UP TO THIS POINT I have shown how mainstream psychological and psychoanalytical models provided the framework for the German Kriegsenkel to explain, explore, and address their emotional suffering. Just as Kerstin did in chapter 4 and Juliane and Anja did in chapter 5, people tended to picture their problems as a parcel of undigested experiences left over from the war, unconsciously handed down by their families and weighing heavily on their present lives. Their dominant desire was to "break the chain of transmission" and extract these unwanted influences from their psyche to achieve happier and healthier lives for themselves and their children. This chapter takes a different approach. It looks at the same experiences through the conceptual lens of absence. Something puzzled me from the beginning: many of the examples that my interviewees brought forward revolved not only around what was actively passed on by parents and grandparents but just as often around a sense of lack or a gap. Many people were feeling pain because of what had not been transmitted by their family or what was more broadly felt to be missing as a result of World War II. There were many grievances about silences in the family communication (explored in chap. 2) that left gaps in knowledge about the past, about an atmosphere of taboos and secrets that swallowed up life force like a black hole. There were grandfathers who had gone missing at the eastern front or who were excluded from family narratives because of their suspected involvement in Nazi war crimes. There were many complaints about cold mothers and their inability to provide nurturing because of an emotional emptiness that their war trauma had left. Lastly, there were feelings of homelessness and lack of attachment related to a family history of forced displacement and loss.

I was fascinated by the emotional charge these gaps exuded in my interviewees' stories and by the images, pains, and desires they produced. I started to ponder on the crucial role that absences play in the construction of Kriegsenkel suffering and in the transgenerational transmission of war experiences more broadly.

Previous research did include some facets of absence in their analysis, such as the impact of silence in families that have experienced a violent past (see chap. 2, and also Baer and Frick-Baer 2010; Kidron 2009a, 2009b; Tatara 1998; Wajnryb 2001), the gaps in attachment due to parental trauma (for example Alberti 2010; Kellermann 2001a), and the intergenerational impact of people killed, missing, or erased from memory as a result of war and political persecution (in particular Cho 2008; but also Baker and Gippenreiter 1998; Hunter-King 1998).

Here, I zoom in on the subtle, highly complex, and shifting experience of absence in a society where this is inextricably linked to a history of aggressive invasion and war crimes. The first part of the chapter homes in on the intergenerational impact of forced migration and the loss of a *Heimat* (homeland) as a result of the German defeat in 1945. The second traces the gaps and breaks in familial relationships resulting from a history of Nazi perpetratorship. While these topics are quite different, I look at all of them through the same analytical lens. In a sense, absence in its different articulations is the protagonist of the chapter. It is the glue that holds the three very different case studies together. This last chapter also closes the circle by drawing a line back to the beginning of the book as I show how Germany's sociopolitical environment crucially alters the shifting perceptions of emotional suffering resulting from World War II.

To trace and illuminate the role of absences in Kriegsenkel life histories, I take the liberty to draw rather eclectically from the ideas of a diverse range of researchers, from the more conceptual contributions to Bille, Hastrup, and Sørensen's (2010a) edited volume *An Anthropology of Absence: Materializations of Transcendence and Loss* to theorists from the fields of sociology (Hetherington 2004; Law 2004; Meyer 2012; Meyer and Woodthorpe 2008); history (LaCapra 2000); and philosophy (Fuery 1995).

On Absence

How can we explore something that is not there? Something that is "by its nature, unstable, unattainable, not present"? (Meyer 2012, 105). Philosopher Patrick Fuery (1995, 2–3) distinguishes between "secondary absence" (something that could potentially be present) and "primary absence" (something that exists without such a relationship). It is the potential of the item's presence that gives absence weight and meaning and makes it painful. "Phantom pains, deceased people, ancestors, destroyed buildings, ghosts, gods, silences. . . . All these absences can have effects on our lives. They matter" (Meyer 2012, 103). Although not (or no longer) physically present, something that is absent can therefore nevertheless have an impact. Writing predominantly about material culture, anthropologist Mikkel Bille and his colleagues (Bille, Hastrup, and Sørensen 2010b, 4) find that "absences are cultural, physical and social phenomena that powerfully influence people's conceptualizations of themselves and the world they engage with." Based on my case study about German Kriegsenkel, I would like to offer three theoretical observations.

Firstly, absences not only affect people's understanding of themselves and the world around them, as Bille and his colleagues note, but also vice versa. The shifting experiences of the absence of Heimat over seventy years of German postwar history and the impact of the public culture of World War II commemoration on family ties with a known Nazi war criminal will show how absences that are constructed and constantly reconstructed in a particular sociopolitical environment may change significantly over time.

Secondly, I will demonstrate what Meyer (2012, 107) notes only theoretically: that absence needs to be conceived of as "not a thing in itself but as something that exists through relations that give absence matter." All three people portrayed in this chapter wrestle intensely with what is absent in their lives as a result of World War II, and they position themselves in relationship to the gap. I will show how an absence is not a fixed entity but can be transformed, sometimes morphing from something material into something immaterial or from something immaterial to something that has "serious immediacy and presence" (Sørensen 2010, 118) that comes quite close to being material.

Thirdly, authors tend to stress the agency of absence, observing, for example, that they "have or take power" (Bille, Hastrup, and Sørensen 2010b, 4) or can "become full participants in the social characterized by their own particular politics and, at times, their own particular emotional and semiotic charge" (Fowles 2010, 27). I will highlight, on the other hand, how people also exert agency over what is missing, by conceptualizing and reconstructing it until it matches their psychological needs. To explore how this translates into practice, let me now introduce you to Charlotte and her search for a place called *Heimat*.

CHARLOTTE: "IT'S LIKE THERE IS NOTHING I CAN STAND ON"; THE LOSSES OF WAR

Charlotte was sitting two rows in front of me at the first-ever Kriegsenkel conference in Göttingen in March 2012, and when she turned around and smiled at me, I recognized her immediately. We had been talking on the phone a few weeks earlier, and her round face and warm smile matched her lively voice. Born in 1966, Charlotte was buoyant and inquisitive, and she had a zest for life that made me want to escape on a Pippi Longstocking adventure with her. She had married young, had completed her university education while also raising three children, and now worked as a research assistant and lecturer. We spent the two days and evenings together in the rainy city, attending workshops and talking about our lives, our families, Germany, and the war, and we stayed in close contact thereafter.

"People Had to Flee"

Charlotte's parents were both born in 1940, and both sides of the family lived as ethnic Germans in Eastern Europe long before Hitler's armies invaded and occupied most of the countries in the East. Her mother's family was originally from Estonia. They were a well-off family that spoke German at home, French in front of guests, and Estonian with the domestic helpers. Her grandparents were not married; Charlotte's grandfather already had another family he did not want to abandon. In 1939, during the large-scale resettlements following the Hitler-Stalin Pact, Charlotte's grandmother was told to pack her belongings; leave her house, friends, and life behind; and move west to Posen (now Poznan/Poland).[1] There she gave birth to Charlotte's mother in 1940. When the Soviet Army moved through the region in 1945, pushing Hitler's soldiers back westward, she again had to leave the home she had only just established. Again, she packed up and made the journey west, this time with her young daughter. They settled in southern Germany, and Charlotte's grandmother rebuilt her life from scratch.

On her father's side, Charlotte's ancestors originated from Böhmen (Bohemia, now Čechy in the Czech Republic). Her grandfather was the director of the local electricity company, and the family belonged to the local upper class, a privileged status that was further cemented with the German annexation of Bohemia in 1938. In 1945, Charlotte's grandfather was arrested and sent to a Russian POW camp. Her grandmother was forced to leave, making the trip west with her two young sons on foot, their belongings reduced to what fit into a small handcart. They shared the fate of millions of other ethnic Germans, who—after being privileged and often profiting heavily during the years of the Nazi occupation—were no longer welcome in the countries where many had lived for generations. There were long trails of people walking through the snow in the cold winter of 1944–45, squeezed into overcrowded trains, or attempting to cross the icy Eastern Sea by boat. In many cases Soviet troops were already in earshot when people grabbed their belongings and fled in panic, as Hitler had demanded by threat of death that they "hold the fort" until the last minute. The chaotic circumstances of the flight contributed to the trauma of losing the place that people had known as home. Between 470,000 (Radebold 2008) and 2 million (Naimark 2010) people, the majority of them women and children, never arrived in Germany. The displacement was often accompanied by traumatizing events such as air raids, combat exposure, looting, mass rapes, and other life-threatening incidents (Kuwert et al. 2009). During the journey, Charlotte's paternal grandmother fell into despair and considered suicide, but the hope of seeing her husband again kept her alive. Their reunion in 1949 was short-lived, however. The grandfather died shortly after his release from a Russian POW camp, his health eroded by the harsh living conditions and exposure to radioactive material. The family first settled in East Germany. In 1958 they packed up one more time and moved to a town in the southwest, where Charlotte's parents later met. Like millions of others, Charlotte's grandmothers both started fresh after the war. They worked hard, focused on their families and the future, and spent little time talking about the past. As mentioned in chapter 2, while growing up Charlotte picked up that "everything used to be better in the past" and that "people had to flee," but she could not put those comments into any meaningful context. As she got older, she slowly found out a bit more about her family history, yet the pictures with which to imagine the past remained few, and they were patchy and disjointed. By choosing to remain silent, Charlotte said, her grandmothers had cut her off from the multitude of stories from another life, from established traditions and customs, and from the vivid descriptions of landscapes, scents, and colors related to a place they called Heimat—homeland. Because they had no hope of ever being able to go back, the idea of Heimat had turned into a fairy tale that had lost all connection with her grandmothers' everyday lives. It had become an absence.

As Fuery (1995) notes, it is the potential of something being present that makes its absent state painful. Charlotte's grandmothers did not openly complain about their loss, but their quietly sighed references to a "past in a better place" implied that they, like many others, experienced what Bille, Hastrup, and Sørensen (2010b, 3) call "phantom pains." Although commonly used in relation to a missing limb that is still aching, in this context the term *phantom pains* is defined as "sensing the presence of people, places and things that have been obliterated, lost, missing or missed, or that have not yet materialized." Members of the grandparent generation in particular were still holding vivid memories of the places where they lived before the war and were filled with varying degrees of nostalgia and longing for what was now missing from their lives.

"People Just Passing Through"

For many Germans of the next generation, the situation was different, depending on their age. Some of my interviewees' parents were already young teenagers in 1945, and their emotional responses resembled those of the grandparents. Others were still small children at the time. They had only a few memories of the places where they were born, and the loss was less painful and tangible. As far as she could tell, Charlotte's parents did not seem to miss the home they left as five-year-olds, but she believed that the experience of forced displacement and the gap it left in their sense of belonging nevertheless played a major role in their lives.

Charlotte's parents were active in the left-wing political movement of 1968.[2] They were eager to create a new society from scratch, one that would radically break with all aspects of the past. Although both were well-educated architects, they moved to the Ruhrgebiet—a region with heavy industry—to be closer to the working class. Charlotte's childhood room overlooked a big car factory. When other people washed their cars on Saturdays, Charlotte's parents were out protesting the Vietnam War and German government policies. "My mum had better things to do than sit at home and knit," Charlotte said with tangible sadness in her voice and a sense of longing for the *Heile Welt*, the idyllic home that so many of my other interviewees hated but that she never had. Yet in spite of their different political outlook, Charlotte's parents resembled the families of my other interviewees in many ways. They too were hardworking and functioned without complaint. When Charlotte was ten, her parents got divorced. In 2012, she attributed the failure of their marriage at least partly to their war experiences. Neither of them knew how to build committed relationships and nurture a family, she believed, because they themselves did not have stabile family lives when they were little. They also did not have any physical roots to rest on in childhood, and the underlying sense of uncertainty and the anticipation of having to pack up again at any given time became part of their emotional makeup. Charlotte's mother later read Sabine Bode's (2004) book *Kriegskinder* but did not feel that the war left a lasting imprint on her biography. Her daughter disagreed. Thinking back to her childhood, Charlotte remembered more than anything an atmosphere of emotional coldness, a "certain emptiness" and lack of connection between her parents and their physical and social environment. "Even today, I would not be able to say where they belong or what place they would call home," she reflected. "Somehow, they remained strangers ['*Fremde*'], people just passing through ['*Menschen auf der Durchreise*']."

Charlotte suspected that the absence in their attachment to a Heimat had a much greater impact on her parents than they acknowledged. Yet it was not a gap they consciously perceived, either as a longing to go back to the old home (also for political reasons, as I will explain in a moment) or as a void in their lives they were actively trying to fill. The absence of Heimat had disappeared from day-to-day consciousness. One could argue that it turned from what Fuery (1995, 2–3) refers to as a "secondary absence"—something that could potentially be present—into a "primary absence" that exists without such a relationship. Or what sociologist John Law (2004, 83–85) calls "otherness"—an absence that is not manifest and that therefore is beyond a person's conscious awareness.

"Mum, Where Do We Belong, Really?": Homelessness across Generations

Growing up, Charlotte did not have any physical link with her family's Heimat. She had no firsthand experience of the regions from which her ancestors on either side of the family originated. None of the Kriegsenkel I interviewed had ever been to the places from which their grandparents were evicted in the wake of World War II. Their families were often not keen to reawaken painful memories and meet the new owners of the houses in which they once lived. While travel restrictions to communist countries in Eastern Europe eased in the 1970s, "homesick tourism"—travel driven by the longing for the homeland—only started to increase in the 1990s, after the collapse of the Soviet Union (Marschall 2015). Even then, many West German families like Charlotte's preferred to take their children to Greece or Italy for the summer holidays rather than visit countries behind the iron curtain in the East.

It went all but unnoticed that for most of Charlotte's life she not only felt disconnected from her ancestral home but also did not have any roots in the place where she herself was born—Germany. The city where she grew up felt familiar, but like her parents she too had no emotional attachment to it. She later moved around a lot, changing places and apartments with an ease that she was initially proud of. However, since reading the Kriegsenkel books, her perspective had changed, and she started to look upon her lack of attachment with sadness: "Where is my place? Where can I draw strength? Where do I belong? I really don't know." Charlotte began to perceive a sense of homelessness and lack of rootedness threaded through her own life, playing out as a constant tension running in the background, a restlessness and agitation. "It is like there is nothing that I can stand on," she told me. "My life was built on a pile of rubble, in spite of the fact that I have not experienced the war myself." Like Anja's infinite sadness and Juliane's negative attitudes toward men, Charlotte's emotions seemed misplaced to her, out of sync with her own experience of having been born and raised in Germany. She put great effort into giving her own children a nurturing and physically anchored home, and she was shocked when her adolescent daughter asked her one day, "Mum, where do we belong, I mean, really?" Once made conscious, Charlotte started to trace how the concept of home, as an absence, was transmitted between generations, from her grandmothers and parents to her and her children. It was transformed from an "otherness" (an absence that is not manifest and that therefore is beyond a person's awareness) to a "manifest absence" (something that is absent but explicit) (Law 2004, 83–85).

The Heimat Elsewhere

Another layer of this experience of absence came through more strongly in other life histories than in Charlotte's. It has to do with the affects (here emotions and atmospheres) that were passed on when families made reference to their Heimat. Growing up, the majority of my interviewees with a background of flight and expulsion had some knowledge that their family had come from somewhere else, but the fact was often not talked about in great detail at home. Marion was already in her thirties when her father, driving around town with her one day, suddenly pointed at a building and said, "Look, that is where we lived when we first arrived in Germany." Up until that moment, Marion had no clue that her father's family was originally from Russia and not from the local region as she had always assumed. She found out, quite literally, in passing. In most other cases, at least basic information about the family's origins would be known and more could be perceived and read between the lines when parents and grandparents talked about home.

In German, *home* can be expressed by two different words: *Zuhause,* meaning the place where you live, and *Heimat,* signifying the place where you are from and to which you have a profound attachment. While Zuhause, as a place of residence or house, can be flexible and temporary, Heimat has long-term, multigenerational connotations. It is a place firmly rooted in a particular region and linked to the land. The notion of Heimat developed in the nineteenth century during the time of romanticism, expressing the attachments and belongings of people to their village, landscape, and dialect (Chalmers 1985). According to German anthropologist Herman Bausinger (1980), Heimat enables people to experience feelings of security, stability, and reliability; it is a place of deep trust. It has been romanticized in popular literature (*Heimatliteratur,* Pott 1986) and movies (*Heimatfilme,* Von Moltke 2005), promoting the idea of an idyllic life close to the land, a world free from the troubles of urbanization and industrialization. Edgar Reitz (born in 1932), the director of *Heimat,* a much watched and discussed 1984 TV film that follows twentieth-century German history from the perspective of three interrelated families in a small fictional village in southern Germany, comments: "Heimat invokes in me the feeling of something lost or very far away, something one cannot easily find or find again" (Birgel and Reitz 1986, 5).

When the parents or, more frequently, the grandparents of my interviewees spoke of Heimat, they referred to a place that they had been forced to leave and that they often yearned for with palpable sadness and nostalgia. Psychoanalyst Günter Jerouschek (2004, 94) describes how he grew up in two different homes: his hometown in southern Germany and a mysterious and imaginary place that his family referred to as *dahoam* ("homeland" in the regional dialect). In her wardrobe, my own grandmother kept two shoeboxes with treasured photos of her home in Łódź (Poland), which she had managed to carry with her as part of her few belongings when she came to Germany with my father after the war. Far into my teenage years, I found myself sitting in her kitchen in the afternoons, looking at these pictures with her, one after another showing family members and friends long dead and places, houses, and landscapes she referred to as "home." It was clear from the inconsolable sadness on her face that this Heimat had ceased to exist and that there was nothing that could be done about it. For many Kriegsenkel who picked up on the strong emotions that resonated with the term in family conversations, Heimat was "somewhere else," a home of the past, not the present, desired but unattainable. Heimat for them was not the place, nor could it ever be the place, where they themselves were born. Writing about the completely different issue of waste disposal, sociologist Kevin Hetherington (2004, 160) made an observation that nevertheless also holds true for this case: "Social relations are performed not only around what is there but also sometimes around the *presence* of what is not" (emphasis in original). While Heimat as a physical experience of place was absent, the notion nevertheless had strong affects (sadness, loss, and nostalgia) attached to it. These affects transpired across generations, passed on through familial everyday interactions, rituals, and communications.

From Absence to Quasi Presence

Half (twenty-seven) of my Kriegsenkel interviewees had a background of displacement of either one or both sides of the family. Feelings of homelessness and lack of attachment are among the first three "symptoms" listed on the Kriegsenkel website as typical signifiers of this generation, always set in direct relationship with a family history of forced migration.[3] Looking back from the standpoint of 2012–13, Charlotte, and many others like her, was tracing how the loss of home, which happened two generations earlier, was still playing out in her life. In my interviews, as well as in the Kriegsenkel books, the support groups, and Facebook groups, people attributed a broad range of their current emotions, life choices, and behaviors to their families' history of losing their homes. The past was felt to play out through an underlying restlessness and hyperalertness or a sense of impending doom, a sense that "everything is suddenly going to end." Some people were reluctant to accumulate material goods, so they could pack up anytime and leave at short notice, or they compulsively hoarded supplies to feel safe. Many reported the urge to constantly move to a new house or frequently change jobs, finding it difficult to commit and settle down. First and foremost, it was experienced as a deep sense of drifting, of being lost, unattached, and unable to belong, and as feelings of loss, grief, and sadness, for which there seemed to be no rational explanation based on their own life experiences. "Almost no one can understand that I often feel so insecure . . . that the world does not stand on solid ground but could collapse any day . . . that there is no permanence, no security, no home," a woman called Anna shared in an interview published on the Forumkriegsenkel.de website.[4]

Through their explorations, either individually or by comparing their life histories with those of their peers in the activities of the Kriegsenkel support community, Charlotte and many others perceived the absence of Heimat more clearly for the first time. They started to describe the contours of the missing piece. In the process Heimat turned into what Fuery (1995, 2) calls a "quasi presence" as "bits of the missing presence are fleshed out, embellished, or signifiers are constructed to provide a presence." Fuery also highlights the close connection between absence and desire: once the absence of a person, thing, or place is made conscious, a strong yearning arises for the gap to be filled. Charlotte's grandparents had still felt this longing for home, but it was unattainable. Her parents had no sense of something missing and politically objected to connecting to the past. Now in the third generation, the desire and longing reemerged, and the search for a sense of Heimat began.

Heimat as a Dirty Word

Additional layers of complexity in the concept of Heimat also explain why its absence went largely unnoticed and only appeared late and with such emotional intensity. For many of the generation of Charlotte's parents and even more for the Kriegsenkel themselves, Heimat has long been a dirty word. It was loaded with such negative connotations that striving to fill the void or searching for the lost home was simply out of the question.

Germans have a complicated and uneasy relationship with the concept. German studies professor Hans-Georg Pott (1986, 7) calls the term "soaked in ideology, discredited and glorified" ("*ideologieträchtig, verrufen und glorifiziert*"). While there is a long tradition of positive romantic connotations, for many Germans Heimat is first and foremost an unpleasant reminder of Nazi propaganda. It was used in their blood-and-soil ideology to glorify the love for the German motherland and to justify the occupation of neighboring countries to create more space for the German *Volksgemeinschaft* (ethnic community). "The term 'Heimat' was a synonym for race (blood) and territory (soil)—a deadly combination that led to the exile or annihilation of anyone who did not 'belong'. Under the National Socialists 'Heimat' meant the murderous exclusion of anything 'un-German'" (Kaes, cited in Morley and Robins 1996, 466). This use brought the word into so much disrepute that it still evokes strong emotional reactions today.

Indulging in nostalgia for a place that was lost as a direct consequence of the war, which Germans had initiated and which had caused so much pain and suffering, was deemed entirely inappropriate. It strongly reeked of the revisionist tendencies promoted by the *Vertriebenenverbände,* the expellee interest groups, which continued their rhetoric against the postwar Eastern borders (*Oder-Neisse-Grenze*) well into the 1980s. No one I talked to admitted to sympathizing with these groups or their politics, perceived to be in the right-wing margins of the political spectrum. In her research Sabine Marschall (2015) also found that descendants of expellees mostly grew up distancing themselves from the entanglement of their family in war and expulsion. To many of this generation, it seemed only fair that Germans had to pay the price for the crimes they had committed or condoned and that the peoples they had subjugated, disowned, and killed during the war had sent them packing. The absence of Heimat, as the place where their ancestors once lived, was felt to be morally justified and imperative.

What made the situation of many Germans, not only those of the Kriegsenkel generation, even more complex was the fact that while they could not connect with a sense of Heimat from their familial past, they often also could not fill the sense of loss transmitted from their parents and grandparents with a new sense of home in the place where they themselves were born and raised. The German war crimes made it extremely difficult to establish a positive sense of belonging to the "fatherland" that was directly responsible for the Holocaust.[5] When I asked whether people were proud to be German, almost every single person shook his or her head. Daniel even had a physical reaction to the question, his body jerking involuntarily as if I had confronted him with a terrifying proposition. As outlined in chapter 1, history lessons at school and public commemorations of the Holocaust and the Nazi war crimes instilled a deep sense of shame in many Germans of the Kriegsenkel generation (in particular in West Germany). A number of them told me that when traveling overseas in their younger years, they used to pretend to be from another country, not wanting to admit that they belonged to the nation of the perpetrators of such terrible crimes.

A turning point came in 2006, when Germany hosted the FIFA World Cup. Germans cheered on their national team with unprecedented enthusiasm and lightheartedness. Visiting Berlin at the time, I was stunned by the previously unimaginable sight of German flags everywhere: on car mirrors, bicycles, balconies, and people's faces. Without exception, all of my interviewees experienced this event with a sense of liberation and relief, even though some of them were still cautiously feeling their way into this newly found national enthusiasm. Reto provided me with a beautiful image for this slow transition. When he went to the stadium to cheer on the German team, he was carrying the German flag for the first time in his life. However, he only wore it as a pair of black, red, and golden socks carefully hidden from public view by long pants. While concepts of pride and being German still do not easily go together in the same sentence, the consensus was that now, more than seventy years after the end of World War II, "it is OK to be German." With that consensus also came an opening in the relationship to the idea of home and the "permission" to start searching for a place to call Heimat.

Looking for a (Re)connection

In "Writing History, Writing Trauma," Dominick LaCapra (2000) calls for a clear delineation between the experiences of loss and lack. Once made conscious and narrativized, the absence of home the Kriegsenkel perceived needs to be viewed as a sense of lack (rather than loss), as no historical trauma or loss has occurred in this particular generation. "Lack nonetheless indicates a felt need or a deficiency; it refers to something that ought to be there but is missing" (LaCapra 2000, 53). When a sense of "something missing" is seen as the source of emotional pain, the desire is not to liberate oneself from the past but to connect to it, to find missing pieces, and to fill in the gaps in one's sense of self. One obvious way for the Kriegsenkel to reconnect with the family history and to trace the elusive "home elsewhere" was to visit the regions where their families originated. In 2012 only a few people I met had ever been to these places. Some were planning trips, either by themselves or with their families, who were now sometimes more willing to undertake this painful journey to the past. Kriegsenkel support groups were also starting to organize excursions to Eastern European areas where ethnic Germans had once lived.

In summer 2012, Charlotte herself journeyed to the Czech Republic, the homeland of her father's family, hoping that the trip would take her closer to her roots. "I am traveling to the past," she wrote on her blog, "to the Czech Republic. In my backpack I have the questions that I am taking on my journey: What does my grandparents' history have to do with me? What does my parents' history have to do with me? What does my own history have to do with me?" After arriving in her grandmother's village, Charlotte, her father, and his new family searched for a long time before they found the right house. Their map was a faded black-and-white photograph, which they showed to the locals, gesturing and asking for directions. Finally, an old woman nodded her head. "Of course," she said in flawless German, "the *P——Haus*! Turn right just before you get to the station and then it is straight ahead of you." Too excited to continue the conversation, they jumped back into the car and followed her directions. They indeed found the beautiful old villa, run down and with the paint peeling off. Charlotte immediately felt a connection with it. Her family did not own the house anymore; other people had lived there for the past seven decades. Somehow it "belonged" to her nevertheless. It was the place where her father was born and of which she had photos with her grandparents standing in front. The current owners spoke a bit of English and invited the small group to come inside. Looking around the old rooms, Charlotte felt torn between the past and the present. "The physical house was still there—our geographical roots—but its history and trajectory have become something else. How many lives may have since passed through here?" she reflected later. They found other traces of the past, an old brewery her family once owned and the cemetery with a few overgrown graves still carrying their name. All relics from a time long gone, yet on some level they were connected to Charlotte's present life. When I asked her later what this journey meant to her, she said: "It is good to know where you are from, but there is also a silver layer of tears on my soul, because the pain of the past has not yet been transformed. But I now feel a sense of calm. It gave me certainty that, yes, there was a past, but that this past does not exist anymore."

For Charlotte, the previously absent home, a place without her own images, memories, and physical experiences, was transformed into a presence she could feel and connect with. Yet paradoxically, when she made the journey to the place that was referred to as Heimat, it also ceased to exist. The Czech Republic was her grandmother's home, and while Charlotte felt a strong emotional relationship to it, it was not hers. For Charlotte, Heimat as a material place became an absence again. Realizing the finality of the loss and once and for all burying her expectation to find a Heimat for herself in the Czech Republic made Charlotte sad, but it also gave her a sense of closure.

Other Kriegsenkel reported similar responses as they visited the places where their families had once lived. Merle Hilbk (2013) described how during her first trip to Kazakhstan, "something in the atmosphere of decay and pride, melancholy and sudden outbursts of energy felt strangely familiar, touching something inside." Another person shared on the Forumkriegsenkel.de website, "I immediately fell in love with the landscape. . . . People come and go, but the land remains. . . . For years now I have had a bowl in my apartment, filled with the soil from the meadows where once the cows of my ancestors were grazing."[6] Marschall (2015, 879) notes that these kinds of "roots-trips" can be intense, immersive, and multisensory experiences as people trace the signs of their forebears in the landscape.[7] Gaining a firsthand experience of the land referred to as "home" can relay a sense of identity and connectedness. She found that the journey to the ancestors' homeland often had a life-changing meaning for descendants of German expellees, resulting in return travel, the establishment of professional and personal relationships, and other ways of maintaining an ongoing connection (Marschall 2015). Unlike in Charlotte's case, here the notion of Heimat was transformed into a present sense of belonging and connection. Ana Dragojlovic (2014) traces a similar phenomenon in her research among descendants of Indonesian Dutch families in the Netherlands, some of whom experienced a powerful sense of reconnection as they traveled to the country their ancestors had once been forced to leave. Applying Marianne Hirsch's (2008) concept of postmemory, Dragojlovic (2014, 12) believes that embodied postmemory of geographies can be awakened, experienced, and integrated, providing a sense of belonging and helping to "forge one's own pathway to an inheritance of loss."

My own "roots trip" was somewhat different and in its final result a bit closer to Charlotte's way of coming to terms. After long discussions, in November 2012 my father finally agreed to take my mother and me to Łódź for the first time, the place that my grandmother had spoken about with so much sadness and nostalgia. I had expected a similarly deep sense of familiarity and connection and was surprised when I felt nothing much at all. Not in the church where my grandparents had married in 1928, or in the house where they lived during the war, or in the attic in which they were cramped after 1945. Not even my great-grandparents' grave, which we miraculously managed to find in the Lutheran cemetery. The only sense of something relatable came as I watched my father chat with taxi drivers, waiters, and hotel staff in still fluent Polish and I found some of his familiar facial expressions and lively gestures mirrored by his counterparts. The trip was an intense and satisfying experience of exploring the city where my family was from. Yet as for Charlotte, it also made me realize that for me Łódź as a Heimat did not exist. Morley and Robins (1996, 459, citing Berman) frame this beautifully: "Heimat is a mythical bond rooted in a lost past, a past that has already disintegrated: 'we yearn to grasp it, but it is baseless and elusive; we look back for something solid to lean on, only to find ourselves embracing ghosts.'"

While the final outcomes vary, the examples above suggest that Germans of the Kriegsenkel generation actively transformed the transmitted absence of home into something present that met their psychological needs. For Charlotte, that entailed realizing what had been absent in her life, mapping and fleshing out the missing connection to a physical Heimat, longing and searching for it, and then ultimately putting it to rest. She realized that the absence she had felt was related to her grandmother's loss of home and not her own, and that it was an absence that could not revert to its original state of presence. Acknowledging the permanency of the absence of Heimat as a physical place permitted her to come to terms with it and opened the possibility for something new to emerge.

Finding the Home Within

I was looking forward to meeting Charlotte again in summer 2013, keen to know how she was traveling on her Kriegsenkel journey. She was relaxed and upbeat as we sat in two old lounge chairs in a park in East Berlin, sipping coffee. The topic had lost a bit of its urgency over the year. Sorting through the past and perceiving the threads of homelessness running through her family, from her grandparents and parents to herself and even her children, put her biography into a new perspective. "My life now has meaning and coherence that stretches back over a number of generations. The idea that the war and the history of my parents and my ancestors live on inside me is also some sort of treasure. I can feel that too." After realizing that there was no physical place that she could call Heimat, she said she now found herself resting on something new: an immaterial home inside herself, a sense of continuity and belonging to a family lineage. Stories of people related to her and images of places where her ancestors once lived had become part of the fabric she was able to stitch together, bit by bit, until it became dense enough to hold her. Her life no longer felt as if it were built on a disjointed pile of rubble. The foundation had become more solid. There now was a piece where she fit into all of this. "If I had to sum it all up," she said, "I would say, I do belong after all. I have my place in this history." Charlotte transformed a material absence of Heimat into a sense of immaterial presence, a space within herself that she called home. At the end it was revealed that what she was really looking for was a sense of rootedness and belonging, of feeling at home, rather than an attachment to the land. This confirms Paul Basu's (2005) observation that roots pilgrimages are ultimately not about the ancestors or the places but about the self. Yet Charlotte's experience contained many of the features that Bausinger (1980) associated with the notion of Heimat: feelings of security, stability, and reliability, a place of deep trust.

Charlotte's story is an example of how absences are constructed and reconstructed in a particular sociopolitical context and how individuals are able to build a relationship with and ultimately exert agency over that which is not present in their lives. I will continue with these observations about the role of absences in my next two very different examples: the stories of Paula and Rainer and their intense psychological wrestling with their Nazi grandfathers.

RAINER AND PAULA: "WHAT OF HIM IS ALSO IN ME?"; THE SHAME OF WAR

Up to this point in the book, I have focused largely on the traumatic World War II experiences of the German majority population, such as the bombardment of cities, forced displacement and sexual violence, and the impact of these across generations, as either an emotional burden or a painful feeling of lack and absence. This was a deliberate choice because the recent public explorations offered a new perspective to explain and address the psychological problems of the Kriegsenkel generation. The (often sudden) realization of the lasting impact that wartime suffering had on Germans born long after the original events lies at the heart of the Kriegsenkel identity construction. These experiences therefore took center stage in my analysis. However, any attempt to provide a rounded picture of the transgenerational transmission of war experiences also needs to include reflections on the long-term impact of Nazi perpetratorship.

There were more than eighteen million German soldiers in the Wehrmacht (Radebold 2008, 46). Particularly on the eastern front, an unknown number of them participated not only in active combat but also in the shooting of women and children and the mass executions of Jews and suspected partisans. They looted and burned down villages, displaced local populations, and coerced them into forced labor (Hamburger Institut für Sozialforschung 2002). An estimated five hundred thousand German men and women were involved in the expulsion and the systematic murder of European Jews, yet less than one thousand were put on trial and convicted for their crimes (Winkler 2014). Most of my interviewees had at least one grandfather and often other men in the extended family who had been soldiers in Hitler's armies. A few were in the SS or the notorious *Sonderkommandos* (special tasks units) in the occupied eastern territories. This means that in most German families there is a history not only of loss and wartime suffering but also of perpetratorship.

Unlike the recent focus on war trauma and its transmission, issues around the transgenerational impact of National Socialist ideology and perpetratorship have been explored in some depth since the 1980s, often describing responses of guilt and shame or denial and avoidance in the younger generation (some of the better known works include Bar-On 1989; Bergmann and Jucovy 1982; Müller-Hohagen 2005; Rosenthal 1998; Roberts 1998; Sichrovsky 1987; Welzer, Moller, and Tschuggnall 2002; and Westernhagen 1987). Continuing with the analytic lens of absence from the first part of this chapter, I will take a different approach. I will venture into an exploration of gaps and absences in family relationships and transgenerational transmission that result from a family history of perpetratorship and Nazi war crimes. I will tell the stories of Rainer and Paula, both grandchildren of high-ranking Nazi officials. They stand out because of the scale of their grandfathers' crimes and because their family's involvement is well documented. However, their responses also lend themselves to connections to members of their generation more broadly.

Much more than is the case with World War II trauma, Nazi perpetratorship is still an extremely sensitive topic in German society. Paula's and Rainer's exploration of their grandfathers' roles in the Third Reich was inextricably entangled with the larger framework of the public culture of commemoration and its contradictory norms. These demand on the one hand a clear distancing from the perpetrator generation while prescribing that the descendants assume a moral responsibility for their forebears' crimes on the other. There is probably no other life history that could exemplify the anguish, emotional burden, and moral binds of transgenerationally transmitted perpetratorship better than that of Rainer Höß, whose name and genes link him directly to the man he mostly refers to as "Rudolf": Rudolf Höß, the *Kommandant* of Auschwitz from 1940–44 and his grandfather.

Rainer: "Ein Höß weint nicht" (A Höß does not cry)

I had a few restless nights before dialing Rainer's number for the arranged interview, tossing and turning as I was trying to imagine what it must be like to have a convicted mass murderer as a grandfather, a man directly linked to a place like Auschwitz, which like no other stands for the evil human beings are capable of. When he picked up the phone, Rainer's voice was warm and friendly, with a strong southern accent and a certain vulnerability that caught me by surprise. He did a lot of the talking in our two-hour conversation. I listened, often holding my breath, but in the end I was still able to ask the questions I was most curious about. Reflecting on his story now brings back the spaces of darkness, heaviness, and incomprehensibly cold cruelty of the Holocaust that I and many other Germans of my generation have been carrying for much of our lives, casting a shadow of guilt and shame over our otherwise relatively carefree existence.

Rainer Höß, former cook and pastry chef, is a well-known public figure. He has devoted his life to researching his grandfather's crimes and to educating the German public about the Holocaust. In 2011, he participated in the Israeli-German documentary *Hitler's Children* (Zeevi 2011), featuring five descendants of high-ranking Nazis and their different responses to growing up in perpetrator families. Höß appeared in a Swedish TV spot for the 2014 elections to the EU parliament, campaigning for a "Nazi-free-Europe" and reminding people to "never forget to vote."[8] He continues to give talks in schools, he accompanies schoolchildren on visits to Auschwitz, and in 2013 he published a book about his struggles as the grandson of Rudolf Höß (Höß 2013). Rainer is using his family name as a powerful tool in his activities and public performances, and he explicitly declined my standard offer to disguise his identity. His purpose in life and sense of identity are inextricably linked to his grandfather as the commander of Auschwitz. Without the name, his activism would lose much of its punch.

Including Rainer's case study in the book was not an easy decision. While all my fifty-three other interviewees are "ordinary citizens," his story stands out and is somewhat sensationalist. I never met him in person, and my analysis relies on a phone conversation and other material that is publicly available (including his autobiography). Rainer is also not without controversy, and his motives and integrity have been questioned. He has been accused, for example, of trying to sell his grandfather's belongings to the Yad Vashem Holocaust Memorial in Jerusalem, a claim that he denies (Beck 2011). On the other hand, he was able to establish close relationships with a number of Holocaust survivors who believed in the sincerity of his efforts. In my view, his account has an important role to play in the general narrative of the book. It offers a different perspective on the Kriegsenkel topic—the transgenerational impact of Nazi perpetratorship. While Höß's case study is indeed unique, it is also an (albeit extreme) example of the ways in which many Germans of this generation are still haunted by their families' involvement with the Nazi regime and the guilt, shame, and responsibility that come with that.

Rainer never met his infamous grandfather. Rudolf Höß, in charge of the systematic murder of at least 1.5 million Jews and other victims of the Nazis, was tracked down after the war by a special unit of the British military (see Harding 2014). He was sentenced to death and hanged outside the crematorium in Auschwitz in April 1947, calm and unapologetic to his last breath. He was forty-six when he was executed, the same age as Rainer when I talked to him in 2012. His mother only found out three years after her wedding who her father-in-law was—through a newspaper article. Rainer's family did not volunteer any information about his grandfather's identity. When asked, they would tell him that his grandfather had died as a "hero for the fatherland." They never revoked their commitment to the National Socialist ideology. There are family photos of Rainer's father, Hans-Jürgen, as a little boy, posing with his brother in the garden of the Höß villa in Auschwitz, propped up in the midst of blossoming flowers. A perfectly idyllic scene if it weren't for the crematorium's chimney clearly visible in the right back corner of the picture. Others show Hans-Jürgen sitting in a toy plane that concentration camp inmates made for the Höß children (Höß 2013). "We had a good life in Auschwitz," Rainer's grandmother continued to say until her death, and she called the concentration camp "just a prison." The fact that she had also reprimanded her children to wash the strawberries they had picked from the garden "because of the ash" exposed her pretended ignorance as a convenient lie. "This is the family I was born into," Rainer wrote in his autobiography. "Sometimes I just want to scream" (Höß 2013, 82). To this day most of his family denies that the Holocaust ever happened, in spite of the historical evidence and the fact that they lived directly on-site. The outrage in Rainer's voice on the phone revealed how their rejection of any responsibility was still cutting him up inside, even though he had severed all contact with his father and the extended family more than twenty years earlier.

As an adult, Rainer started to obsessively research the Holocaust, collecting as much information as possible to disprove his family's claims and trying to comprehend and to distance himself from his grandfather's motives. He said: "I never got closer to my grandfather than his uniform on the tailor's dummy. I only know his face from photos, his character through his deeds and his clumsy autobiography. I can despise him mercilessly without it hurting much. Yet since I have become an adult, I have been trying to understand his life. What drove him to kill millions of people? We, his children and grandchildren, have always lived with this dead man. Absent, he was always standing there, right next to us" (Höß 2013, 78).

Here, the experience of absence in relationship to World War II and the transmission of experiences in the family is quite different from Charlotte's. For her the absence of Heimat went unnoticed in her everyday life because of her family's silences. In Rainer's case, it was clear early on that his grandfather had died after the war. However, it was the framing of his absence that created discord, because the family distorted the historical role his grandfather had played. Yet similarly to Charlotte's elaborations, which sharpened the contours of the missing home, Rainer's investigation turned Rudolf into a "quasi presence" (Fuery 1995, 2) that he related to almost as if the man were still alive. His grandfather was an integral feature of every aspect of Rainer's everyday experience, fleshed out by historical documents, photos, and survivors' stories and woven together in his imagination. The more Rainer brought his grandfather back to life, the more Rudolf became a specter that haunted him. Rainer constantly put himself in relationship to his absent grandfather, comparing character traits and habits. Did he get his meticulousness and compulsive orderliness from Rudolf? His strict sense of duty? The way he folded up his clothes before going to bed? His need to keep his hair cut short and neat? He even considered Rudolf when tying his shoelaces. "I am spending my life searching for resemblances with my grandfather," he said to me. His main worry was that he might have inherited the Auschwitz commander's "evil genes." Other descendants of high-ranking Nazi war criminals share this fear that a disposition to commit heinous crimes is transmitted through the DNA. Bettina Göring, great-niece of Hermann Göring, Hitler's notorious Reich Marshal, famously opted for sterilization in order to prevent the "Göring genes" from getting passed on to yet another generation (Lebovic 2012). Monika Hertwig, the daughter of Amon Göth, the sadistic commander of the Plaszów concentration camp depicted in the movie *Schindler's List,* was worried that she may be a "bad seed" like her father (Livingston 2010, 212). Here, concepts of transgenerational transmission of trauma and of perpetratorship intersect with the assumed determinism of a genetic inheritance, where character traits are seen as being handed down through the DNA. "There is one question that haunts me to this day: What of him is also in me? Is there a resemblance, an alikeness, a genetic inheritance?" Rainer wrote in this book (Höß 2013, 31) A vignette he shared with me shows how great his fear of this biological legacy was. Visiting Auschwitz for the first time in 2010, he met his grandfather's former barber. The old man asked Rainer to walk up and down in front of him and then concluded, "You walk like your grandfather, and you look like your grandfather; you are just a bit taller." After coming home, Rainer locked himself up in a room for two weeks, too distraught to talk to his family. While on the one hand Rainer was haunted by his grandfather's presence and the threat of their genetic similarity, "fleshing out the ghost" (Cho 2008) of the *Kommandant* served an important purpose: it enabled Rainer to distance himself. Step by step, he cut all ties with his father's family. He publicly denounced his grandfather's crimes, and he told his four children that he would rather sacrifice them and die himself than subscribe to the National Socialist ideology should he ever be forced to choose. However, the key moment for him in this respect happened, of all places, in Auschwitz. When Rainer was interviewed for *Hitler's Children,* he found himself surrounded by a group of Israeli teenagers who stared at him in shock when they heard that he was a direct descendant of the *Kommandant.* Suddenly, a Holocaust survivor appeared from among the group. He walked up to Rainer, put his arms around him, and said, "It is not your fault." Both men cried. "At that very moment," Rainer said to me, "I stepped out of the family line." When he was little, his father used to beat him and his siblings mercilessly when he found them "whining about something" as he came home. *"Ein Höß weint nicht"* (A Höß does not cry) was the abiding rule. It was also a motto with which his grandfather had raised his children. Showing emotions went against the National Socialist ideology of hardness, strength, and tenacity. Even at the gallows Rudolf did not divert from this path. In that moment in Auschwitz, Rainer realized, tears rolling down his face, that he was "not an animal" like his grandfather. He was able to show emotions, even with everyone, including TV cameras, watching. Rainer stressed how liberating that moment was for him, to break with his family tradition and prove to himself that he was not a victim of his grandfather's "evil genes." *"Ich bin nicht Rudolf"* (I am not Rudolf), he repeated emphatically a few times.

After wrestling with the absent presence of his grandfather, Rainer felt able to break the line of transgenerational transmission of perpetratorship. However, while the gap that he managed to carve out between himself and Rudolf seemed liberating, he remained tightly bound to his grandfather in other ways. As someone of his generation, who had internalized and accepted the German culture of commemoration, he was committed to remembering the past and to making sure that crimes like the Holocaust would never be repeated. It is a mission that is particularly binding for him as a direct descendant of one of the worst perpetrators of the Third Reich. Unlike Charlotte, Rainer could not put the past to rest, and unlike Anja and Juliane, his liberation from the past could only go a certain distance. He accepted this willingly, devoting himself to raising public awareness about the Nazi crimes. "At least in this way, the Höß family and I will leave something positive behind. I can live better with that," he said, summing up his own way of coming to terms with his family history. He acknowledged that the specter of Rudolf would haunt him for the rest of his life. "I wake up every morning with the Holocaust and I go to bed every night with the Holocaust," he responded when I asked him that question. After I hung up the phone, his last sentence kept echoing in my head: "In spite of everything, I am actually quite a cheerful person."

Paula, whose story I turn to now, agreed with this approach for most of her life, firmly rejecting the Nazi side of her family. In 2012, however, she was starting to question whether this attitude did not come at a price, leaving a gap in the relationship and in the transmission between the generations that ultimately negatively affected her sense of self and identity.

Paula: "Den Ball flach halten" (Keep your head down)

Like Rainer, Paula used to resolutely distance herself from her father's family and in particular from her grandfather, a high-ranking member of the SS and official of the Nazi regime. He had known Hitler personally, a fact that half of the family still talked about with a sense of pride, while the other half despised him as an "opportunistic, drunken Nazi thug." According to Paula, a German court convicted her grandfather in 1947 for his involvement with the Third Reich and forever banned him from practicing any kind of profession that would allow him to continue spreading the Nazi ideology among the German population (i.e., lawyer, teacher, pastor, journalist). Learning about the horrors of the Holocaust at school, Paula was ashamed of the man, whom she referred to as "*der böse Opa*" (the bad grandpa) or "*mein SS Opa*" (my SS grandpa). Among the five siblings, Paula was the one most interested in the family history, and her mother often said that she had "started asking questions before she could talk." Paula admitted that, particularly when she was a teenager, her enquiries about the family's National Socialist past were often aggressive and judgmental, and her interrogations were met with equally fierce rebuttals and denials. She held unpleasant memories of her grandparents scaring her with their strictness and verbal reprimands, such as "girls like you belong in a concentration camp," and of her grandmother fiercely brushing her unruly curly hair to a point where she feared her scalp would come off. She said the Nazi spirit was also still tangible in her own family home. The children were not allowed to talk during meals, and chewing gum was forbidden as something American. In their own accounts, her family had been treated badly after the war. Her father and his siblings were bullied at school as "Nazi children." The lesson that they, in Paula's view, took away from this was that "it is better to keep your head down" ("*den Ball flach halten*"). The same message was also passed on to her. She had internalized and never really challenged it.

After reading the Kriegsenkel books, however, Paula started to explore how much her upbringing had prevented her from "stepping into her own strength and power." She attributed her lack of self-confidence to a number of different factors: the gaps and denials around Nazi perpetratorship, the life lessons ("keep your head down") transmitted by her family, and the history lessons at school that compounded her sense of shame for coming from a perpetrator family. This deeply embedded sense of guilt, shame, and insecurity is a common feature among members of this generation, often stemming from a similar mix of denial of responsibility for or knowledge of Nazi crimes and reinforced by public narratives, TV documentaries, and history lessons at school (see chap. 2). Paula used words like *wackelig* (shaky), *unsicher* (uncertain or insecure) to describe her sense of self. She always added that that was not the "real her," that somewhere underneath she was a strong person. She could not accept or express her strength because "everything had to be kept under wraps." To me, her stifled life force was very palpable. Conversations with her were never less than three hours long, and they were extremely intense. She had a sharp, analytical mind and demanded full concentration and attention, holding me captured with her gaze, probing into every word, always a bit on edge.

Early in our discussions a new question opened up. Was it possible that her feeling of shakiness was further compounded by the fact that she had deliberately cut herself off from her family, and in particular from her grandfather, because of his involvement with the National Socialist regime? Had this left a gap in her sense of self and confidence? Paula was a regular participant in shamanistic family constellations workshops, in which, as she explained, the ancestors are viewed as a source of strength, transmitting their support and encouragement to their descendants. She had always felt a particularly close connection to this grandfather. Her family often commented on how much she resembled him: her height and straight posture, her stubbornness, the way she sat and walked. Like Rainer, she had always found these similarities troubling, pushing them as far away from herself as possible. Yet somehow her grandfather's absent presence was always close by, a frequent appearance in her vivid dreams and daytime visions.

Over the course of 2012, Paula devoted herself to researching her grandfather's history. She was studying the historical documents about his trial and was reading books about the SS. For the first time, she was trying to look at his involvement through a more open lens, exploring and enquiring rather than condemning him outright. Paula was hoping to create a context for the few stories and bits of fragmented information she had and to fill in the gaps, including in relation to the crimes her grandfather may have committed. As she was methodically sorting through the past, Paula's absent grandfather was more and more brought back to life with every bit of information she found (although unlike Rainer she had childhood memories of him). He became an "entity-like presence" (Fowles 2010, 25) that she, like Rainer, fleshed out and interacted with. Paula had an extremely rich inner life of vivid, fluid spaces, where past and present often merged into one. The war and her "SS grandpa" were constant features in her visions during this period. She often felt him standing close behind her, his hands on her shoulder, always still wearing his SS uniform. While for Rainer, his intense relationship with his absent grandfather was aimed at creating the greatest possible distance between them, Paula was cautiously looking for a way to generate a sense of continuity between the generations, in spite of her grandfather's perpetratorship. She had started to feel the absence of this connection as undermining her sense of self. Her previous rejection of her grandfather in her view had not allowed her to accept some of the character traits that she had inherited from him—determination, strength, tenacity, willpower, and idealism—because he had put them in the service of the Hitler regime.

Over the space of the year, things were starting to change for her. She said that she was beginning to come to terms with her grandfather's presence and the active relationship between them. "After I talked to you, I suddenly had this image of a bathtub. Someone pulled the plug, things started flowing again, and all the stagnant water was flushed out," she said to me. Rather than a haunting ghost, as was the case for Rainer, he turned into a source of strength in her everyday life, often appearing and backing her up in difficult situations. When I saw Paula again in 2013, her mind was elsewhere, caught up in an unhappy love affair that she talked about with familiar intensity and passion. Asked how she felt more generally, she said that all in all she was more stable, with "more trust in life." She said that this was the first time that she had ever explored her family history in such a way, something she could not have done with a "real German." She was pointing to the fact that while I am of the same age and of a similar upbringing, I had been away from Germany for twenty years and was now doing my PhD in Australia. In her eyes this made me less bound by the tight norms of the German culture of commemoration. I did indeed follow Paula's exploration with as much openness as possible, often admiring her bravery. However, when she said things like "some people really were just nominally kept on the SS membership list without really being active," or told me that she could not find any evidence that he had committed any major crimes, I could not help thinking that the grandfather she had brought back to life had moved away from the historical figure. Was she starting to make excuses for him to help her maintain their newly found bond?[9] Yet, it was clear how liberating this process was for her, even though it was an extremely delicate undertaking, one that she still felt to be very much taboo. One time, when I turned off the voice recorder after a particularly intense conversation, she glanced at it and said, "Make sure you don't lose that, or we will both get arrested." She was half joking, but her comment showed that even if German society is now more open to reassessing the past and World War II, a desire to reconnect with a grandfather who is a known Nazi perpetrator is still perceived to be a long way outside the limits of accepted norms and attitudes. Along similar lines, Kathy Livingston (2010) showed in her case study that sons and daughters of high-ranking Nazis lacked permission, social acknowledgment, sympathy, and support to grieve for their deceased parents because of the stigma surrounding their fathers' crimes. This "disenfranchisement of grief" (Livingston 2010, 209) forced them to carry the burden of their loss alone and in silence and diminished their opportunities to mourn and come to terms with their loss.

Rainer's and Paula's stories were exceptions, and they overshadowed those of all my other interviewees when it came to Nazi perpetratorship. Yet quite a number of other Kriegsenkel were also haunted by the (suspected) crimes of their grandparents. All of them took Rainer's approach, trying to distance themselves from their families (to varying degrees). As explored in chapter 2, knowledge about the grandparents' involvement in the Hitler regime was never passed on voluntarily. In an atmosphere of taboos and secrets at home, inklings of perpetratorship were perceived only through the cracks of interrupted conversations, blocked off questions, and family members present on photos but never openly talked about. To the grandchildren generation, who grew up with a strong awareness of the Holocaust and the Nazi crimes, the unresolved mysteries around a direct involvement of their families had often troubled their imaginations since teenage years. Many Kriegsenkel, like Rainer and Paula, were trying to fill in the gaps in their family histories by tapping into historical archives or by interviewing their extended families, yet that rarely yielded satisfactory results. The grandfathers lived on in Kriegsenkel lives as absent presences, embellished by fantasies and unanswered questions about their possible crimes, not clearly outlined enough to allow for a positioning of oneself in the relationship. For Rainer there was sufficient historical information to bring the absent grandfather back to life, allowing him to distance himself and gain a sense of agency. In many other cases the unformed and haunting absences took power away and left the descendant stuck, fearful, and uncertain.

In her grandfather's Wehrmacht book, Isabelle found an entry explaining that for a short time he had been part of the *Sonderkommando 19* somewhere in Eastern Europe. As a historian she was well aware that the term meant *special duties*, more often than not participation in the execution of Jews or partisans. Yet she could not find any further information about this particular unit, and the uncertainty about what her grandfather had done during those unaccounted weeks would not let her rest. "I want to know what kind of a family I am from," she said to me, a sentence I heard a few times. It implies that one would feel the need to take a moral stance and distance oneself from a family of known perpetrators or supporters of the Nazi regime. For the group of people of this generation who, like Rainer and Paula, had internalized and shared the values of the public culture of commemoration, known or assumed Nazi perpetratorship directly affected their relationships with their families. This led to varying degrees of separation, sometimes to the extent that ties were severed. Taking a moral stance meant cutting oneself off from a potential transmission of Nazi perpetratorship. It was a conscious choice, often felt as a step toward individuation and separation, as was the case for Rainer.

Absence Revisited

Charlotte's, Rainer's, and Paula's stories illuminate in quite different ways the dynamic role that absences play in Kriegsenkel experiences. Each of the three protagonists was wrestling with something that was not there yet was still perceived to have a direct impact on everyday life—a place in Charlotte's case, a family member in Paula's and Rainer's. My research supports Bille, Hastrup, and Sørensen's (2010b, 4) observation that "absences are cultural, physical and social phenomena that powerfully influence people's conceptualizations of themselves and the world they engage with." Charlotte felt that her lack of attachment to a place called home and the gap she initially detected in her sense of belonging directly affected her sense of identity and emotional stability. Paula's and Rainer's understanding of themselves and the way they acted in their lives was closely linked to their absent grandfathers and a feared inheritance of perpetrator genes.

Their trajectories furthermore illustrate Meyer's theoretical claim that absences are not things in themselves but things that come to matter through relationships. "Absence, in this view, is something performed, textured and materialized through relations and processes, and via objects" (Meyer 2012, 103). In all three examples the person entered into an intense engagement with what was felt to be absent. For most of Charlotte's life, she did not have any conscious awareness of her lack of attachment to a Heimat. The absence of home "did not matter" until she became aware and started building a relationship with it. All three were actively tracing, framing, and fleshing out what was missing until firm contours emerged that allowed them to perceive the absent bit as a "quasi presence" (Fuery 1995, 2). Charlotte's path was through the framework of the Kriegsenkel movement, which enabled her to source and clearly define the gaps in her sense of self and to start searching for a Heimat. Rainer and Paula predominantly looked to historical sources to provide the material that allowed them to "flesh out the ghost" (Cho 2008) of their grandfathers, a process they both undertook to a great level of depth and detail. The creation of "quasi presences" (Fuery 1995, 2) that act as stand-ins for the absent place or person permitted Charlotte, Rainer, and Paula to position themselves in relationship to what was absent in a way that met their psychological needs and desires. For Charlotte and Paula that meant relating more closely to what was missing in their lives, in order to bridge the gap and allow for a sense of continuity and transmission between the generations, an act that they understood as strengthening their sense of self. For Rainer, on the other hand, engaging with Rudolf meant moving further and further away from him, to break the family ties and interrupt a possible transmission of perpetratorship. In spite of their different directions, by going through this process, all three ultimately found a meaning for what was absent that suited their psychological wants.

Interestingly, it became clear that in this process of transformation, these psychological needs were far more important than the physical absence or presence of the place or person itself, which could easily morph from one state to another. Charlotte was initially looking for a sense of home and attachment to a material place. Yet what she later found and defined as *Heimat* was an immaterial sense of belonging inside herself and as part of her family history, which provided her with much of what she had been looking for. For Paula and Rainer, on the other hand, both grandfathers were fleshed out in their imagination to an extent that the men were transformed from something immaterial to something that had "serious immediacy and presence" (Sørensen 2010, 118), that came quite close to being material, and that they engaged with almost as if the "SS Grandpa" and the *Kommandant* were alive.

Authors have also highlighted the agency that absences possess (Bille, Hastrup, and Sørensen 2010b; Fowles 2010; Meyer 2012; Meyer and Woodthorpe 2008). Meyer (2012, 104), for example, comments that "via various kinds of places, objects and practices the absent can have an important effect on the social world—in other words, that absence has agency." Absences were observed to "have or take power" (Bille, Hastrup, and Sørensen 2010b, 4) or to be "full participants in the social characterized by their own particular politics" (Fowles 2010, 27). While the observation that absences can have or take power holds true also for the German Kriegsenkel, my case study showed how people exert agency over what is absent in a way that strengthens their subjectivity.

The last point I would like to make is that absences not only influence people's conceptualizations of themselves and the world they engage with, as

Bille, Hastrup, and Sørensen note, but also vice versa. My German case studies highlight the crucial impact of the social and political environment on the construction of and relationship to what is absent as well as on the potentiality of it becoming present. Charlotte's grandmothers experienced the loss of their homeland firsthand, and the political situation of postwar Germany left no hope for a return. This turned Heimat into an absence surrounded by nostalgia, sadness, and longing. For Charlotte's radically left-wing parents, Heimat became a dirty word, as their aim was to cut all physical and ideological ties to a prewar society. For most of Charlotte's life, the absent home also did not have the potential to be returned into a presence, for political as much as for psychological reasons. However, the recent opening in the political situation and the emergence of more positive attitudes toward German national identity allowed her to search for a reconnection with the "lost home." Yet, while she (and other people who undertook "roots trips") was able to transform the sense of lack into some form of presence, the construction of that presence was still limited by historical realities and moral imperatives. Revisionist demands for a return of the territories in the East were out of the question. The "new" owners will continue to live in the house, which Charlotte knew as her family's home. Finding a "home within" is her way of coming to terms with this reality. Other Kriegsenkel, as described above, chose other ways to reframe the absence of Heimat for themselves. Yet they all found a solution that respected the European post-1945 borders. Paula and Rainer were also affected by Germany's political environment, and more specifically by the public culture of commemoration of World War II. They clearly defined the boundaries for the transformation of their relationship to their grandfathers. Rainer, and many others who suspected their grandparents' support for the Hitler regime, strictly stayed within the limits set by this moral framework while coming to terms with his absent grandfather and his legacy. Paula, as the only exception, cautiously tried to move beyond them, highly aware of the taboos she was breaking and conducting her exploration largely in secret.

By enabling us to show in detail how each individual or each generation constructs and addresses war-related transmitted legacies differently in a historical context where loss is directly linked to a history of aggressive invasion and war crimes, the conceptual lens of absence contributes to our understanding of the interface among individual, familial, and national contexts in the construction of emotional suffering. It becomes clear that it is not only what passes within the bounds of the family unit that determines whether and how individuals perceive and evaluate processes of transgenerational transmission. The sociopolitical environment also crucially influences individual experiences of suffering and the perception of what is missing, and it moderates the desire to alleviate emotional distress.

ON HEALING THE PAST

When it comes to the long-term psychological impact of war and violence, the most common approach is to conceptualize and address it as a transgenerationally transmitted emotional burden. The underlying objective of therapeutic treatment is to create an awareness of such influences and to relieve the individual from the burden of forebears' traumatic pasts. Kriegsenkel like Kerstin, Anja, and Juliane perceived the familial past predominantly in line with these narratives. The chosen therapeutic interventions were aimed at working through the familial legacy to break the chain of transmission and to build happier, more independent, and healthier futures. Rainer also fit into this approach to some extent, although his "liberation" was restricted by the moral responsibility to carry the burden of his grandfather's crimes. As described in chapter 4, the tools selected for working through these issues usually ranged from traditional psychotherapy and psychoanalysis to self-help groups, specialized seminars, and workshops, and to more alternative approaches, such as family constellations, dance, spiritual healings, homeopathy, and bodywork.

For Charlotte and Paula, it was the gaps in the family history and in the transmission between the generations that caused them pain and a gap in their sense of self. They aimed to fill the void, reconnect with the past, and feel their lives embedded in a family line that stretched back over multiple generations. Many of my other interviewees shared this desire (more in line with Charlotte's story rather than Paula's, as I explained). Here the chosen interventions were slightly different. Rather than (or often in addition to) making an appointment with a healer or a therapist, Kriegsenkel were consulting historical archives, interviewing relatives, or traveling to the Heimat of their ancestors to create a sense of continuity, identity, and belonging.

While still moving within the broader framework of Western therapeutic culture and its goals, this endeavor links the Kriegsenkel to another Western middle-class pursuit: the tracing and collecting of genealogical information. Genealogy, or family history research, is one of the most popular hobbies in many Western countries, including mainland Europe, Canada, and Australia (Cannell 2011), and is allegedly the second most common use of the internet—after pornography (Basu 2007). Individual hobby genealogists have different reasons for their interests, yet a common driving force is a yearning for a sense of belonging to a particular place, culture, and family (for example, see Basu 2007; Dragojlovic 2014; Marschall 2015). Fenella Cannell (2011, 462) argues that one of the central aspects of the appeal of family history research is that it gives people the opportunity to remake kinship relations with the departed and to care for the related dead. This is also true for someone like Charlotte, who through her travels to the Czech Republic found "a sense of re-containment within a personalized family history" (Kidron 2013, 177, citing Santos and Yan 2009). For other Germans, however, the situation is quite different. Tracing historical information about the family is extensively used not to connect with and care for but to morally distance oneself from one's forebears. Rainer is the most striking example. Here, identity and belonging are strengthened by breaking ties with the ancestors.

Evidently, the strategies are not mutually exclusive, and in fact many of my more active interviewees, like Kerstin, followed both paths, working through and reconnecting with or repositioning themselves vis-à-vis the past, although they were usually more passionate about one than the other. The aims are the same: to identify, explore, and alleviate the causes of emotional suffering, to create meaning for one's life history, and to achieve a greater sense of peace, acceptance, and happiness.

Kerstin, Anja, Juliane, Charlotte, Rainer, and Paula, whose life histories I have told in more detail, were able to find some degree of resolution and closure with the Kriegsenkel topic. Many others still found themselves traveling somewhere on their Kriegsenkel journey when I talked to them. Some were just starting after the first big eureka moment, excited, shocked, and keen to explore every aspect of this newly found issue. Many were stuck in depression, loneliness, and hopelessness, or they were angry and judgmental toward their parents. Others were looking for comfort and camaraderie in the support groups and other activities of the Kriegsenkel scene. While searching for themselves, two people found each other and love along the way.

NOTES

1. The Hitler-Stalin Pact, signed in August 1939, was a German-Soviet treaty on nonaggression that divided Eastern Europe into German and Soviet spheres of influence. See http://www.britannica.com/EBchecked/topic/230972/German-Soviet-Nonaggression-Pact (accessed November 9, 2019).

2. This refers to a generation of Germans born roughly between 1940 and 1950. Their members protested against the continuity between the political, bureaucratic, and educational elite of the National Socialist regime and that of the Federal Republic of Germany.

3. Forumkriegsenkel. n.d. "Studie." Accessed November, 9 2019. http://www.forumkriegsenkel.de/Studie.htm.

4. Forumkriegsenkel. n.d. "Lebensgeschichten." Accessed November, 9 2019. http://www.forumkriegsenkel.de/Lebensgeschichten.htm.

5. Some of the complexities and contradictions around the German national identity are well captured by Dirk Moses's 2007 article "The Non-German German and the German German: Dilemmas of Identity after the Holocaust," *New German Critique* 34, no. 2 (Summer): 45–94.

6. Forumkriegsenkel. n.d. "Lebensgeschichten." Accessed November 9, 2019. http://www.forumkriegsenkel.de/Lebensgeschichten.htm.

7. *Roots tourism* is an umbrella term for different kinds of travel in search of origin and identity, named after Alex Haley's 1976 novel *Roots* and the subsequent US TV series with the same name, which resulted in a wave of African Americans traveling to Africa to reconnect with the land of their ancestors. See Sabine Marschall, "'Homesick Tourism': Memory, Identity and (Be)Longing" (2015).

8. "Never Forget to Vote: A Nazi-Free Europe feat. Rainer Höss." *YouTube* video, May 13, 2014. http://youtu.be/KicA_oLNrsw.

9. A similar psychological mechanism was observed in the well-known book *Opa war kein Nazi* (Grandpa was not a Nazi). There the grandchildren also downplayed their grandparents' support for the Nazi regime—even if there was clear evidence otherwise—in order to maintain strong and positive family ties. See Harald Welzer, Sabine Moller, and Karoline Tschuggnall. 2002. *Opa war kein Nazi: Nationalsozialismus und Holocaust im Familiengedächtnis.*

CONCLUSION

This book is about the recent emergence of the Kriegsenkel generation—the grandchildren of World War II—in Germany. Searching for the roots of their indistinct and often therapy-resistant malaise, growing numbers of Germans in their forties and fifties have embarked on a journey to explore the indirect yet fundamental impact of World War II on their present lives and mental health. Their parents and grandparents had lived through the bombardment of German cities, the loss of family members, the pain of forced displacement, and the long-lasting shame of the Nazi war crimes. As a result of best-selling popular literature, the Kriegsenkel now feel that their own psychological struggles—from depression, anxiety disorders, and burnout to relationship breakups and career problems—are the direct consequences of these unresolved war experiences that their families passed down to them. People identifying as Kriegsenkel are now meeting across the country in self-help groups, in workshops, and on internet platforms such as Facebook, sharing personal stories and discussing ways to overcome the burden of their emotional inheritance.

Chapters 1 and 2 set the emergence of the Kriegsenkel movement into the broader sociopolitical context of postwar Germany. Chapters 3 and 4 offered an analysis of the movement as a social phenomenon and documented the construction and management of Kriegsenkel identities in the framework of contemporary therapeutic culture. Lastly, chapters 5 and 6 delved deeper into individual narratives of the transgenerational transmission of trauma and of perpetratorship. After briefly summarizing the findings of the three parts of the book and providing updates on more recent developments, I will here advance some more general points and discuss their relevance beyond the German case study.

FROM SILENCE TO TALK?: TACKLING THE HIDDEN LEGACY OF WAR

For many decades, to speak openly of German wartime suffering, to claim victimhood in a country that had victimized so many, was felt to be a moral taboo. Out of shame about the inconceivable crimes Germans had committed in the name of the Third Reich, the suffering of the majority population was largely excluded from public discourses and psychotherapeutic practices alike. While some parents and grandparents were more comfortable with sharing their personal war stories in the privacy of their homes, in the vast majority of German families the war was also not much of a topic around the dinner table.

I traced this complex history back to postwar Germany's attempts to publicly come to terms with its responsibility for the Holocaust on the one hand and its own losses on the other (chap. 1). I showed that while West Germany considered its responsibility for the crimes committed by the Nazi regime, East Germany understood itself on the side of the "victors of history." It focused on building a better socialist future rather than dwelling on the past. In both parts of the divided country, however, most aspects of wartime suffering were excluded from the culture of public commemoration, in particular in the 1970s and 1980s, when the Kriegsenkel started to watch TV and attend history lessons at school. In recent years the issue has moved into the limelight of public debate. Since 2000, a flood of memories of the firebombing of German cities, the forced displacement of ethnic Germans from Eastern Europe, and the systematic sexual violence of the occupying forces at the end of the war have swept into the public sphere. For the first time Germans have also started to consider the long-term psychological impact on the eyewitness generation and their descendants.

From the public discourses I turned my focus to the family environment, in which my interviewees grew up. Chapter 2 systematically mapped the whole spectrum of communication about World War II. From almost complete silence to incessant talking, it showed how public silences around wartime suffering were often compounded by silences in the private sphere. Taboos, denials, and an unwillingness to share painful and shameful memories created an atmosphere of secrecy and suppression that left the Kriegsenkel generation without a clear sense of the familial past, a family dynamic in which they often played an active role. The book illuminated how these overlapping layers of silences, gaps, and blind spots kept questions about a possible transgenerational influence of the war hidden from public and private awareness until the late 2000s. It explained why the topic only emerged then and why it was taken up with such great emotional intensity.

The broader question that remains for me at the end of my exploration is how to appropriately "master the past" (Herf 1997) in the aftermath of conflict, war, and violence, particularly in a situation where a population—or today more commonly certain parts of a population—needs to reconcile both the atrocities committed and their own traumatic losses. Across cultures, the eyewitness generation tends to remain silent about a difficult past. Could this be seen as a nonpathological response to mass violence, as Carol Kidron (2009a, 2009b, 2012) argued? Or do silences need to be broken, as psychologists demand, "because what cannot be talked about can also not be put to rest; and if it is not, the wounds continue to fester from generation to generation" (Bettelheim 1985, 166)? There may not be a simple answer.

In the case of Germany after 1945, respect for the millions of victims of the German aggression, including the six million European Jews systematically murdered in the Holocaust, was the context for an extended period of public silencing of the suffering of the German majority population. In my view, this was the only morally acceptable path, even if it meant that some of the war's traumatic impact receded into the background and remained largely unseen and unaddressed. To reiterate Henryk M. Broder's quote from the introduction, "Everything the Germans had to go through during the war and after was mere discomfort compared with what the Nazis did to their victims" (in Crossland 2008). Accepting responsibility for and attempting to come to terms with the crimes Germans had committed was the highest priority.

However, the international landscape has changed since the time of the Nuremberg trials. Since the 1980s, new instruments, such as Truth and Reconciliation Commissions (TRCs), have become available to deal with the aftermath of conflicts, civil wars, and dictatorial regimes. Although they are not without controversy (see, for example, Wilson 2001 for the TRC in South Africa), they do seem to offer an opportunity for different voices to be heard and for complex narratives of recent pasts, including aspects of both perpetratorship and victimhood, to emerge without long delays. This may also positively affect communication patterns within families. It is clear from my case study that while both spheres can follow slightly different norms, public discourses significantly influence private conversations about the past, either encouraging or discouraging the sharing of memories.

When it comes to dealing with the reluctance of the eyewitness generation to privately discuss their experiences with their children and grandchildren, there may not be a one-size-fits-all approach. In Kidron's (2009b, 2010) case studies, there was a level of respect for the decision by survivors of the Holocaust and the Cambodian genocide to remain silent and not to verbally pass on their painful memories to their offspring. Few of my interviewees demonstrated this kind of respect for their families. Raised in the age of therapeutic culture, the Kriegsenkel had a clear expectation of what "healthy talk" would have looked like. They expected open and age-appropriate communication that would have allowed them to learn about all aspects of the family history without being overwhelmed in the process. In the German case, the need to know was furthermore driven by the desire to position oneself in relationship to a potential family history of Nazi perpetratorship, which made private silence even more unacceptable.

However, it also became apparent in my research that the interest in the past and the pain of not knowing about it only affected certain members of the family. The siblings of my interviewees almost never shared the same concerns. For example, I was the only one among thirteen grandchildren to keep asking my grandparents about the war, whereas my brothers and cousins would probably not have felt any sense of loss had my grandparents decided to keep their memories to themselves. These individual differences would also occur in other countries.

Lastly, drawing on my German case study, silence seemed to be more easily accepted in situations where the parents were perceived as having adapted reasonably well to their war experience and as being able to function as parents. In view of today's victims of conflict, violence, and forced displacement, this acceptance points to the importance of providing tools to help them come to terms with traumatic experiences—whether through counseling or other, culturally appropriate approaches. Helping the first generation adjust may increase the chance for healthy talk, in which the younger generation can explore their family history without being overburdened by too much talk in the process. I do not believe that there is a blanket approach to the question of talk and silence in family communication about the past but think that it depends on cultural norms, as well as individual needs, desires, and abilities, to be negotiated for each family.

NOT JUST NARRATIVES OF SUFFERING: THE KRIEGSENKEL MOVEMENT AND THERAPEUTIC CULTURE

The second part of the book was devoted to the Kriegsenkel movement as a social phenomenon and as an emergent illness identity. Chapter 3 provided an overview of the movement's short history, its self-understanding, and its range of activities. It showed that the core function of the collective Kriegsenkel practices is to contextualize and validate emotional distress. In a situation where research on the transgenerational impact of World War II and related psychotherapeutic practices were only just starting to emerge, the Kriegsenkel were de facto diagnosing themselves as sufferers of transmitted war trauma. They extracted common psychological symptoms from life histories collected in popular books, contributed to internet forums, and continuously negotiated in closed Facebook groups. Through these practices, participants in this self-help community were slowly and organically assembling a cluster of symptoms associated with a new psychological profile. By doing that, they transformed their image as seemingly unjustified middle-class "whiners" into one of legitimate sufferers of transmitted trauma and ultimately into victims of war. They preferred to be labeled *sick* rather than *strange*, even though this meant pushing toward a medicalization of growing up in families affected by war.

I subsequently set the construction of Kriegsenkel identities into the context of Western therapy culture. Chapter 4 followed Kerstin's transformation from a middle-aged woman with emotional problems to a Kriegsenkel. From her story I drew out common elements that are typical for the broader experiences of this group. The Kriegsenkel identified their families as the roots of their emotional suffering. They diagnosed their parents and grandparents as traumatized and themselves as sufferers of war-transmitted trauma. They contextualized and confirmed their identities through the practices of the self-help community, and they attempted to liberate themselves from their inherited burden with therapeutic techniques. All of these actions firmly link them into the cultural framework of contemporary Western therapeutic culture. Sociologists have long critiqued therapy culture as cultivating vulnerability and victimhood and as promoting political disengagement and narcissistic self-concern. However, the subjective Kriegsenkel experiences as consumers of therapy and self-help culture also suggest that such narratives produce empowerment and facilitate agency. Therapeutic discourses give meaning to emotional distress, provide safe spaces to discuss issues that are still considered politically sensitive, and offer therapeutic interventions that relay hope for a better and happier future. Kerstin captured this sentiment in her seemingly odd statement "Hooray, I am a Kriegsenkel!"

The Kriegsenkel Movement Five Years On

When I left Germany at the end of 2012, the scope of the Kriegsenkel scene did not reach very far beyond their closed circles and self-help groups. Since then, the movement has grown considerably, not only in terms of its public exposure and participation but also in regard to its resources, diversification, and therapeutic responses. When talking to members of the public or even therapists during my time in Berlin, I found that only a small minority was familiar with the word *Kriegsenkel*. In 2017, the term and the concept behind it have become much more widely known. Over the last few years, a steady stream of media articles, TV programs, and talk show discussions have greatly added to their exposure. A first wave came in March 2013 because of the nationwide broadcasting of the three-part TV feature film *Unsere Mütter, unsere Väter* (Our mothers, our fathers). The series portrayed the different trajectories of five German friends in their early twenties through the chaos of World War II and their entanglement with the National Socialist ideology. Around seven million Germans watched each episode. The series was surrounded by extensive public discussions about the impact of the war, including on the later generations. Public interest in the Kriegsenkel topic continued to increase and peaked in May 2015 around the seventieth anniversary of the end of World War II. That same year, *Nebelkinder* (Children of Fog; Schneider and Süss 2015), a third book with war grandchildren's life histories and more general essays on the topic, topped the list of nonfiction books about World War II sold on www.Amazon.de. within two months of its publication.[1]

Other popular books have also recently appeared. They are largely accounts of individual Kriegsenkel journeys, documenting personal attempts to trace and come to terms with one's family history. Among them are Matthias Lohre's (2016) *Das Erbe der Kriegsenkel: Was das Schweigen der Eltern mit uns macht* (The inheritance of the Kriegsenkel: How our parents' silence affects us); Jens Orback's (2015) *Schatten auf meiner Seele: Ein Kriegsenkel entdeckt die Geschichte seiner Familie* (Shadows on my soul: A war grandchild discovers the history of his family); and Raymond Unger's (2016) novel *Die Heimat der Wölfe: Ein Kriegsenkel auf den Spuren seiner Familie* (Homeland of the wolves: A war grandchild traces his family history).

The Kriegsenkel scene has evolved from a handful of support groups in 2012 to something that considers itself to be an "emerging social movement."[2] More than twenty groups are now meeting regularly across the country, and, judging from the slowly expanding membership in the various Facebook groups, it seems that an increasing number of people identify as Kriegsenkel today. While the special websites and the media coverage have helped to raise awareness of the particular emotional issues of the Kriegsenkel, as far as I am aware, there is no coordinated push for a formal diagnosis or recognition of a "Kriegsenkel syndrome" yet. However, one of the key drivers to demand formal acknowledgment of emerging conditions (as in the case of the Vietnam veterans in the United States, for example) is access to specialized treatment. In Germany, on the other hand, an official diagnosis as a sufferer of transmitted war trauma is not required for one to have access to counseling. Also, the psychological profession has started to respond to the particular needs of an already therapy-experienced Kriegsenkel clientele. A number of German psychotherapists have recently published books that promoted different pathways and techniques to help alleviate the symptoms associated with the Kriegsenkel experience (Baer and Frick-Baer 2015; Reddemann 2015; Meyer-Legrand 2016; Wüstel 2017). Thirty-seven psychotherapists with a special focus on Kriegsenkel issues are now offering their services on Kriegsenkel.de.[3] Considering that Germany had 44,310 registered psychotherapists in 2017, that number should still be considered marginal.[4] It does show, however, a growing awareness among psychologists that being a Kriegsenkel implies a particular psychopathology and requires specialized therapeutic interventions. Therapists are also increasingly involved in the running of Kriegsenkel support groups, with around a quarter of the groups promoted on Kriegsenkel.de now organized by psychotherapists or alternative healers.[5]

The Kriegsenkel movement has evolved, but I believe it will ultimately remain a therapeutic subculture. With around twenty-one million Germans in this age group, only a small fraction of them publicly identify with the Kriegsenkel topic or participate in the organized activities. Many others do not. The most striking observation in this regard is that the new collective identity has found substantially less resonance among East Germans. This is in spite of the fact that they come from families with historical experiences very similar to those of their Western counterparts. While the recent establishment of the Leipzig (2015) and Dresden (2016) support groups may be a first step toward stronger participation, it remains that they are significantly lagging behind. My research clearly points to the fact that the construction and adoption of a Kriegsenkel identity requires more than a family history of war and violence. It only tends to happen under certain conditions. A number of potential variables that come into play were discussed at the end of chapter 4: differential exposure to Kriegsenkel books, varying degrees of parental war trauma, individual differences in responses among siblings. However, I believe the key factor is the degree of embeddedness in the therapeutic culture. The unequal exposure to therapy culture in the two Germanys may well have altered the enlistment of the trauma profile. This could explain the dissimilar uptake in either part of the country (which has now been reunited for almost thirty years!), highlighting the importance of discursive macro contexts for the construction of subjective identities, including illness identities. To pursue this point further, it would be interesting to compare Kriegsenkel experiences with those of people of the same generation across Europe (and beyond). How do Italians, French, or English people of that age group relate to growing up in families that lived through World War II? Are there those who explain their current emotional problems in a similar way? Of particular interest would be interviewing members of the second generation in Japan, as one of the German allies of World War II.

Complementing Narratives of Victimhood

One recent development in the Kriegsenkel movement is relevant in the context of the critique of therapeutic culture as encouraging narratives of suffering and victimhood. In chapter 4 I argued that while therapeutic narratives indeed encouraged the German Kriegsenkel to understand themselves as victims of their dysfunctional families, the same therapeutic culture was also seen as providing the tools to exert agency and overcome emotional suffering.

Most recently another aspect has come into this mix, putting the spotlight on the positive character traits, strengths, and life skills associated with a Kriegsenkel existence. The first phase of the Kriegsenkel movement revolved strongly around the negative impact of growing up in World War II survivor families. In 2012, Forumkriegsenkel.de had published a list of issues and problems that the contributors understood to be typical for their generation (see chap. 3). At the end of 2014, the same website added a second posting. This time interested Kriegsenkel contributed what they saw as their personal resources and positive characteristics that "make life worth living." The list included empathy, the ability to set boundaries, creative expression, and appreciation for the life skills their families had passed on.[6] The theme of the 2017 annual meeting of the Kriegsenkel Association was *Vermächtnis und Vermögen*, which could be translated as *Legacy and Wealth/Patrimony*. The title captures the duality of the Kriegsenkel experience as an inherited burden on the one hand and as a resource on the other. This duality was also reflected in the individual contributions. In her talk *Die Kraft der Kriegsenkel* (The strength of the Kriegsenkel, based on her 2016 book with the same title), psychotherapist Ingrid Meyer-Legrand pointed out that typical Kriegsenkel challenges such as parentification (assuming responsibility for one's emotionally impaired parents) do not necessarily have to be detrimental to the children's development. They can also encourage the cultivation of strength, determination, and practical intelligence. Along similar lines, Joachim Süss's argued in his latest book, *Die entschlossene Generation* (The determined generation, 2017), that with quiet but unwavering determination the Kriegsenkel generation is now actively contributing their resources, aspirations, and values to create a more peaceful, stable, and conciliatory German society. I would therefore amend the critique of therapeutic culture further to say that while it may support narratives of trauma and victimhood in the first instance, it later on encourages a broadening of the focus to include aspects of resilience resulting from the same upbringing. These two aspects—trauma and resilience—are also found in the research on Holocaust survivor families, and they constitute an integral part of trauma studies more broadly (see Agaibi and Wilson 2005 for an overview and literature review).

Therapeutic Practices as Protected Spaces

I would like to come back to the second critique of therapeutic culture: that it discourages social and political action. I believe the Kriegsenkel movement will most likely continue to frame itself as therapeutic rather than turning into a movement with broader social ambitions. While, as I explained in chapter 4, this focus was not a conscious decision, therapeutic culture is quite simply by far the most dominant framework within which problems of the self are explored and addressed. Nonetheless, there is a political dimension to this choice. It could, for example, be argued that the culture of commemoration in both German states systematically discouraged public discourses of wartime suffering and consequently produced an environment in which the war trauma of the majority population remained hidden and thus unaddressed. The Kriegsenkel could frame their families and themselves as victims of this "conspiracy of silence" (Danieli 1998).

However, most people I talked to in Germany would be intensely uncomfortable with any public statement that may put them in the same political corner as those claiming German victimhood to minimize the Holocaust and the many other Nazi war crimes. To an extent, framing one's problems as psychological avoids the need to navigate this minefield. An article in the Swiss *Neue Zürcher Zeitung* (Plamper 2015) voiced the suspicion that the Kriegsenkel topic, disguised as a psychotherapeutic discourse, may bring in claims of German victimhood "through the backdoor." Demarcating Kriegsenkel topics as therapeutic provides protected spaces where issues can be raised without fear of public criticism. It would be interesting to investigate this aspect further in other countries. Do therapeutic environments there similarly allow people to explore the transgenerational consequences of past violence that cannot easily be discussed in public without the fear of repercussions? China comes to mind, where therapeutic culture is now booming, while at the same time the immense human suffering caused by the political campaigns of the Maoist era and after still remain very sensitive issues (for an overview of the recent psycho-boom and a discussion of other aspects of therapeutic culture in the Chinese context, see Huang 2014; Yang 2013; and Zhang 2014, 2016). Do Chinese people use therapeutic practices and vocabulary to raise issues that could be considered social and political? Do patients talk to their therapists about the impact the Cultural Revolution or the massacre on Tiananmen Square in 1989 had on them and their families? Are therapeutic spaces considered private, confidential, and beyond government reach?

MAKING SENSE AND ACCEPTING THE PAST

Part three of the book delved more deeply into five Kriegsenkel life histories. Anja and Juliane were the protagonists of chapter 5. Both women felt the continuing and devastating impact of World War II on their families and, by extension, themselves. As a child Anja's father narrowly survived the nightly bombardment of his hometown, attacks by low-flying Allied warplanes, and the violence and chaos in the wake of the Nazi downfall. What he saw and lived through scarred for life not only him but also his daughter, who struggled with severe anxiety, panic attacks, and depression. Juliane's family had fled from their home in Eastern Europe at the end of the war. In 2012, she was starting to suspect that the women in her family had experienced or witnessed sexual violence during the flight and that they had passed their trauma on to her. The chapter problematized the way in which processes of transgenerational transmission of trauma are commonly explained and how Kriegsenkel apply them to their own cases. I argued that while psychological models of transgenerational transmission provide a convincing explanation for emotional suffering, they also pathologize the relationship between generations. Transgenerational transmission is understood to be a compartmentalized process, cordoning off the undesirable and ultimately "sick" aspects of the relationship with the parents from the overall transfer of cultural and psychosocial resources that happens as part of raising children. I suggested that ideas from the field of affect theory could help normalize these processes. Affect theory understands human beings as open systems, invariably interacting with and influenced by people and the environment around them.

Normalizing Transgenerational Transmission?

I would like to return to the negative side effects, discussed in chapter 5, that common models of transgenerational transmission of trauma can have. Listening to my many German interviewees talk about their struggles and frustrations,

I realized that they needed to overcome more than just their individual suffering. There was also significant room for improvement in the relationships between the generations. I would argue that in many cases "becoming" a Kriegsenkel made already-strained family relationships worse. The pain of coming to terms with one's own emotional issues was compounded by anger, resentment, and judgment vis-à-vis the parents. In my participants' view, their parents had not done their "duty" of working through their war trauma but had instead passed on their problems to their children. Therapeutic norms and truth rules fueled the fire and provided the ammunition for the intergenerational conflict. Relationship cutoffs were seen as an accepted means of protecting oneself from negative parental influences and focusing on one's own healing. As Eva Illouz (2008) observed for the United States, this kind of therapeutic thinking is so ingrained in Germany's society today that it is never really challenged. However, I believe that taking a step back could be beneficial to members of the Kriegsenkel generation and to those who are dealing with similar questions in other contexts, including therapists. I have two main considerations.

Firstly, I would suggest starting from the premise that processes of transgenerational transmission are normal rather than pathological. I would challenge the expectation that there should not be a transmission of experiences in families where the parent generation has lived through war or mass loss and that, with the right therapy, such a transmission can be avoided. Parents inevitably raise their children with the values, worldviews, and emotional makeup that they themselves have acquired over the course of their own lives. Sociologists Bertaux and Thompson (1993, 1) state that "transmission between generations is as old as humanity itself." They believe that family therapists have underestimated the normality of the processes they describe, focusing mainly on their negative consequences (8). The family, in their view, is the main channel not only for the transmission of language, social standing, and religion but also for social values and aspirations, fears, worldviews, and ways of behaving.

The second point I would like raise is a reminder that by clicking into their Kriegsenkel identities, members of this generation were de facto rewriting the past, in the way that philosopher Ian Hacking (1995) explored in the context of multiple personality disorder (now called dissociative identity disorder). Kriegsenkel tended to take today's therapeutic worldview absolute. It was the yardstick with which they measured their upbringing and looked back into their families' pasts. However, while they clearly experienced suffering, Germans of the war generation were not instructed to conceive of themselves as traumatized at the time of the war or for decades after. They had no knowledge that they should work through their painful and shameful memories in order to "break the chain of transmission" and to avoid passing their emotional burden on to their children. The pervasiveness of therapeutic thinking is a recent development, and concepts of transmission of trauma are "retroactive re-descriptions" (Hacking 1995, 241). They superimpose ideas on the past on the basis of today's norms, which did not exist in this form at the time. The judgment of Kriegsenkel vis-à-vis their families is based on expectations that in my view were impossible to fulfill.

Needless to say, these caveats do not discount the subjective experience of suffering or take away from the fact that the Kriegsenkel would have benefited from a more nurturing and emotionally healthy family environment. However, I hope that by bringing up these points, I may be able to contribute to more understanding, empathy, and ultimately forgiveness between the generations. I like to think that our parents did their best raising us with the resources and the knowledge they had available at the time.

I admit, at the end of my exploration of processes of transgenerational transmissions, that they still remain somewhat mysterious and elusive. They are hard to notice and difficult to pinpoint, in particular since many observations are constructed retrospectively and with long time lags. They are complex to diagnose even with current psychological assessment tools, and they are expressed in highly abstract models that defy direct observation. However, what remains is the subjective perception of the Kriegsenkel themselves, their embodied and often nonverbal knowing that this explanation for their problems fits and makes sense. What matters in the end is not whether every single issue can be traced back to the war but that making this connection is meaningful to the individual. As Hacking (1995, 250–51) said: "We constitute our souls by making up our lives, that is, by weaving stories about our past, by what we call memories. The tales we tell of ourselves and to ourselves are not a matter of recording what we have done and how we have felt. They must mesh with the rest of the world and with other people's stories, at least in externals, but their real role is in the creation of a life, a character, a self."

Navigating Suffering in the Context of War Trauma and Perpetratorship

The final chapter of the book (chap. 6) traced the long-term, intergenerational impact of expulsion and forced migration on the one hand and of Nazi perpetratorship on the other. Rather than applying the more conventional understanding of transgenerational transmission as an emotional burden passed down the family line, this chapter analyzed descendants' accounts through the anthropological lens of absence. Charlotte's story showed how her family's loss of their *Heimat* (homeland) at the end of World War II impacted the lives of three generations, leaving the youngest generation with a gap where an attachment to home was expected to be. Paula and Rainer were both struggling with the legacy of being the offspring of high-ranking Nazi perpetrators. Their grandfathers still played major roles in their grandchildren's lives, in spite of the fact that they were no longer physically present. I showed how people were able to exert agency over absences, either by actively attempting to reconnect with what was missing or by consciously widening the gap between family members and familial transmission.

As I explained in the introduction, one particularity of the German Kriegsenkel movement sets it apart from most other second-generation identities: it ventures out to explore the long-term traumatic impact of a war in which their country was the main perpetrator. The challenge of exploring the psychological pain of the majority population without being disrespectful to the pain of the victims of the German aggression was palpable throughout this book. My research clearly revealed the crucial influence of the sociohistorical context on the perception, construction, and management of individual emotional suffering.

This influence was palpable in the taboos and "humiliated silence" (Connerton 2008) in public and private memories of World War II and the way that the Kriegsenkel define their newly found identity as illness and address it with therapeutic techniques, carefully staying away from all political claims or ambitions. The final chapter of the book brings this aspect even more explicitly into the analysis of descendants' narratives. Charlotte's story (told only from her perspective) illustrated how each of the three generations involved perceived the absence of Heimat very differently: as an irrecoverable loss, a political necessity, or an (unconscious) lack of attachment to one's country of birth. In each case, the individual experience of suffering was substantially altered by the political realities of Germany's postwar borders and the way the loss of the territories in the East was framed in public narratives and commemoration. More recent, positive attitudes to German national identity enabled Charlotte to find a personally satisfying resolution for her yearning for a Heimat—her home within herself. The Kriegsenkel movement could therefore be seen as an example of how the intergenerational impact of war and violence can successfully be addressed in a so-called perpetrator society. The framework of therapeutic culture allowed Germans of this generation to choose from an array of mainstream and alternative techniques to address the damage from their family's difficult pasts while at the same time treading carefully and respectfully around the memory of the war and the Holocaust.

When it comes to the transgenerational impact of high-level Nazi perpetratorship, the choices are much more limited. The current culture of commemoration does not easily accommodate the concept of working through or therapeutically extracting the past in order to achieve an emotionally healthier future. (Opting for childlessness or sterilization in order to "break the chain of transmission" of Nazi perpetratorship makes an extreme point of this.) Having a known or suspected Nazi perpetrator in the family, one is expected to take a clear moral and political stance and distance oneself from the person to the extent that family ties are severed. While for someone like Rainer this was a psychologically satisfactory solution, Paula experienced it with a degree of loss. The other option is to maintain the emotional connection to the grandfathers (or grandparents) but then deny or downplay their role during the Third Reich (see, for example, Senfft 2015; Welzer, Moller, and Tschuggnall 2002).

Is there another way? While this is currently difficult to fathom, there may be a slightly different nuance, which Alexandra Senfft recently described. Senfft, a well-known German book author and journalist (Senfft 2016, 2008), is the granddaughter of Hanns Ludin, Hitler's ambassador (*Gesandter*) to Slovakia. Ludin signed the deportation orders that sent thousands of Jews to Auschwitz, and he was executed for war crimes in 1947. Like Rainer and Paula, Alexandra Senfft intensively researched her family history, much to her extended family's dismay.[7] As it did for them, working through the historical documents brought the ghost of her grandfather back to life and closer to her. She claims that confronting the truth of his involvement with the Nazi regime, as challenging and sickening as it was, also helped her on another level to accept him as her grandfather. She said she integrated him into her personal narrative and into a truthful and realistic family narrative she now passes on to her own children (Senfft 2015, 119–20). Yet, while she did find a degree of liberation and, to an extent, made peace with her past, she also continues to be haunted by the details of the horrific crimes her grandfather committed.

ANZAC DAY REVISITED

As I am concluding my book, Anzac Day—the anniversary of the first major military action fought by Australian and New Zealand forces during the World War I—passes by again. It is celebrated with the same public ceremonies and testimonies of military heroism as ever. I am still not any more comfortable with these sentiments than I was six years ago, nor do I ever aspire to be. I do understand better now, though, how strengthening it may be for descendants to connect to their grandfathers and great-grandfathers as heroes who gave their lives fighting for their country. For us Germans, thinking about our own grandfathers going to war will never have the same pathos. Maybe in its place we have a more sober view of how destructive and dehumanizing war is.

My own Kriegsenkel journey was there throughout this entire project, sometimes explicitly, often in the background. Over time, it became more and more mixed with, and ultimately superseded by, other life events. I am grateful to my parents for their active interest, love, and support, and in particular for my father's courage to make the difficult trip to Poland, the old *Heimat*, with my mother and me. I am thankful to my grandparents for the stories they shared, the few additional things I found out about them along the way, and the many questions that will remain forever unanswered. May they rest in peace.

I have learned a lot about my country, about my generation, and about the difficult long-term consequences that wars have—even on the populations of the perpetrators. Yet watching the news at night hits home again, reminding me that war is, of course, by no means an issue of the past. There are still children today who are attacked by machine-gun fire and who have to clear the streets of dead bodies after air raids, just as Anja's father had to more than seventy years ago. There are still people who are forced to leave their homes like Charlotte's grandmothers, girls and women who are raped like the women in Juliane's family, and people who try to make their way on shaky boats in desperate hope of reaching a welcoming country. It pains me immensely to think that seventy years from now another generation of anthropologists will set out to explore the ways this trauma was passed on to their children and grandchildren.

On the other hand, when I was back in Berlin in 2015, Germany was about to take one million refugees who had fled from the war in Syria—just in that one year. To me, as someone who lives in Australia with its extremely restrictive refugee policy, this was a gesture of immense generosity and humanitarianism. There surely were some economic motives behind accepting such a large number of predominantly young people to a country with an aging population. However, the media also made frequent reference to World War II and pointed to Germany's particular moral responsibility to help alleviate human suffering. Newspaper articles drew a direct line from the trains that took Jewish citizens to Auschwitz to the "trains of hope" that were now traveling in the opposite direction. As they were bringing food, clothes, and toys to the shelters for newly arrived refugees, German seniors talked on TV about their own experiences of having to leave their homes in 1945. I won't deny that Germany's open-arms policy has resulted in social problems and has boosted the following of right-wing parties and their antiforeigner rhetoric. Still, it gives me confidence that we have learned something from our history after all.[8]

When I spoke to Kriegsenkel book author Sabine Bode in 2012, she suspected that the Kriegsenkel scene would never turn into a mainstream social movement with common goals and ambitions. While this may well be the case, I would like to think that encouraging our parents and grandparents to tell their stories and exploring our own Kriegsenkel identities has made us more empathetic to the lasting damage that war and forced migration leave behind. Bode also expressed hope that this generation would eventually work through their present, more introverted, phase of self-discovery and soul-searching to play a more active role in society, even if only on an individual basis.[9] As I watched middle-aged Germans waiting at the stations with signs welcoming refugees or heard that people had donated money or volunteered their time to teach German language courses, I found comfort in thinking that they were doing just that.

NOTES

1. Private email exchange with Joachim Süss on May 6, 2015.
2. Wikipedia, The Free Encyclopedia. "Kriegsenkel". Accessed November 9, 2019. http://de.wikipedia.org/wiki/Kriegsenkel#cite_note-6.
3. Kriegsenkel e.V. n.d. "Beratung, Therapie, Coaching, Mediation." Accessed November 9, 2019. https://www.kriegsenkel.de/gespraech-und-begleitung/.
4. Deutsche Gesellschaft für Psychiatrie und Psychotherapie, Psychosomatik und Nervenheilkunde e.V. n.d. Accessed November 9, 2019. https://www.dgppn.de/_Resources/Persistent/154e18a8cebe41667ae22665162be21ad726e8b8/Factsheet_Psychiatrie.pdf.
5. Kriegsenkel e.V. n.d. "Gesprächsgruppen." Accessed November 9, 2019. http://www.kriegsenkel.de/gespraechsgruppen/.
6. Forumkriegsenkel. n.d. "Studie." Accessed November 9, 2019. http://www.forumkriegsenkel.de/Studie.htm.
7. Alexandra Senfft is the niece of Malte Ludin, the producer of a well-known documentary about his father, Hanns Ludin: *2 oder 3 Dinge, die ich von ihm weiss* (*2 or 3 Things I Know about Him*). The film graphically shows the family's stoic determination to deny Ludin's role in the Holocaust, even when faced with a wealth of historical documents proving the opposite.
8. This is well captured in comedian Jan Böhmermann's song "Be Deutsch." *YouTube* video. March 31, 2016. https://www.youtube.com/watch?v=HMQkV5cTuoY.
9. Interview with Sabine Bode on May 30, 2012.

APPENDIX: INTERVIEW STRUCTURE AND SAMPLE QUESTIONS

1. Biographical information
   - Date of birth, place of birth (East or West Germany, city or rural area), occupation, date of birth of both parents
2. Family history
   - What do you know of your family's history during and immediately after World War II?
3. Family communication about World War II
   - Did your parents and/or grandparents talk about their war experiences, and to what extent?
   - Did you ask questions?
   - Did you have a sense of taboos and secrets surrounding the war, and if so, how did you respond to them?
4. Perceived impact of World War II on parents and grandparents
   - How did your family deal with their war experiences?
   - Do you think they affected your family life and their parenting, and if so, how?
5. Perceptions and impact of transgenerational transmission
   - Do you feel that some of your family's World War II experiences were passed on to you? If so, what and how?
   - If so, how do you feel this impacted on your life?
6. The social and political environment
   - Did you talk about your family history outside the immediate family, with friends, etc.?

- What did you learn about World War II at school and when growing up?
- How do feel about being German? Has this changed over time?

7. The Kriegsenkel movement
    - Are you familiar with the term *Kriegsenkel,* and if so, do you identify with it?
    - Have you read the Kriegsenkel books?
    - If so, how did you come across them?
    - Do you participate in Kriegsenkel activities, such as support groups, internet discussions, etc.?

BIBLIOGRAPHY

Aarts, Petra G. H. 1998. "Intergenerational Effects in Families of World War II Survivors from the Dutch East Indies: Aftermath of Another Dutch War." In *International Handbook of Multigenerational Legacies of Trauma,* edited by Yael Danieli, 175–90. New York: Plenum.

Abraham, Nicolas, and Maria Torok. 1994. *The Shell and the Kernel: Renewals of Psychoanalysis.* Chicago: University of Chicago Press.

Agaibi, Christine E., and John P. Wilson. 2005. "Trauma, PTSD, and Resilience: A Review of the Literature." *Trauma, Violence, & Abuse* 6, no. 3 (July): 195–216.

Alberti, Bettina. 2010. *Seelische Trümmer: Geboren in den 50er—und 60er—Jahren: Die Nachkriegsgeneration im Schatten des Kriegstraumas.* München: Kösel.

Altounian, Janine. 1999. "Putting into Words, Putting to Rest and Putting Aside the Ancestors: How an Analysand Who Was Heir to the Armenian Genocide of 1915 Worked through Mourning." *International Journal of Psychoanalysis* 80, no. 3 (June): 439–48.

Ancharoff, Michelle R., James F. Munroe, and Lisa Fisher. 1998. "The Legacy of Combat Trauma: Clinical Implications of Intergenerational Transmission." In *International Handbook of Multigenerational Legacies of Trauma,* edited by Yael Danieli, 257–76. New York: Plenum.

Anonyma. 2003. *Eine Frau in Berlin: Tagebuchaufzeichnungen vom 20. April bis 22. Juni 1945.* Frankfurt am Main: Eichborn.

Argenti, Nicolas, and Katharina Schramm. 2010. *Remembering Violence: Anthropological Perspectives on Intergenerational Transmission.* New York: Berghahn Books.

Aron, Elaine. 1996. *The Highly Sensitive Person.* New York: Broadway Books.

Ashplant, T. G., Graham Dawson, and Michael Roper. eds. 2000. "The Politics of War Memory and Commemoration." *Routledge Studies in Memory and Narrative* 7. London: Routledge.

Assmann, Aleida. 2006a. *Der lange Schatten der Vergangenheit—Erinnerungskultur und Geschichtspolitik*. München: Beck.

———. 2006b. "On the (In)Compatibility of Guilt and Suffering in German Memory." *German Life & Letters* 59, no. 2 (April): 187–200.

Aubry, Timothy, and Trysh Travis, eds. 2015. *Rethinking Therapeutic Culture*. Chicago: University of Chicago Press.

Auerhahn, Nanette C., and Dori Laub. 1998. "Intergenerational Memory of the Holocaust." In *International Handbook of Multigenerational Legacies of Trauma*, edited by Yael Danieli, 21–41. New York: Plenum.

Bachofen, Andreas. 2012. "Heile Welten. Der unbewusste Verzicht der Kriegsenkel auf ein eigenes Leben." In *Die Kinder der Kriegskinder und die späten Folgen des NS-Terrors*, edited by Heike Knoch, Winfried Kurth, Heinrich J. Reiß, and Götz Egloff, 13: 101–12. Jahrbuch für psychohistorische Forschung. Heidelberg: Mattes.

Baer, Udo, and Gabriele Frick-Baer. 2010. *Wie Traumata in die nächste Generation wirken-Untersuchungen, Erfahrungen, therapeutische Hilfen*. Neukirchen-Vluyn: Affenkönig.

———. 2015. *Kriegserbe in der Seele: Was Kindern und Enkeln der Kriegsgeneration wirklich hilft*. 3rd ed. Weinheim, Bergstr: Beltz.

Baker, Katherine B., and Julia Gippenreiter. 1998. "Stalin's Purge and Its Impact on Russian Families." In *International Handbook of Multigenerational Legacies of Trauma*, edited by Yael Danieli, 403–34. New York: Plenum.

Barker, Kristin. 2002 "Self-Help Literature and the Making of an Illness Identity: The Case of Fibromyalgia Syndrome (FMS)." *Social Problems* 49, no. 3 (August): 279–300.

———. 2008 "Electronic Support Groups, Patient-Consumers, and Medicalization: The Case of Contested Illness." *Journal of Health and Social Behavior* 49, no. 1 (March): 20–36.

Bar-On, Dan. 1989. *Legacy of Silence: Encounters with Children of the Third Reich*. Cambridge, MA: Harvard University Press.

Barth, Anne. 2012. "Schwarze Schafe finden zueinander. Selbstbehauptung und Solidarität über das Internetforum für Kriegsenkel." In *Die Kinder der Kriegskinder und die späten Folgen des NS-Terrors*, edited by Heike Knoch, Winfried Kurth, Heinrich J. Reiß, and Götz Egloff, 13: 173–81. Jahrbuch für psychohistorische Forschung. Heidelberg: Mattes.

Basu, Paul. 2005. "Roots-Tourism as Return Movement: Semantics and the Scottish Diaspora." In *Emigrant Homecomings: The Return Movement of Emigrants, 1600–2000*, edited by Marjory Harper, 131–50. Manchester: Manchester University Press.

———. 2007. *Highland Homecomings: Genealogy and Heritage Tourism in the Scottish Diaspora*. London: Routledge.

Baumert, Jürgen, Kai S. Cortina, Achim Leschinsky, and Karl Ulrich Mayer. 2003. *Das Bildungswesen in der Bundesrepublik Deutschland: Strukturen und Entwicklungen im Überblick*. Reinbek bei Hamburg: Rowohlt.

Bausinger, Hermann, and Deutsche Gesellschaft für Volkskunde. 1980. "Kulturelle Identität—Schlagwort und Wirklichkeit." In *Heimat und Identität, Probleme regionaler Kultur: 22. Deutscher Volkskunde-Kongress in Kiel vom 16. bis 21. Juni 1979*, edited by Konrad Köstlin and Hermann Bausinger, 9–24. Neumünster: Wachholtz.

Beck, Edald. 2011. "The Nazi's Grandson." *Jewish World*, May 18, 2011. http://www.ynetnews.com/articles/0,7340,L-4070115,00.html.

Becker, David, and Margarita Diaz. 1998. "The Social Process and the Transgenerational Transmission of Trauma in Chile." In *International Handbook of Multigenerational Legacies of Trauma*, edited by Yael Danieli, 435–45. New York: Plenum.

Becker, Jurek. 1969. *Jakob der Lügner*. Berlin: Aufbau.

Bendick, Rainer. 2001. "Zweierlei Entlastung des deutschen Volkes: die Darstellung des Zweiten Weltkriegs in Schulgeschichtsbüchern der DDR und der BRD." In *Schuld und Sühne? Kriegserlebnis und Kriegsdeutung in deutschen Medien der Nachkriegszeit (1945–1961): Internationale Konferenz vom 01.–04.09.1999 in Berlin*, edited by Ursula Heukenkamp, vol. 50.2. Amsterdamer Beiträge zur neueren Germanistik. Amsterdam.

Ben-Ze'ev, Efrat, Ruth Ginio, and Jay Winter, eds. 2010. *Shadows of War: A Social History of Silence in the Twentieth Century*. Cambridge: Cambridge University Press.

Bergmann, Martin S., and Milton E. Jucovy. 1982. *Generations of the Holocaust*. New York: Basic Books.

Bertaux, Daniel, and Paul Thompson. 1993. *Between Generations: Family Models, Myths, and Memories*. Oxford: Oxford University Press.

Best, Dieter. 2012. "Mythen und Fakten zur Psychotherapie." *Psychotherapie Aktuell*, no. 1, 7–10.

Bettelheim, Bruno. 1985. Afterword to *I Didn't Say Goodbye: Interviews with Children of the Holocaust*, by Claudine Vegh, 166–171. Translated by Ros Schwartz. New York: E. P. Dutton.

Bille, Mikkel, Frida Hastrup, and Tim Flohr Sørensen. 2010a. *An Anthropology of Absence: Materializations of Transcendence and Loss*. New York: Springer.

———. 2010b. Introduction to *An Anthropology of Absence: Materializations of Transcendence and Loss*, 3–22. New York: Springer.

Birgel, Franz A., and Edgar Reitz. 1986. "You Can Go Home Again: An Interview with Edgar Reitz." *Film Quarterly* 39, no. 4 (Summer): 2–10.

Bode, Sabine. 2004 *Die vergessene Generation: Die Kriegskinder brechen ihr Schweigen*. 8th ed. Stuttgart: Klett-Cotta.

———. 2006. *Die deutsche Krankheit—German Angst*. Stuttgart: Klett-Cotta.

———. 2009. *Kriegsenkel: Die Erben der vergessenen Generation*. Stuttgart: Klett-Cotta.

Brähler, Elmar, Oliver Decker, and Hartmut Radebold. 2004. "Ausgebombt, vertrieben, vaterlos." In *Kindheiten im II. Weltkrieg und ihre Folgen*, edited by Hartmut Radebold, 111–36. Psyche und Gesellschaft. Reinbek bei Hamburg: Psychosozial.

Brähler, Elmar, Heide Glaesmer, Philipp Kuwert, and Christoph Muhtz. 2011. "Transgenerationale Übertragung traumatischer Erfahrungen: Wissensstand und theoretischer Rahmen und deren Bedeutung für die Erforschung transgenerationaler Folgen des Zweiten Weltkrieges in Deutschland." *Trauma und Gewalt* 5, no. 4 (November): 330–43.

Brave Heart, Maria Yellow Horse, and Lemyra M. DeBruyn. 1998. "The American Indian Holocaust: Healing Historical Unresolved Grief." *American Indian and Alaska Native Mental Health Research* 8 (2): 56.

Brennan, Teresa. 2004. *The Transmission of Affect*. Ithaca, NY: Cornell University Press.

Brown, Phil. 1995. "Naming and Framing: The Social Construction of Diagnosis and Illness." *Journal of Health and Social Behavior* (Extra Issue): 34–52.

Buck, Chris, and Jennifer Lee. 2013. *Frozen*. Animated movie. Walt Disney.

Bundespsychotherapeutenkammer. n.d. "Paths to Psychotherapy". Accessed November 9, 2019. https://www.bptk.de/wp-content/uploads/2019/09/2019-09_bptk_patientenbroschuere_englisch_web.pdf.

Cain, Carole. 1991. "Personal Stories: Identity Acquisition and Self-Understanding in Alcoholics Anonymous." *Ethos* 19, no. 2 (June): 210–53.

Cannell, Fenella. 2011. "English Ancestors: The Moral Possibilities of Popular Genealogy." *Journal of the Royal Anthropological Institute* 17, no. 3 (September): 462–80.

Chalmers, Martin. 1985. "Heimat: Approaches to a Word and a Film." *Framework; Coventry, Eng.* 0 (26): 90–101.

Chamberlain, Sigrid. 2004. "The Nurture and Care of the Future Master Race." *Journal of Psychohistory* 31, no. 4 (Spring): 367–94.

Cho, Grace M. 2008. *Haunting the Korean Diaspora: Shame, Secrecy, and the Forgotten War*. Minneapolis: University of Minnesota Press.

Chriss, James J. 1999. *Counseling and the Therapeutic State*. New York: Aldine de Gruyter.

Connerton, Paul. 2008. "Seven Types of Forgetting." *Memory Studies* 1, no. 1 (January): 59–71.

Conrad, Peter. 2005. "The Shifting Engines of Medicalization." *Journal of Health and Social Behavior* 46, no. 1 (March): 3–14.

Cotten, Christopher, and John Ridings. 2011. "Getting Out/Getting In: The DSM, Political Activism, and the Social Construction of Mental Disorders." *Social Work in Mental Health* 9, no. 3 (April): 181–205.

Crapanzano, Vincent. 2011. *The Harkis: The Wound That Never Heals*. Chicago: University of Chicago Press.

Cross, William E. 1998. "Black Psychological Functioning and the Legacy of Slavery: Myth and Reality." In *International Handbook of Multigenerational Legacies of Trauma*, edited by Yael Danieli, 387–401. New York: Plenum.

Crossland, David. 2008. "Germany Reflects on Its Own Agony." *National*, October 28, 2008. https://www.thenational.ae/world/europe/germany-reflects-on-its-own-agony-1.493922.

Cushman, Philip. 1990. "Why the Self Is Empty: Toward a Historically Situated Psychology." *American Psychologist* 45, no. 5 (May): 599–611.

Danieli, Yael. 1998. Introduction to *International Handbook of Multigenerational Legacies of Trauma*, edited by Yael Danieli, 1–17. New York: Plenum.

———. 2007. "Assessing Trauma across Cultures from a Multigenerational Perspective." In *Cross-Cultural Assessment of Psychological Trauma and PTSD*, edited by John P. Wilson and Catherine So-Kum Tang, 65–90. New York: Springer.

Danyel, Jürgen. 1995a. *Die Geteilte Vergangenheit: Zum Umgang mit Nationalsozialismus und Widerstand in beiden Deutschen Staaten*. Berlin: Akademie.

———. 1995b. "Die Opfer—und Verfolgtenperspektive als Gründungskonsens? Zum Umgang mit der Widerstandstradition und der Schuldfrage in der DDR." In *Die Geteilte Vergangenheit: Zum Umgang mit Nationalsozialismus und Widerstand in beiden Deutschen Staaten*, edited by Jürgen Danyel, 31–46. Berlin: Akademie.

Derrida, Jacques. 1976. "Fors: Les mots anglés de Nicolas Abraham et Maria Torok, Preface." In *Cryptonomanie: Le Verbier de l'Homme aux Loups*, by Nicolas Abraham and Maria Torok, 7–73. Paris: Aubier Flammarion.

Dickson-Gómez, Julia. 2002. "The Sound of Barking Dogs: Violence and Terror among Salvadoran Families in the Postwar." *Medical Anthropology Quarterly* 16, no. 4 (September): 415–38.

Diner, Dan. 2003. "Anthropologisierung des Leidens." *Phase* 2 (9). http://docupedia.de/zg/Literatur:Diner_Anthropologisierung_des_Leidens_2003.

Donzelot, Jacques. 1979. *The Policing of Families*. New York: Pantheon Books.

Dragojlovic, Ana. 2014. "The Search for Sensuous Geographies of Absence." *Bijdragen Tot de Taal-, Land- En Volkenkunde* 170 (4): 473–503.

Drost, Nicola, and Ulrich Lamparter. 2013. "Das Tableau diagnostischer Urteile. Ein qualitativ-quantitative Auswertung der Zeitzeugeninterviews."

In *Zeitzeugen des Hamburger Feuersturms 1943 und ihre Familien: Forschungsprojekt zur Weitergabe von Kriegserfahrungen*, edited by Ulrich Lamparter, Silke Wiegand-Grefe, and Dorothee Wierling, 167–92. Göttingen: Vandenhoeck & Ruprecht.

Edelman, Lucila, Diana Kordon, and Dario Lagos. 1998. "Transmission of Trauma: The Argentine Case." In *International Handbook of Multigenerational Legacies of Trauma*, edited by Yael Danieli, 447–63. New York: Plenum.

Eichhorn, Svenja, and Philipp Kuwert. 2011. *Das Geheimnis unserer Großmütter: Eine empirische Studie über sexualisierte Kriegsgewalt um 1945*. Gießen: Psychosozial.

Ermann, Michael. 2007. "Kriegskinder im Forschungsinterview." *Zeitschrift für Individualpsychologie* 32, no. 4 (December): 304–11.

European Commission. 2013. "Mental Health Systems in the European Union Member States, Status of Mental Health in Populations and Benefits to Be Expected from Investments into Mental Health: European Profile of Prevention and Promotion of Mental Health (EuroPoPP-MH)." European Commission. http://ec.europa.eu/health/mental_health/docs/europopp_full_en.pdf.

Färberböck, Max. 2008. *Anonyma—eine Frau in Berlin*. Movie. München: Constantin Film.

Fass, Paula S. 2016. *The End of American Childhood: A History of Parenting from Life on the Frontier to the Managed Child*. Princeton, NJ: Princeton University Press.

Fassin, Didier, and Richard Rechtman. 2009. *The Empire of Trauma: An Inquiry into the Condition of Victimhood*. Princeton, NJ: Princeton University Press.

Felsen, Irit. 1998. "Transgenerational Transmission of Effects of the Holocaust: The North American Research Perspective." In *International Handbook of Multigenerational Legacies of Trauma*, edited by Yael Danieli, 43–68. New York: Plenum.

Ferrari, Alize J., Fiona J. Charlson, Rosana E. Norman, Scott B. Patten, Greg Freedman, Christopher J. L. Murray, Theo Vos, and Harvey A. Whiteford. 2013. "Burden of Depressive Disorders by Country, Sex, Age, and Year: Findings from the Global Burden of Disease Study 2010." *PLoS Medicine* 10, no. 11 (November).

Feuchtwang, Stephan. 2009. "The Transmission of Traumatic Loss: A Case Study in Taiwan." In *Remembering Violence: Anthropological Perspectives on Intergenerational Transmission*, edited by Nicolas Argenti and Katharina Schramm, 229–50. New York: Berghahn Books.

———. 2011. *After the Event: The Transmission of Grievous Loss in Germany, China and Taiwan*. New York: Berghahn Books.

Fischer, C. J., J. Struwe, and M. R. Lemke. 2006. "Langfristige Auswirkungen traumatischer Ereignisse auf somatische und psychische Beschwerden: Am Beispiel von Vertriebenen nach dem 2. Weltkrieg." *Nervenarzt* 77: 58–63.

Fischer, Torben, and Matthias N. Lorenz. 2007. *Lexikon der "Vergangenheitsbewältigung" in Deutschland. Debatten—und Diskursgeschichte des Nationalsozialismus nach 1945*. Bielefeld: Transcript.

Förster, Alice, and Birgit Beck. 2003. *Post-Traumatic Stress Disorder and World War II. Life after Death: Approaches to a Cultural and Social History of Europe during the 1940s and 1950s*. New York: Cambridge University Press.

Foucault, Michel. 1995. *Discipline and Punish: The Birth of the Prison*. New York: Vintage Books.

Fowles, Severin. 2010. Introduction to *An Anthropology of Absence: Materializations of Transcendence and Loss*, edited by Mikkel Bille, Frida Hastrup, and Tim Flohr Sørensen, 23–41. New York: Springer.

Freemann, Mark. 2010. "Telling Stories: Memory and Narrative." In *Memory: Histories, Theories, Debates*, edited by Susannah Radstone and Bill Schwarz, 263–77. New York: Fordham University Press.

Friedrich, Jörg. 2002. *Der Brand. Deutschland im Bombenkrieg 1940–1945*. Berlin: Propyläen.

Fuery, Patrick. 1995. *The Theory of Absence: Subjectivity, Signification, and Desire*. Westport, CT: Greenwood.

Furedi, Frank. 2004. *Therapy Culture: Cultivating Vulnerability in an Uncertain Age*. London: Routledge.

Gaines, Atwood D. 1992. "From DSM-I to III-R; Voices of Self, Mastery and the Other: A Cultural Constructivist Reading of U.S. Psychiatric Classification." In "The Cultural Construction of Diagnostic Categories: The Case of American Psychiatry," special issue, *Social Science & Medicine* 35, no. 1 (July): 3–24.

Giordano, Ralph. 1987. *Die zweite Schuld: Oder on der Last ein Deutscher zu sein*. Hamburg: Rasch & Röhring.

Glaesmer, Heide, Elmar Brähler, Steffi G. Riedel-Heller, Harald J. Freyberger, and Philipp Kuwert. 2011. "The Association of Traumatic Experiences and Posttraumatic Stress Disorder with Health Care Utilization in the Elderly: A German Population Based Study." *General Hospital Psychiatry* 33, no. 2 (March–April): 177–84.

Glaesmer, Heide, Thomas Gunzelmann, Elmar Brähler, Simon Forstmeier, and Andreas Maercker. 2010. "Traumatic Experiences and Post-Traumatic Stress Disorder among Elderly Germans: Results of a Representative Population–Based Survey." *International Psychogeriatrics* 22, no. 4 (June): 661–70.

Goldhagen, Daniel Jonah. 1996. *Hitler's Willing Executioners: Ordinary Germans and the Holocaust*. New York: Alfred A. Knopf.

Goldstein, Diane. 2004. "Emerging Illnesses and the Internet." In *Emerging Illnesses and Society: Negotiating the Public Health Agenda*, edited by Randall M. Packard, Ruth L. Berkelman, Howard Frumkin, and Peter J. Brown, 121–38. Baltimore: Johns Hopkins University Press.

Goltermann, Svenja. 2010. "On Silence, Madness, and Lassitude: Negotiating the Past in Post-War West Germany." In *Shadows of War: A Social History of Silence in the Twentieth Century*, edited by Efrat Ben-Ze'ev, Ruth Ginio, and Jay Winter, 91–112. Cambridge: Cambridge University Press.

———. 2017. *Opfer die Wahrnehmung von Krieg und Gewalt in der Moderne*. Frankfurt am Main: S. Fischer.

Grass, Günter. 2002. *Im Krebsgang. Eine Novelle*. Göttingen: Steidl.

Grundmann, Matthias, Dieter Hoffmeister, and Sebastian Knoth. 2009. *Kriegskinder in Deutschland zwischen Trauma und Normalität: Botschaften einer beschädigten Generation*. Berlin: LIT.

Haarer, Johanna. 1934. *Die deutsche Mutter und ihr erstes Kind*. München: Lehmanns.

Hacking, Ian. 1995. *Rewriting the Soul: Multiple Personality and the Sciences of Memory*. Princeton, NJ: Princeton University Press.

Hamburger Institut für Sozialforschung, ed. 2002. *Verbrechen der Wehrmacht. Dimensionen des Vernichtungskrieges 1941–1944*. Ausstellungskatalog. 2nd ed. Hamburg: Hamburger.

Harding, Thomas. 2014. *Hanns and Rudolf: The True Story of the German Jew Who Tracked Down and Caught the Kommandant of Auschwitz*. Reprint. New York: Simon & Schuster.

Heer, Hannes, and Stiftung Hamburger Institut für Sozialforschung, eds. 1997. *Vernichtungskrieg. Verbrechen der Wehrmacht 1941 bis 1944 Ausstellungskatalog*; Katalog zur Ausstellung "Vernichtungskrieg. Verbrechen der Wehrmacht 1941 bis 1944." Hamburg: Hamburger Edition.

Heimannsberg, Barbara, and Christoph J. Schmidt. 1992. *Das Kollektive Schweigen: Nationalsozialistische Vergangenheit und gebrochene Identität in der Psychotherapie*. 2nd ed. Köln: Humanistische Psychologie.

Herf, Jeffrey. 1997. *Divided Memory: The Nazi Past in the Two Germanys*. Cambridge, MA: Harvard University Press.

Hetherington, Kevin. 2004. "Secondhandedness: Consumption, Disposal, and Absent Presence." *Environment and Planning D: Society and Space* 22, no. 1 (February): 157–73.

Hettwer, Hubert. 1976. *Das Bildungswesen in der DDR: Strukturelle und inhaltliche Entwicklung seit 1945*. Köln: Kiepenheuer & Witsch.

Hilbk, Merle. 2013. "Das schönste Dorf am schönsten Fluss der Erde." *die tageszeitung (TAZ)*, April 6.

Hildebrandt, Tina, and Giovanni Di Lorenzo. 2012. "Joachim Gauck: 'Meine Seele hat Narben.'" *Die Zeit*, May 31, sec. Deutschland.

Hirsch, Marianne. 1996. "Past Lives: Postmemories in Exile." *Poetics Today* 17, no. 4 (Winter): 659–86.

———. 2001. "Surviving Images: Holocaust Photographs and the Work of Postmemory." *Yale Journal of Criticism* 14, no. 1 (Spring): 5–37.

———. 2008. "The Generation of Postmemory." *Poetics Today* 29, no. 1 (Spring): 103.

Hirsch, Marianne, and Leo Spitzer. 2006. "Testimonial Objects: Memory, Gender, and Transmission." *Poetics Today* 27, no. 2 (Summer): 353–83.

Holstein, Christa, and Ulrich Lamparter. 2013. "Die Zweite Generation: Die Kinder der Zeitzeugen." In *Zeitzeugen des Hamburger Feuersturms 1943 und ihre Familien: Forschungsprojekt zur Weitergabe von Kriegserfahrungen*, edited by Ulrich Lamparter, Silke Wiegand-Grefe, and Dorothee Wierling, 231–55. Göttingen: Vandenhoeck & Ruprecht.

Hondrich, C. 2011. *Vererbte Wunden: Traumata des Zweiten Weltkriegs-die Folgen für Familie, Gesellschaft und Kultur.* Lenderich: Pabst Science.

Horwitz, Allan V. 2003. *Creating Mental Illness.* Chicago: University of Chicago Press.

Höß, Rainer. 2013. *Das Erbe des Kommandanten.* München: Belleville.

Huang, Hsuan-Ying. 2014. "The Emergence of the Psycho-Boom in Contemporary Urban China." In *Psychiatry and Chinese History*, edited by Howard Chiang, 183–204. London: Pickering & Chatto.

Hunter-King, Edna J. 1998. "Children of Military Personnel Missing in Action in Southeast Asia." In *International Handbook of Multigenerational Legacies of Trauma*, edited by Yael Danieli, 243–56. New York: Plenum.

Hurley, Dan. 2013. "Grandma's Experiences Leave Epigenetic Mark on Your Genes." *Discover Magazine*, June 11. http://discovermagazine.com/2013/may/13-grandmas-experiences-leave-epigenetic-mark-on-your-genes.

Illouz, Eva. 2008. *Saving the Modern Soul: Therapy, Emotions, and the Culture of Self-Help.* Berkeley: University of California Press.

Irvine, Leslie. 1999. *Codependent Forevermore: The Invention of Self in a Twelve Step Group.* Chicago: University of Chicago Press.

Jablinski, Anke. 2012. *Klettermax: Der Roman einer Aufwärtsbewegung.* Frankfurt: Dielmann.

Janus, Ludwig, ed. 2006. *Geboren im Krieg: Kindheitserfahrungen im 2. Weltkrieg und ihre Auswirkungen.* Gießen: Psychosozial.

Jerouschek, Günter. 2004. "Vertreibungsschicksale in Psychoanalysen." In *Kindheiten im II. Weltkrieg und ihre Folgen*, edited by Hartmut Radebold, 91–99. Psyche und Gesellschaft. Reinbek bei Hamburg: Psychosozial.

Josselson, Ruthellen. 1995. "Imagining the Real: Empathy, Narrative, and the Dialogical Self." In *The Narrative Study of Lives*, edited by Ruthellen Josselson and Amia Lieblich, 3: 27–44. Newbury Park, CA: SAGE.

Jureit, Ulrike, and Christian Schneider. 2010. *Gefühlte Opfer: Illusionen der Vergangenheitsbewältigung*. Stuttgart: Klett-Cotta.

Kaes, Anton. 1989. *From Hitler to Heimat: The Return of History as Film*. Cambridge, MA: Harvard University Press.

Kanon, Joseph. 2005. "'A Woman in Berlin': My City of Ruins." *New York Times*, August 14, 2005. http://www.nytimes.com/2005/08/14/books/review/14KANONL.html.

Kellermann, Natan P. F. 2001a. "Perceived Parental Rearing Behavior in Children of Holocaust Survivors." *Israel Journal of Psychiatry and Related Sciences* 38, no. 1 (February): 58–68.

———. 2001b. "Transmission of Holocaust Trauma: An Integrative View." *Psychiatry Interpersonal & Biological Processes* 64, no. 3 (February): 256–67.

———. 2008. "Transmitted Holocaust Trauma: Curse or Legacy? The Aggravating and Mitigating Factors of Holocaust Transmission." *Israel Journal of Psychiatry and Related Sciences* 45, no. 4 (February): 263–70.

Keppler, Angela. 1994. *Tischgespräche: Über Formen kommunikativer Vergemeinschaftung am Beispiel der Konversation in Familien*. Frankfurt am Main: Suhrkamp.

Keseling, Uta. 2013. "Wie der Zweite Weltkrieg die Enkelgeneration beeinflusst." *Berliner Morgenpost*, March 19.

Kidron, Carol A. 2003. "Surviving a Distant Past: A Case Study of the Cultural Construction of Trauma Descendant Identity." *Ethos* 31, no. 4 (December): 513–44.

———. 2009a. "Silent Legacies of Trauma: A Comparative Study of Cambodian Canadian and Israeli Holocaust Trauma Descendant Memory Work." In *Remembering Violence: Anthropological Perspectives on Intergenerational Transmission*, edited by Nicolas Argenti and Katharina Schramm, 193–228. New York: Berghahn Books.

———. 2009b. "Toward an Ethnography of Silence: The Lived Presence of the Past in the Everyday Life of Holocaust Trauma Survivors and Their Descendants in Israel." *Current Anthropology* 50, no. 1 (February): 5–19.

———. 2010. "Silent Legacies of Trauma: A Comparative Study of Cambodian Canadian and Israeli Holocaust Trauma Descendent Memory Work." In *Remembering Violence: Anthropological Perspectives on Intergenerational Transmission*, edited by Nicolas Argenti and Katharina Schramm, 193–228. New York: Berghahn Books.

———. 2012. "Alterity and the Particular Limits of Universalism: Comparing Jewish-Israeli Holocaust and Canadian-Cambodian Genocide Legacies." *Current Anthropology* 53, no. 6 (December): 723–54.

———. 2013. "Being There Together: Dark Family Tourism and the Emotive Experiences of Co-Presence in the Holocaust Past." *Annals of Tourism Research* 41.

Kinzie, J. David, J. Boehnlein, and William H. Sack. 1998. "The Effects of Massive Trauma on Cambodian Parents and Children." In *International Handbook of Multigenerational Legacies of Trauma*, edited by Yael Danieli, 211–21. New York: Plenum.

Kitano, Harry H. L. 1985. "The Effects of the Evacuation on Japanese Americans." In *Japanese Americans: From Relocation to Redress*, edited by Roger Daniels, Sandra C. Taylor, and Harry H. L. Kitano, 151–58. Seattle: University of Washington Press.

Klungel, Janine. 2009. "Rape and Remembrance in Guadeloupe." In *Remembering Violence: Anthropological Perspectives on Intergenerational Transmission*, edited by Nicolas Argenti and Katharina Schramm, 43–62. New York: Berghahn Books.

Knoch, Heike, and Winfried Kurth. 2012. "Kriegsenkel—Ein spätes Erwachen? Die Kinder der Kriegskinder aus der Sicht der Psychohistorie." In *Die Kinder der Kriegskinder und die späten Folgen des NS-Terrors*, edited by Heike Knoch, Winfried Kurth, Heinrich J. Reiß, and Götz Egloff 13: 39–55. Jahrbuch für psychohistorische Forschung. Heidelberg: Mattes.

Knoch, Heike, Winfried Kurth, Heinrich J. Reiß, and Götz Egloff, eds. 2012. *Die Kinder der Kriegskinder und die späten Folgen des NS-Terrors*. Jahrbuch für psychohistorische Forschung 13. Heidelberg: Mattes.

Koski, Jessica Powers. 2014. "'I'm Just a Walking Eating Disorder': The Mobilisation and Construction of a Collective Illness Identity in Eating Disorder Support Groups." *Sociology of Health & Illness* 36 (1): 75–90.

Kupelian, Diane, Annie Sanentz Kalayjian, and Alice Kassabian. 1998. "The Turkish Genocide of the Armenians: Continuing Effects on Survivors and Their Families Eight Decades after Massive Trauma." In *International Handbook of Multigenerational Legacies of Trauma*, edited by Yael Danieli, 191–209. New York: Plenum.

Kutchins, Herb, and Stuart A. Kirk. 1997. *Making Us Crazy: DSM: The Psychiatric Bible and the Creation of Mental Disorders*. New York: Free Press.

Kuwert, Philipp, Elmar Brähler, Heike Glaesmer, Harald Freyberger, and Ottmar Decker. 2009. "Impact of Forced Displacement during World War II on the Present-Day Mental Health of the Elderly: A Population-Based Study." *International Psychogeriatrics / IPA* 21, no. 4 (August): 748–53.

Kuwert, Philipp, and Harald Freyberger. 2007. "The Unspoken Secret: Sexual Violence in World War II." *International Psychogeriatrics / IPA* 19, no. 4 (August): 782–84.

Kuwert, Philipp, Thomas Klauer, and Svenja Eichhorn. 2010. "Trauma and Current Posttraumatic Stress Symptoms in Elderly German Women Who Experienced Wartime Rapes in 1945." *Journal of Nervous and Mental Disease* 198, no. 6 (June): 450–51.

Kuwert, Philipp, Carsten Spitzer, Anna Träder, Harald Freyberger, and Michael Ermann. 2007. "Sixty Years Later: Post-Traumatic Stress Symptoms and Current Psychopathology in Former German Children of World War II." *International Psychogeriatrics / IPA* 19, no. 5 (October): 955–61.

LaCapra, Dominick. 2000. *Writing History, Writing Trauma*. Baltimore: Johns Hopkins University Press.

Lamparter, Ulrich. 2013. "Aufbau und Struktur des Forschungsprojekts." In *Zeitzeugen des Hamburger Feuersturms 1943 und ihre Familien: Forschungsprojekt zur Weitergabe von Kriegserfahrungen*, edited by Ulrich Lamparter, Silke Wiegand-Grefe, and Dorothee Wierling. Göttingen: Vandenhoeck & Ruprecht.

Lamparter, Ulrich, Valeska Buder, Veronique Sydow, Stefan Nickel, and Silke Wiegand-Grefe. 2013. "Psychometrische Befunde in der Generation der Zeitzeugen." In *Zeitzeugen des Hamburger Feuersturms 1943 und ihre Familien: Forschungsprojekt zur Weitergabe von Kriegserfahrungen*, edited by Ulrich Lamparter, Silke Wiegand-Grefe, and Dorothee Wierling, 124–46. Göttingen: Vandenhoeck & Ruprecht.

Lamparter, Ulrich, and Christa Holstein. 2013. "Was ist gefolgt? Erste Ergebnisse zur Transmission der Erfahrung des 'Hamburger Feuersturms' (1943) zwischen der ersten und der zweiten Generation." In *Zeitzeugen des Hamburger Feuersturms 1943 und ihre Familien: Forschungsprojekt zur Weitergabe von Kriegserfahrungen*, edited by Ulrich Lamparter, Silke Wiegand-Grefe, and Dorothee Wierling, 274–94. Göttingen: Vandenhoeck & Ruprecht.

Lasch, Christopher. 1991. *The Culture of Narcissism: American Life in an Age of Diminishing Expectations*. New York: W. W. Norton.

Law, John. 2004. *After Method: Mess in Social Science Research*. New York: Routledge.

Lebovic, Matt. 2012. "When Family Ties Lead Straight to Hitler." *Times of Israel*, November 16, 2012. http://www.timesofisrael.com/when-family-ties-lead-straight-to-hitler/.

Lemke, Thomas, Monica J. Casper, and Lisa Jean Moore. 2011. *Biopolitics: An Advanced Introduction*. New York: New York University Press.

Lifton, Robert Jay. 1973. *Home from the War: Vietnam Veterans: Neither Victims nor Executioners*. New York: Simon & Schuster.

Lindt, Martijn W. J. 1998. "Children of Collaborators: From Isolation toward Integration." In *International Handbook of Multigenerational Legacies of Trauma*, edited by Yael Danieli, 163–74. New York: Plenum.

Livingston, Kathy. 2010. "Opportunities for Mourning When Grief Is Disenfranchised: Descendants of Nazi Perpetrators in Dialogue with Holocaust Survivors." *OMEGA: Journal of Death and Dying* 61, no. 3 (November): 205–22.

Lohre, Matthias. 2016. *Das Erbe der Kriegsenkel: Was das Schweigen der Eltern mit uns macht.* Gütersloh: Gütersloher.

Ludin, Malte. 2005. *2 oder 3 Dinge, die ich von ihm weiß: Die Gegenwart der Vergangenheit in einer deutschen Familie* [2 or 3 things I know about him]. TV documentary. Berlin: Absolut Medien.

Maercker, Andreas, Simon Forstmeier, Bettina Wagner, Heide Glaesmer, and Elmar Brähler. 2008. "Posttraumatische Belastungsstörungen in Deutschland." *Der Nervenarzt* 79, no. 5 (May): 577–86.

Mannheim, Karl. 1928. "Das Problem Der Generationen." *Kölner Vierteljahreshefte zur Soziologie* 7: 157–85, 309–30.

Marschall, Sabine. 2015. "'Homesick Tourism': Memory, Identity and (Be)Longing." *Current Issues in Tourism* 18 (9): 876–92.

Martin, Emily. 2009. *Bipolar Expeditions: Mania and Depression in American Culture.* Princeton, NJ: Princeton University Press.

Maynes, Mary Jo, Jennifer L. Pierce, and Barbara Laslett. 2008. *Telling Stories: The Use of Personal Narratives in the Social Sciences and History.* Ithaca, NY: Cornell University Press.

McLeod, Julie, and Katie Wright. 2009. "The Talking Cure in Everyday Life: Gender, Generations and Friendship." *Sociology* 43, no. 1 (February): 122–39.

Merridale, Catherine. 1996. "Death and Memory in Modern Russia." *History Workshop Journal* 42, no. 1 (Autumn): 1–18.

———. 1999. "War, Death and Remembrance in Soviet Russia." In *War and Remembrance in the Twentieth Century,* edited by J. M. Winter and Emmanuel Sivan, 61–83. Cambridge: Cambridge University Press.

———. 2010. "Soviet Memories: Patriotism and Trauma." In *Memory: Histories, Theories, Debates,* edited by Susannah Radstone and Bill Schwarz, 376–89. New York: Fordham University Press.

Messerschmidt, James W. 2006. "Review Symposium: The Forgotten Victims of World War II Masculinities and Rape in Berlin, 1945." *Violence against Women* 12, no. 7 (July): 706–12.

Meyer, Morgan. 2012. "Placing and Tracing Absence: A Material Culture of the Immaterial." *Journal of Material Culture* 17 (1): 103–10.

Meyer, Morgan, and Kate Woodthorpe. 2008. "The Material Presence of Absence: A Dialogue between Museums and Cemeteries." *Sociological Research Online* 13 (5): 127–35. http://www.socresonline.org.uk/13/5/1.html.

Meyer-Legrand, Ingrid. 2016. *Die Kraft der Kriegsenkel: Wie Kriegsenkel heute ihr biografisches Erbe erkennen und nutzen.* Berlin: Europa.

Miller, Alice. 1979. *The Drama of the Gifted Child: The Search for the True Self.* New York: Basic Books.

Moeller, Robert G. 1996. "War Stories: The Search for a Usable Past in the Federal Republic of Germany." *American Historical Review* 101, no. 4 (October): 1008–48.

———. 2005. "Germans as Victims?: Thoughts on a Post–Cold War History of World War II's Legacies." In "Histories and Memories of Twentieth-Century Germany," special issue, *History and Memory* 17, no. 1–2 (Spring–Winter): 147–94.

———. 2006. "Victims in Uniform: West German Combat Movies from the 1950s." In *Germans as Victims: Remembering the Past in Contemporary Germany,* edited by B. Niven, 43–61. New York: Palgrave Macmillan.

Möller, Birgit, and Ulrich Lamparter. 2013. "Erlebnis und Verarbeitung des 'Feuersturms' im Lebenslauf. Ein typologischer Ansatz." In *Zeitzeugen des Hamburger Feuersturms 1943 und ihre Familien: Forschungsprojekt zur Weitergabe von Kriegserfahrungen,* edited by Ulrich Lamparter, Silke Wiegand-Grefe, and Dorothee Wierling, 67–103. Göttingen: Vandenhoeck & Ruprecht.

Moller, Sabine. 2003. *Vielfache Vergangenheit. Öffentliche Erinnerungskulturen und Familienerinnerungen an die NS-Zeit in Ostdeutschland. Studien zum Nationalsozialismus in der edition diskord 8.* Tübingen: diskord.

Morley, David, and Kevin Robins. 1996. "No Place like Heimat: Images of Home(Land) in European Culture." In *Becoming National: A Reader,* edited by Geoff Eley and Ronald Grigor Suny, 456–78. New York: Oxford University Press.

Moses, A. Dirk. 2007. "The Non-German German and the German German: Dilemmas of Identity after the Holocaust." *New German Critique* 34, no. 2 (Summer): 45–94.

Moskowitz, Eva S. 2001. *In Therapy We Trust: America's Obsession with Self-Fulfillment.* Baltimore: Johns Hopkins University Press.

Müller, Meike. 2013. "Das seelische Erbe des Krieges." *Weser Kurier,* February 2. https://www.weser-kurier.de/bremen/stadtteile/stadtteile-bremen-mitte_artikel,-Das-seelische-Erbe-des-Krieges-_arid,493635.html.

Müller-Hohagen, Jürgen. 2005. *Verleugnet, verdrängt, verschwiegen: Seelische Nachwirkungen der NS-Zeit und Wege zu ihrer Überwindung.* München: Kösel.

Münyas, Burcu. 2008. "Genocide in the Minds of Cambodian Youth: Transmitting (Hi)Stories of Genocide to Second and Third Generations in Cambodia." *Journal of Genocide Research* 10 (3): 413–39.

Nagata, Donna K. 1998. "Intergenerational Effects of the Japanese American Internment." In *International Handbook of Multigenerational Legacies of Trauma,* edited by Yael Danieli, 125–39. New York: Plenum.

Naimark, Norman M. 2010. "The Persistence of the 'Postwar.'" In *Histories of the Aftermath: The Legacies of the Second World War in Europe,* edited by Frank Biess and Robert G. Moeller, 13–29. New York: Berghahn Books.

Navaro-Yashin, Yael. 2009. "Affective Spaces, Melancholic Objects: Ruination and the Production of Anthropological Knowledge." *Journal of the Royal Anthropological Institute* 15: 1–18.

Niederland, William G. 1968. "Clinical Observations on the 'Survivor Syndrome.'" *International Journal of Psycho-Analysis* 49: 313–15.

Niven, Bill, ed. 2006a. *Germans as Victims: Remembering the Past in Contemporary Germany*. New York: Palgrave Macmillan.

———. 2006b. "Introduction: German Victimhood at the Turn of the Millennium." In *Germans as Victims: Remembering the Past in Contemporary Germany*, edited by Bill Niven, 1–25. New York: Palgrave Macmillan.

Novick, Peter. 1999. *The Holocaust and Collective Memory: The American Experience*. London: Bloomsbury.

Nowak, Jessica. 2012. "Wie entstand die Redewendung einen Persilschein ausstellen?" *Hamburger Abendblatt*, March 9, sec. Wissen. https://www.abendblatt.de/ratgeber/wissen/article107754913/Wie-entstand-die-Redewendung-einen-Persilschein-ausstellen.html.

Op den Velde, Wybrand. 1998. "Children of Dutch War Sailors and Civilian Resistance Veterans." In *International Handbook of Multigenerational Legacies of Trauma*, edited by Yael Danieli, 147–61. New York: Plenum.

Orback, Jens. 2015. *Schatten auf meiner Seele: Ein Kriegsenkel entdeckt die Geschichte seiner Familie*. Translated by Regine Elsässer. 2nd ed. Freiburg: Herder.

Peikert, Gregor, Jürgen Hoyer, Andrea Mrazek, Wolfram Rosendahl, Hans-Joachim Hannich, and Frank Jacobi. 2011. "Ambulante Psychotherapeutische Versorgung in Ostdeutschland." *Psychotherapeutenjournal* 1: 43–50.

Peuckert, Rüdiger. 2002. *Familienformen im sozialen Wandel*. 4th ed. Leverkusen: Leske & Budrich.

Plamper, Jan. 2015. "Erinnerung an Den Zweiten Weltkrieg: Die Deutschen als Opfer." *Neue Zürcher Zeitung*. Accessed January 9, 2019. http://www.nzz.ch/meinung/debatte/die-deutschen-als-opfer-1.18557580.

Pott, Hans-Georg. 1986. "Der 'neue Heimatroman'? Zum Konzept der 'Heimat' in der neueren Literatur." In *Literatur und Provinz: Das Konzept "Heimat" in der neueren Literatur*, edited by Hans-Georg Pott, 7–21. Paderborn: F. Schöningh.

Radebold, Hartmut. 2000. *Abwesende Väter: Folgen der Kriegskindheit in Psychoanalysen*. Göttingen: Vandenhoeck & Ruprecht.

———. ed. 2004. *Kindheiten im II. Weltkrieg und ihre Folgen. Psyche und Gesellschaft*. Reinbek near Hamburg: Psychosozial.

———. 2005. *Die dunklen Schatten unserer Vergangenheit: Ältere Menschen in Beratung, Psychotherapie, Seelsorge und Pflege. Konzepte der Humanwissenschaften*. Stuttgart: Klett-Cotta.

———. 2008. "Kriegsbedingte Kindheiten und Jugendzeit, Teil 1: Zeitgeschichtliche Erfahrungen, Folgen und trangenerationale Auswirkungen." In *Transgenerationale Weitergabe kriegsbelasteter Kindheiten:*

Interdisziplinäre Studien zur Nachhaltigkeit historischer Erfahrungen über vier Generationen, edited by Hartmut Radebold, Werner Bohleber, and Jürgen Zinnecker, 45–55. Weinheim: Juventa.

———. 2012. Interview with Andrea Frey, unpublished interview transcript.

Radebold, Hartmut, Werner Bohleber, and Jürgen Zinnecker. 2008. *Transgenerationale Weitergabe kriegsbelasteter Kindheiten: Interdisziplinäre Studien zur Nachhaltigkeit historischer Erfahrungen über vier Generationen*. 2nd ed. Kinder des Weltkrieges. Weinheim: Juventa.

Radstone, Susannah. 2005. "Reconceiving Binaries: The Limits of Memory." *History Workshop Journal* 59, no. 1 (Spring): 134–50.

Raphael, Beverley, Pat Swan, and Nada Martinek. 1998. "Intergenerational Aspects of Trauma for Australian Aboriginal People." In *International Handbook of Multigenerational Legacies of Trauma*, edited by Yael Danieli, 327–39. New York: Plenum.

Reddemann, Luise. 2015. *Kriegskinder und Kriegsenkel in der Psychotherapie: Folgen der NS-Zeit und des Zweiten Weltkriegs erkennen und bearbeiten-Eine Annäherung*. 2nd ed. Stuttgart: Klett-Cotta.

Reulecke, Jürgen, and Barbara Strambolis. 2008. "Kindheiten und Jugendzeit im Zweiten Weltkrieg. Erfahrungen und Normen der Elterngeneration und ihre Weitergabe." In *Transgenerationale Weitergabe kriegsbelasteter Kindheiten: Interdisziplinäre Studien zur Nachhaltigkeit historischer Erfahrungen über vier Generationen*, 2nd ed., edited by Hartmut Radebold, Werner Bohleber, and Jürgen Zinnecker, 13–31. Kinder des Weltkrieges. Weinheim: Juventa.

Rieff, Philip. 1966. *The Triumph of the Therapeutic: Uses of Faith after Freud*. Chicago: University of Chicago Press.

Roberts, Ulla. 1998. *Spuren der NS-Zeit im Leben der Kinder und Enkel: Drei Generationen im Gespräch*. München: Kösel.

Rose, Nikolas. 1990. *Governing the Soul: The Shaping of the Private Self*. London: Routledge.

———. 1997. "Assembling the Modern Self." In *Rewriting the Self: Histories from the Renaissance to the Present*, edited by R. Porter. London: Routledge.

———. 1998. *Inventing Our Selves: Psychology, Power, and Personhood*. Cambridge: Cambridge University Press.

Rosenheck, Robert, and Alan Fontana. 1994. "Posttraumatic Stress Disorder among Vietnam Theater Veterans: A Causal Model of Etiology in a Community Sample." *Journal of Nervous and Mental Disease* 182, no. 12 (December): 677–84.

Rosenheck, Robert, and Pramila Nathan. 1985. "Secondary Traumatization in the Children of Vietnam Veterans with Post-Traumatic Stress Disorder." *Hospital and Community Psychiatry* 36: 538–39.

Rosenthal, Gabriele. 1998. *The Holocaust in Three Generations: Families of Victims and Perpetrators of the Nazi Regime*. London: Cassell.

Rothberg, Michael. 2009. *Multidirectional Memory: Remembering the Holocaust in the Age of Decolonization*. Stanford, CA: Stanford University Press.

Rousseau, Cecile, and Aline Drapeau. 1998. "The Impact of Culture of the Transmission of Trauma: Refugees' Stories and Silence Embodied in Their Children's Lives." In *International Handbook of Multigenerational Legacies of Trauma*, edited by Yael Danieli, 465–86. New York: Plenum.

Sagi-Schwartz, Abraham, Marinus H. van IJzendoorn, Klaus E. Grossmann, Tirtsa Joels, Karin Grossmann, Miri Scharf, Nina Koren-Karie, and Sarit Alkalay. 2003. "Attachment and Traumatic Stress in Female Holocaust Child Survivors and Their Daughters." *American Journal of Psychiatry* 160, no. 6 (June): 1086–92.

Sander, Helke, and Barbara Johr. 2008. *BeFreier und Befreite: Krieg, Vergewaltigung, Kinder*, 3rd ed. Frankfurt am Main: Fischer Taschenbuch.

Schneider, Michael, and Joachim Süss, eds. 2015. *Nebelkinder: Kriegsenkel treten aus dem Traumaschatten der Geschichte*. München: Europa.

Schneider, Norbert. 1994. *Familie und private Lebensführung in West- und Ostdeutschland: Eine vergleichende Analyse des Familienlebens, 1970–1992*. Stuttgart: F. Enke.

Schwab, Gabriele. 2010. *Haunting Legacies: Violent Histories and Transgenerational Trauma*. New York: Columbia University Press.

Sebald, Winfried G. 2001. *Luftkrieg und Literatur*. Frankfurt am Main: Fischer Taschenbuch.

Seegers, Lu, and Jürgen Reulecke. 2009. *Die "Generation der Kriegskinder." Historische Hintergründe und Deutungen. Psyche und Gesellschaft*. Giessen: Psychosozial.

Seidler, Christoph, and Michael Froese. 2009. *Traumatisierungen in (Ost-) Deutschland*. Gießen: Psychosozial.

Senfft, Alexandra. 2008. *Schweigen tut weh: Eine deutsche Familiengeschichte*. Berlin: List Taschenbuch.

———. 2015. "Lasten der Vergangenheit—Chancen für die Zukunft." In *Nebelkinder: Kriegsenkel treten aus dem Traumaschatten der Geschichte*, edited by Michael Schneider and Joachim Süss, 108–25. München: Europa.

———. 2016. *Der lange Schatten der Täter: Nachkommen stellen sich ihrer NS-Familiengeschichte*. München: Piper.

Sichrovsky, Peter. 1987. *Schuldig geboren: Kinder aus Nazifamilien*. Köln: Kiepenheuer & Witsch.

Solomon, Zahava. 1998. "Transgenerational Effects of the Holocaust: The Israeli Research Perspective." In *International Handbook of Multigenerational Legacies of Trauma*, edited by Yael Danieli, 69–95. New York: Plenum.

Sommers, Christina Hoff, and Sally Satel. 2005. *One Nation under Therapy: How the Helping Culture Is Eroding Self-Reliance*. New York: St. Martin's Press.

Sørensen, Tim Flohr. 2010. "A Saturated Void: Anticipating and Preparing Presence in Contemporary Danish Cemetery Culture." In *An Anthropology of Absence: Materializations of Transcendence and Loss*, edited by Mikkel Bille, Frida Hastrup, and Tim Flohr Sørensen, 115–30. New York: Springer.

Spitzer, Carsten, S. Barnow, H. Volzke, and U. John. 2008. "Trauma and Posttraumatic Stress Disorder in the Elderly: Findings from a German Community Study." *Journal of Clinical Psychiatry* 69, no. 5 (May): 693–700.

Spock, Benjamin. 1946. *The Common Sense Book of Baby and Child Care*. New York: Duell, Sloan and Pearce.

Stein, Arlene. 2009. "Feminism, Therapeutic Culture, and the Holocaust in the United States: The Second-Generation Phenomenon." *Jewish Social Studies* 16, no. 1 (Fall): 27–53, 145.

Summerfield, Derek. 1996. "The Psychological Legacy of War and Atrocity: The Question of Long-Term and Transgenerational Effects and the Need for a Broad View." *Journal of Nervous and Mental Disease* 184, no. 6 (June): 375–76.

Süss, Joachim. 2015. "Wir Nebelkinder." In *Nebelkinder: Kriegsenkel treten aus dem Traumaschatten der Geschichte*, edited by Michael Schneider and Joachim Süss, 20–41. München: Europa.

———. 2017. *Die entschlossene Generation*. Berlin: Europa.

Swoboda, Debra A. 2006. "The Social Construction of Contested Illness Legitimacy: A Grounded Theory Analysis." *Qualitative Research in Psychology* 3, no. 3 (July): 233–51.

Szasz, Thomas. 2007. *The Medicalization of Everyday Life: Selected Essays*. Syracuse, NY: Syracuse University Press.

Tatara, Mikhachiro. 1998. "The Second Generation of Hibakusha, Atomic Bomb Survivors: A Psychologist's View." In *International Handbook of Multigenerational Legacies of Trauma*, edited by Yael Danieli, 141–46. New York: Plenum.

Teegen, F., and V. Meister. 2000. "Traumatic Experiences of German Refugees at the End of World War II and Present Stress Disorders." *Zeitschrift für Gerontopsychologie und Psychiatrie* 13: 112–24.

Trifan, T. A., H. Stattin, and L. Tilton-Weaver. 2014. "Have Authoritarian Parenting Practices and Roles Changed in the Last 50 Years?" *Journal of Marriage and Family* 76, no. 4 (August): 744–61.

Trouillot, Michel-Rolph. 1995. *Silencing the Past: Power and the Production of History*. Boston: Beacon.

Tschuggnall, Karoline, and Harald Welzer. 2002. "Rewriting Memories: Family Recollections of the National Socialist Past in Germany." *Culture & Psychology* 8, no. 1 (March): 130–45.

Unger, Raymond. 2016. *Die Heimat der Wölfe: Ein Kriegsenkel auf den Spuren seiner Familie Eine Familienchronik*. Berlin München: Europa.

Ustorf, Anne-Ev. 2008. *Wir Kinder der Kriegskinder: Die Generation im Schatten des Zweiten Weltkriegs*. Freiburg: Herder.

Vees-Gulani, Susanne. 2008. *Trauma and Guilt: Literature of Wartime Bombing in Germany*. Berlin: Walter de Gruyter.

Vermes, Timur. 2012. *Er ist wieder da: Der Roman*. Köln: Eichborn.

Vesper, Ingrid, and Andrea Weber. 1991. *Familien-Geschichten: Mündliche Überlieferung von Zeitgeschichte in Familien*. Hamburg: Dölling & Galitz.

Volkan, Vamik D. 1997. *Bloodlines: From Ethnic Pride to Ethnic Terrorism*. New York: Farrar, Straus and Giroux.

Volkan, Vamik D., Gabriele Ast, and William F. Greer. 2002. *The Third Reich in the Unconscious: Transgenerational Transmission and Its Consequences*. New York: Brunner-Routledge.

Völter, Bettina. 2008. "Generationenforschung und 'transgenerationale Weitergabe' aus biografietheoretischer Perspektive." In *Transgenerationale Weitergabe kriegsbelasteter Kindheiten: Interdisziplinäre Studien zur Nachhaltigkeit historischer Erfahrungen über vier Generationen*, edited by Hartmut Radebold, Werner Bohleber, and Jürgen Zinnecker, 95–106. Weinheim: Juventa.

Von Borries, Bodo. 2004. "Vernichtungskrieg und Judenmord in den Schulbüchern beider deutscher Staaten seit 1949 (2000)." In *Lebendiges Geschichtslernen*, 386–415. Schwalbach: Wochenschau.

Von Issendorff, Philipp. 2013. "Transgenerationale Weitergabe von Kriegstraumata. Eine psychometrische Untersuchung." In *Zeitzeugen des Hamburger Feuersturms 1943 und ihre Familien: Forschungsprojekt zur Weitergabe von Kriegserfahrungen*, edited by Ulrich Lamparter, Silke Wiegand-Grefe, and Dorothee Wierling, 256–73. Göttingen: Vandenhoeck & Ruprecht.

Von Moltke, Johannes. 2005. *No Place like Home: Locations of Heimat in German Cinema. Weimar and Now 36*. Berkeley: University of California Press.

Wagner, Roland. 2012. "Kriegsenkel." *Südwestrundfunk 2*, October 18. Radio broadcast. SWR2 Tandem Hörer live.

Wajnryb, Ruth. 2001. *Silence: How Tragedy Shapes Talk*. Crows Nest, NSW: Allen & Unwin.

Walendzik, Anke, Cornelia Rabe-Menssen, Gerald Lux, Jürgen Wasem, and Rebecca Jahn. 2010. "Erhebung zur ambulanten psychotherapeutischen Versorgung 2010." https://www.mm.wiwi.uni-due.de/fileadmin/fileupload/BWL-MEDMAN/Forschung/Gutachten_DPtV_finalfinalkorr.pdf.

Weizsäcker, Richard von. 1985. "Speech in the Bundestag on 8 May 1985 during the Ceremony Commemorating the 40th Anniversary of the End of War in Europe and of National-Socialist Tyranny." Accessed November 9, 2019.

https://www.bundespraesident.de/SharedDocs/Downloads/DE/Reden/2015/02/150202-RvW-Rede-8-Mai-1985-englisch.pdf?__blob=publicationFile.

Welzer, Harald. 2008. "Die Nachhaltigkeit historischer Erfahrungen: Eine sozialpsychologische Perspektive." In *Transgenerationale Weitergabe kriegsbelasteter Kindheiten: Interdisziplinäre Studien zur Nachhaltigkeit historischer Erfahrungen über vier Generationen*, edited by H. Radebold, W. Bohleber, and J. Zinnecker, 75–93. Weinheim: Juventa.

Welzer, Harald, Sabine Moller, and Karoline Tschuggnall. 2002. *Opa war kein Nazi: Nationalsozialismus und Holocaust im Familiengedächtnis*. 3rd ed. Die Zeit des Nationalsozialismus. Frankfurt am Main: Fischer Taschenbuch.

Westernhagen, Dörte von. 1987. *Die Kinder der Täter: Das Dritte Reich und die Generation danach*. München: Kösel.

Wierling, Dorothee. 2010. "Generations as Narrative Communities: Some Private Sources of Official Cultures of Remembrance in Postwar Germany." In *Histories of the Aftermath: The Legacies of the Second World War in Europe*, edited by Frank Biess and Robert G. Moeller, 100–122. New York: Berghahn Books.

———. 2013. "Das 'Feuersturm'-Projekt." In *Zeitzeugen des Hamburger Feuersturms 1943 und ihre Familien: Forschungsprojekt zur Weitergabe von Kriegserfahrungen*, edited by Ulrich Lamparter, Silke Wiegand-Grefe, and Dorothee Wierling, 45–57. Göttingen: Vandenhoeck & Ruprecht.

Wilson, Richard. 2001. *The Politics of Truth and Reconciliation in South Africa: Legitimizing the Post-Apartheid State*. Cambridge: Cambridge University Press.

Winkler, Willi. 2014. "ARD-Doku 'Akte D'-Vorwärts und alles vergessen." *Die Süddeutsche*, October 13, 2014. http://www.sueddeutsche.de/medien/ard-doku-akte-d-vorwaerts-und-alles-vergessen-1.2170107.

Winter, Jay. 2010. "Thinking about Silence." In *Shadows of War: A Social History of Silence in the Twentieth Century*, edited by Efrat Ben-Ze'ev, Ruth Ginio, and Jay Winter, 3–31. Cambridge: Cambridge University Press.

Wittlinger, Ruth. 2006. "Taboo or Tradition? The 'Germans as Victims' Theme in West Germany until the Early 1990s." In *Germans as Victims: Remembering the Past in Contemporary Germany*, edited by Bill Niven, 62–75. New York: Palgrave Macmillan.

Wolf, Christa. 1976. *Kindheitsmuster*. Berlin: Aufbau.

Wortmann, Sönke. 2004. *Das Wunder von Bern*. Movie. Hamburg: Universal Pictures Germany.

Wright, Katie. 2008. "Theorizing Therapeutic Culture: Past Influences, Future Directions." In "Cultural Sociology: Australian Perspectives and Themes," special issue, *Journal of Sociology* 44, no. 4 (December): 321–36.

Wüstel, Jens-Michael. 2017. *Traumakinder: Warum der Krieg immer noch in unseren Seelen wirkt*. Bergisch Gladbach: Bastei Lübbe.

Yang, Jie. 2013. "'Fake Happiness': Counseling, Potentiality, and Psycho-Politics in China." *Ethos* 41, no. 3 (September): 292–312.

Yehuda, Rachel, ed. 2006. *Psychobiology of Posttraumatic Stress Disorder: A Decade of Progress*. Boston: Blackwell.

Yehuda, Rachel, and Linda M. Bierer. 2007. "Transgenerational Transmission of Cortisol and PTSD Risk." In *Stress Hormones and Post Traumatic Stress Disorder: Basic Studies and Clinical Perspectives*, edited by Melly S. Oitzl, Eric Vermetten, and E. Ronald De Kloet, 121–35. Oxford, UK: Elsevier.

Yehuda, Rachel, Jim Schmeidler, Abbie Elkin, George Skye Wilson, Larry Siever, Karen Binder-Brynes, Milton Wainberg, and Dan Aferiot. 1998. "Phenomenology and Psychobiology of the Intergenerational Response to Trauma." In *International Handbook of Multigenerational Legacies of Trauma*, edited by Yael Danieli, 639–55. New York: Plenum.

Yehuda, Rachel, James Schmeidler, Milton Wainberg, Karen Binder-Brynes, and Tamar Duvdevani. 1998. "Vulnerability to Posttraumatic Stress Disorder in Adult Offspring of Holocaust Survivors." *American Journal of Psychiatry* 155 (9): 1163–71.

Young, Allan. 1995. *The Harmony of Illusions: Inventing Post-Traumatic Stress Disorder*. Princeton, NJ: Princeton University Press.

———. 1996. "Suffering and the Origins of Traumatic Memory." *Daedalus* 125, no. 1 (Winter): 245–60.

Yuh, Jennifer. 2011. *Kung Fu Panda 2*. Animated movie. DreamWorks.

Zeevi, Chanoch. 2011. *Hitler's Children*. TV documentary. Jerusalem: Channel 2.

Zerubavel, Eviatar. 2010. "The Social Sound of Silence: Towards a Sociology of Denial." In *Shadows of War: A Social History of Silence in the Twentieth Century*, edited by Efrat Ben-Ze'ev, Ruth Ginio, and Jay Winter, 32–44. Cambridge: Cambridge University Press.

Zhang, Li. 2014. "Bentuhua: Culturing Psychotherapy in Postsocialist China." *Culture, Medicine and Psychiatry* 38 (2): 283–305.

———. 2016. "The Rise of Therapeutic Governing in Postsocialist China." *Medical Anthropology* 35 (2): 119–31.

Zinnecker, Jürgen. 2008. "Die 'transgenerationale Weitergabe' der Erfahrung des Weltkrieges in der Familie. Der Blickwinkel der Familien-, Sozialisations-, und Generationenforschung." In *Transgenerationale Weitergabe kriegsbelasteter Kindheiten-Interdisziplinäre Studien zur Nachhaltigkeit historischer Erfahrungen über vier Generationen*, edited by Hartmut Radebold, Werner Bohleber, and Jürgen Zinnecker, 141–54. Weinheim: Juventa.

INDEX

LINA JAKOB is a cultural anthropologist with a PhD from the Australian National University. She lives and works in Sydney.

www.ingramcontent.com/pod-product-compliance
Lightning Source LLC
LaVergne TN
LVHW090807070826
844660LV00022B/1106

* 9 7 8 0 2 5 3 0 4 8 2 5 7 *